READING POWER

Second Edition

Reading for Pleasure • Comprehension Skills • Thinking Skills • Reading Faster

Beatrice S. Mikulecky / Linda Jeffries

Longman

Acknowledgments

Our sincere thanks to the teachers around the world who took the time to give us valuable feedback for this revision. We are especially grateful to Charlotte Seeley, Newton, Massachusetts; Barbara Swartz, Boston, Massachusetts; Masako Kirihara, Osaka, Japan; and Ronald Bixler, Cordelia Chang, Jay Durighello, Mo Tam, and Bill VanderWerf, San Francisco, California.

Reading Power, Second Edition

Pearson Education, 10 Bank Street, White Plains, NY 10606

Acquisitions editor: Janet Aitchison
Development editor: Françoise Leffler
Production editor: Christine Cervoni
Photo research: Amy Durfy
Cover design adaptation: Kathleen Marks
Text design adaptation: Kathleen Marks
Text composition: ElectraGraphics
Text art: Len Shalansky

Text Credits: **p. 4,** "The First Day of School" by William Saroyan. Permission to reprint is granted by the Stanford University Libraries; **p. 15,** "Murder in the Language Lab" from *Who Done It?* by Yorio/Morse, © 1980. Adapted by permission of Prentice-Hall, Inc., Upper Saddle River, NJ; **p. 23,** table of contents of *Sanctuary* Magazine, July/August 1996. Reprinted with the permission of *Sanctuary* Magazine, Massachusetts Audubon Society, Lincoln, MA; **p. 27,** "Schedules and Fares for the San Juan Explorer and Victoria Clipper III." Reprinted with the permission of Clipper Navigation, Inc., Seattle, WA; **p. 30,** "14 Yonkers Stores Damaged by Fire." Copyright © 1985 by The New York Times Co. Reprinted by permission; **p. 31,** "Philippines Sends Aid for Typhoon Damage." Reprinted with permission from The Associated Press; **p. 139,** excerpt from *Project Omega* by Elaine O'Reilly. Reprinted by permission of Addison Wesley Longman, Ltd.; **p. 140,** excerpt from *Girl against the Jungle* by Monica Vincent. Reprinted by permission of Addison Wesley Longman, Ltd.; **p. 141,** excerpt from *Sarah, Plain and Tall* by Patricia MacLachlan. Copyright © 1985 by Patricia MacLachlan. Used by permission of HarperCollins Publishers; **p. 142,** excerpt from *Snow Treasure* by Marie McSwigan. Copyright 1942 by E.P. Dutton & Co., Inc., renewed © 1970 by Kathryn McSwigan Laughlin and Andrew McSwigan. Used by permission of Dutton Children's Books, a division of Penguin Books USA Inc.

Photo Credits: **p. 2,** Suzanne Arms/Jeroboam, Inc.; **p. 8,** International Tennis Hall of Fame & Museum, Newport, RI; **p. 20,** Jane Scherk/Jeroboam, Inc.; **p. 32,** Bill Kostroun/AP Wide World Photos; **p. 37,** Kaz Mori/The Image Bank; **p. 38,** Copyright 1996 Tom Neiman/First Image West, Inc.; **p. 48,** Courtesy of the American Foundation for the Blind/Helen Keller Archives; **p. 63,** Stephan Savoia/AP Wide World Photos; **p. 156,** NASA; **p. 197,** Paulo Friedman/International Stock Photo; **p. 245,** Copyright Doug Corrance/Still Moving Pic. Co.; **p. 259,** Archive Photos/Popperfoto; **p. 263,** © Derek Laird/Still Moving Pic.Co.

ISBN: 0-201-84674-8

9 10 11 12 13 14 – CRS – 07060504

Contents

Why is reading in English important?

- Reading in English helps you learn to think in English.
- Reading in English helps you build your English vocabulary.
- Reading in English makes you more comfortable with writing in English. You can write better in English if you feel comfortable with the language.
- Reading in English may be the only way for you to use English if you live in a non-English-speaking country.
- Reading in English can help if you plan to study in an English-speaking country.

How to use Reading Power to become a better reader

This book has four parts. In each part you will work on reading in a different way. Be sure to work on each part every time you use *Reading Power*.

Part One. Reading for Pleasure

The best way to become a better reader is to read for pleasure. You will read books that you choose—books that are interesting to you. The more you read, the better you will read.

Part Two. Reading Comprehension Skills

Reading comprehension skills help you understand and remember what you read. In this part you will learn to use some important skills.

Part Three. Thinking Skills

You will work on understanding English sentences. You will learn how to get the meaning of what you read and will find out how ideas follow each other in English.

Part Four. Reading Faster

In this part you will learn to read faster. You will find that you can understand many texts better when you read faster.

Reading for Pleasure

Reading for pleasure

Reading for pleasure is the easiest way to become a better reader in English. It is also the most important way. That's why it is the first part of *Reading Power*.

Some students say they don't want to read for pleasure. They say they want to use their time with grammar lessons and vocabulary drills. They say that pleasure reading is too easy.

According to many experts, pleasure reading is very important for learning English. Dr. Stephen Krashen, a famous expert on learning language, says that pleasure reading helps you learn many important things about English. Students learn more grammar and vocabulary when they read for pleasure. They also learn more about good writing.

Professor Krashen explains that pleasure reading helps each student in a different way. Each student needs to learn something different. Pleasure reading makes it possible for each student to learn what he or she needs.

Reading for pleasure is not the same as studying. When you read for pleasure, you choose your own books, and you do not have to remember everything. There are no tests on your pleasure reading books.

Remember

Reading for pleasure is very important for learning English. It will help you:

- learn how English speakers use English.
- read faster in English.
- find examples of good writing in English.
- learn new words.
- learn about the cultures of English speakers.

Talking about your pleasure reading

It is important to talk about your pleasure reading. English speakers have special ways of talking about books and stories. To practice, you will read two passages. One is fiction (not true) and one is nonfiction (true).

A. Short story (fiction)

➤ *Follow these steps as you read.*

1. Read the title. Then talk with another student. What do you think the story is about? How can you tell? Write your guess here.

_____

2. Read the story all the way to the end. Do not stop for new words. You will have another chance to read the story.

3. Now talk about the story with another student. Ask each other:

   • Where does it take place?
   • Who are the people in the story?
   • What happens in the story?

4. Read the story again. Mark the new words that you need to learn. (You may not need to learn all the new words. Some of them are not important for the story, and you may not need them again.)

5. Talk to another student about the new words. Guess the meanings. Write them here.

_____

_____

_____

_____

_____

_____

6. Work with a group of three or four students. Retell the story from beginning to end. Ask one another:

   • Did you like the story? Why?
   • Which person did you like best? Why?
   • Did you like the ending? Why?
   • Try to think of a different ending.

The First Day of School

by William Saroyan

He was a little boy named Jim, the first and only child of Dr. Louis Davy, 717 Mattei Building, and it was his first day at school. His father was French, a small heavy-set man of forty whose boyhood had been full of poverty and unhappiness and ambition. His mother was dead: she died when Jim was born, and the only woman he knew intimately
5 was Amy, the Swedish housekeeper.

It was Amy who dressed him in his Sunday clothes, and took him to school. Jim liked Amy, but he didn't like her for taking him to school. He told her so. All the way to school he told her so.

I don't like you, he said. I don't like you any more.

10 I like *you,* the housekeeper said.

Then why are you taking me to school? he said.

He had taken walks with Amy before, once all the way to the Court House Park for the Sunday afternoon band concert, but this walk to school was different.

What for? he said.

15 Everybody must go to school, the housekeeper said.

Did you go to school? he said.

No, said Amy.

Then why do I have to go? he said.

You will like it, said the housekeeper.

20 He walked on with her in silence, holding her hand. I don't like you, he said. I don't like you any more.

I like you, said Amy.

Then why are you taking me to school? he said again.

Why?

25 The housekeeper knew how frightened a little boy could be about going to school.

You will like it, she said. I think you will sing songs and play games.

I don't want to, he said.

I will come and get you every afternoon, she said.

I don't like you, he told her again.

30 She felt very unhappy about the little boy going to school, but she knew that he would have to go.

The school building was very ugly to her and to the boy. She didn't like the way it made her feel, and going up the steps with him she wished he didn't have to go to school.

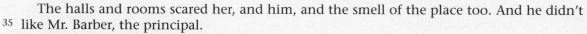

The halls and rooms scared her, and him, and the smell of the place too. And he didn't
35 like Mr. Barber, the principal.

Amy despised Mr. Barber.

What is the name of your son? Mr. Barber said.

This is Dr. Louis Davy's son, said Amy. His name is Jim. I am Dr. Davy's housekeeper.

James? said Mr. Barber.
40 Not James, said Amy, just Jim.

All right, said Mr. Barber. Any middle name?

No, said Amy. He is too small for a middle name. Just Jim Davy.

All right, said Mr. Barber. We'll try him out in the first grade. If he doesn't get along all
right we'll try him out in kindergarten.
45 Dr. Davy said to start him in the first grade, said Amy. Not kindergarten.

All right, said Mr. Barber.

The housekeeper knew how frightened the little boy was, sitting on the chair, and she
tried to let him know how much she loved him and how sorry she was about everything,
but she couldn't say anything, and she was very proud of the nice way he got down from
50 the chair and stood beside Mr. Barber, waiting to go with him to a classroom.

On the way home she was so proud of him she began to cry.

Miss Binney, the teacher of the first grade, was an old lady who was all dried out. The
room was full of little boys and girls. School smelled strange and sad. He sat at a desk and
listened carefully.
55 He heard some of the names: *Charles, Ernest, Alvin, Norman, Betty, Hannah, Juliet, Viola, Polly.*

He listened carefully and heard Miss Binney say, Hannah Winter, what *are* you chewing? And he saw Hannah blush. He liked Hannah Winter right from the beginning.

Gum, said Hannah.

Put it in the waste-basket, said Miss Binney.
60 He saw the little girl walk to the front of the class, take the gum from her mouth, and
drop it into the waste-basket.

And he heard Miss Binney say, Ernest Gaskin, what are *you* chewing?

Gum, said Ernest.

And he liked Ernest Gaskin too.
65 They met in the schoolyard, and Ernest taught him a few jokes.

Amy was in the hall when school ended. She was sullen and angry at everybody until she
saw the little boy. She was amazed that he wasn't changed, that he wasn't hurt, or perhaps
utterly unalive, murdered. The school and everything about it frightened her very much. She
took his hand and walked out of the building with him, feeling angry and proud.
70 Jim said, What comes after twenty-nine?

Thirty, said Amy.

Your face is dirty, he said.

His father was very quiet at the supper table.

What comes after twenty-nine? he said.
75 Thirty, said his father.

Your face is dirty, he said.

In the morning he asked his father for a nickel.

What do you want a nickel for? his father said.

Gum, he said.
80 His father gave him a nickel and on the way to school he stopped at Mrs. Riley's store
and bought a package of Spearmint.

Do you want a piece? he asked Amy.

Do you want to give me a piece? the housekeeper said.

Jim thought about it a moment, and then he said, Yes.
85 Do you like me? said the housekeeper.

I like you, said Jim. Do you like me?

Yes, said the housekeeper.

Do you like school?

Jim didn't know for sure, but he knew he liked the part about gum. And Hannah Win-
90 ter. And Ernest Gaskin.

I don't know, he said.

Do you sing? asked the housekeeper.

No, we don't sing, he said.

Do you play games? she said.
95 Not in the school, he said. In the yard we do.

He liked the part about gum very much.

Miss Binney said, Jim Davy, what are you *chewing?*

Ha ha ha, he thought.

Gum, he said.
100 He walked to the waste-paper basket and back to his seat, and Hannah Winter saw him, and Ernest Gaskin too. That was the best part of school.

It began to grow too.

Ernest Gaskin, he shouted in the schoolyard, *what* are you *chewing?*

Raw elephant meat, said Ernest Gaskin. Jim Davy, what are *you* chewing?
105 Jim tried to think of something funny to be chewing, but he couldn't.

Gum, he said, and Ernest Gaskin laughed louder than Jim laughed when Ernest Gaskin said raw elephant meat.

It was funny no matter what you said.

Going back to the classroom Jim saw Hannah Winter in the hall.
110 Hannah Winter, he said, *what in the world* are you *chewing?*

The little girl was startled. She wanted to say something nice that would honestly show how nice she felt about having Jim say her name and ask her the funny question, making fun of school, but she couldn't think of anything that nice to say because they were almost in the room and there wasn't time enough.
115 Tutti-frutti, she said with desperate haste.

It seemed to Jim he had never before heard such a glorious word, and he kept repeating the word to himself all day.

Tutti-frutti, he said to Amy on the way home.

Amy Larson, he said, *what, are, you, chewing?*
120 He told his father about it at the supper table.

He said, Once there was a hill. On the hill there was a mill. Under the mill there was a walk. Under the walk there was a key. What is it?

I don't know, his father said. What is it?

Milwaukee, said the boy.
125 The housekeeper was delighted.

Mill. Walk. Key, Jim said.

Tutti-frutti.

What's that? said his father.

Gum, he said. The kind Hannah Winter chews.
130 Who's Hannah Winter? said his father.

She's in my room, he said.

Oh, said his father.

After supper he sat on the floor with the small red and blue and yellow top that hummed while it spinned. It was all right, he guessed. It was still very sad, but the gum
135 part of it was very funny and the Hannah Winter part very nice. Raw elephant meat, he thought with great inward delight.

Raw elephant meat, he said aloud to his father who was reading the evening paper. His father folded the paper and sat on the floor beside him. The housekeeper saw them together on the floor and for some reason tears came to her eyes.

B. Biography (nonfiction, a life story)

➤ *Follow these steps as you read.*

1. Read the title. Then talk with another student. What can you guess from the title? Do you know anything about this person?

2. Read the biography all the way to the end. Don't stop for new words. You will have another chance to read the biography.

3. Now talk about the biography with another student. Ask each other:

   - Whose biography is it?
   - When did the person live? Is he or she still alive?
   - What can you remember about the person's life?
   - Who are some other people in the biography?

4. Read the biography again. Mark the new words that you need to learn.

5. Talk to another student about the new words. Guess the meanings. Write them here.

   _____

   _____

   _____

   _____

6. Work with a group of three or four students. Retell the biography from beginning to end. Ask one another:

   - Did you like the biography? Why?
   - Which part did you like best? Why?
   - Would you like to meet this person? Why?
   - Would you like to be this person? Why?

Arthur Ashe, American Hero
by Enid Brooks

When Arthur Ashe was growing up, there were very few black tennis players. African-Americans were not even allowed to play on the tennis courts in many cities. Arthur helped change this. He was the first African-American champion tennis player. In fact, he was the first black person to become a world tennis champion.

Arthur was born in Richmond, Virginia, in 1943. When he was only seven years old, his mother died. After that, his father was both mother and father to him. His father supervised the tennis courts in a park near their home. As a young boy, Arthur liked to watch the players. One day, one of the players, Ron Charity, asked him if he wanted to learn how to play. At that moment, Arthur's life changed forever.

Ron Charity helped Arthur in his early years as a tennis player. Arthur's dream was to win a place on the U.S. Davis Cup Tennis Team. But in Richmond at that time, most tennis courts were for white people only, and all of the tennis officials were white. They did not encourage Arthur to play. However, he did not let them stop him from playing.

Arthur Ashe

He continued to play tennis at the University of California at Los Angeles. Then, in 1963, the captain of the U.S. Davis Cup Tennis Team invited him to join the team. Arthur was the first black player on the team. For the next 15 years, he played and won many Davis Cup matches for the team. During those years, he also won many tennis tournaments around the world.

In 1969, Arthur heard that there would be a tennis match in South Africa and he wanted to play in it. In those days, South Africa was still under the control of an all-white government. It did not allow blacks and whites to meet as equals. Because of this, many Africans and black Americans said that Arthur should not play in the match. But Arthur believed he could be a good example for young black tennis players around the world.

For many years, however, the South African government did not even allow Arthur into the country. Then, in 1973, he was allowed to play in matches against white South Africans. After that, he returned to South Africa for three more tennis matches. He felt that he was helping change the South Africans' ideas about blacks. During his matches, he made sure that black and white people could sit together and did not have to sit separately. Once, while he was in Johannesburg, a 14-year-old black boy followed him around everywhere. When Arthur asked him why, the boy replied, "You're the first one I've ever seen." Arthur asked, "The first what?" "The first free black man," the boy said.

In 1977, Arthur married Jeanne Moutoussamy. Two years later, the U.S. Tennis Association made Arthur the captain of the U.S. Davis Cup Tennis Team. Arthur was at the top of his career and was winning large amounts of money. That year, however, was also the last of his career. He be-

gan to suffer from serious heart problems and had to have a major operation. With Jeanne to help him, he became healthy again. But his career as a professional tennis player was over.

Arthur continued to work in sports as a TV commentator. He also worked for several companies that made sports equipment and clothing. But he still was having trouble with his heart. In 1983, Arthur had another big heart operation. During the operation, he lost a lot of blood, and the hospital had to give him blood from their blood bank. This blood was not healthy. It had the HIV virus, which causes AIDS.

After the operation, Arthur went back to work. He also began to help some organizations for youth and for black people. In 1986, he and Jeanne had a little daughter named Camera. Then, in 1988, Arthur had another health problem and he had to have another operation. When the doctors tested him for this operation, they found the HIV virus in his blood. Arthur and Jeanne were shocked and scared.

They soon learned that Jeanne and Camera did not have the virus. And they learned how Arthur had caught it—from the hospital blood given to him in 1983. Arthur and Jeanne kept the illness a secret as long as possible. Only their families and a few other people knew until 1992. At that time, a newspaper reporter heard about the secret and wanted to write a story. So Arthur held a news conference. He told everyone that he had AIDS.

Once again, Arthur's name was in the news. His family could not live quietly and peacefully any more. Arthur learned how to live with pain. He learned how to talk about AIDS and dying. As in his tennis matches and in his work with young people, Arthur Ashe continued to be a champion. He died in December 1993.

Finding good books

On the next few pages, you will find a list of some good books. Your teacher may have some of them in the classroom. Your school may have some in the school library.

You can go to the town or city library. You may be able to find a good book in the young adults department. Many books for young adults are easy to read. They are in very easy English.

You can also go to a large bookstore. Ask the clerk to help you find the young people's books. Some bookstores also have books called "graded readers" for ESL/EFL students. Ask a clerk for books at Level 2 or Level 3.

Look for some stories and novels. Look for some books with facts and information. If you read both kinds of books, you will learn English faster and better.

Choosing a book

1. Read the front cover and back cover of the book. Do you think the book is interesting?
2. How many pages are there in the book? It is better to begin with a short book.
3. Are there pictures in the book? Pictures can help you understand the book.
4. If you think you like the book, find out if you can understand it. You should read a book that is not too difficult and not too easy for you. Read one page. If you know all the words on the page, the book may be too easy. If you find more than 10 new words, the book may be too difficult for you.
5. The most important thing is this: *The book should be interesting to you.*

Getting the most from pleasure reading

Read your book every day. Write down how many pages you read on the Reading for Pleasure Progress Charts (pages 269–270). Try to read your book quickly.

You may find some new words in your book. Do not use a dictionary for every new word. Try to guess the meaning or skip over the word. Using a dictionary often will make it harder to follow the story.

After you finish the book, tell your teacher. She may talk to you about it. She may ask you to tell the class or write a letter about your book. This way you can learn more English.

If you liked your book, tell a friend about it, too.

Book list

The books on this list are not just for ESL/EFL students. But they are easy to read. Many speakers of English in the United States enjoy these books. You can find these books in many libraries and bookstores.

This list has two main sections: **Fiction** and **Nonfiction.** Fiction books are not true stories. The stories are made up by the authors. Nonfiction books are written to give facts and information. They are about every kind of topic: biography, history, travel, adventure, nature, science, technology, and many others.

Fiction

A Lantern in Her Hand, by Bess Streeter Aldrich. The story of Abby MacKenzie Deal, who lived in the American West during the Civil War. (251 pages)

Under the Domim Tree, by Gila Almagor. Three teenage girls learn to become women in 1953 in Israel. (164 pages)

Sometimes I Think I Hear My Name, by Avi. The story of a 13-year-old boy who tries to understand his parents. Humorous. (139 pages)

If Beale Street Could Talk, by James Baldwin. The story of a young black American family. A man is in jail, but he did not do anything wrong. A sad love story. (197 pages)

The Squared Circle, by James Bennett. Sonny Youngblood is a star basketball player. But who is he, really? (247 pages)

Forever, by Judy Blume. The famous story of teenage love. The question is, Can you love two people at the same time? A best-seller. (220 pages)

Paper Moon, by Joe David Brown. The story of an 11-year-old girl in the American South during the 1930 Depression years. (308 pages)

SOS Titanic, by Eve Bunting. A young man tries to rescue his friends as the ship Titanic sinks into the cold sea. (246 pages)

The Incredible Journey, by Sheila Burnford. Two dogs and a cat travel many miles to return to their home. (146 pages)

The White Mountains, by John Christopher. One hundred years from now, Switzerland is the only free country. This is science fiction and a thriller. (214 pages)

The House on Mango Street, by Sandra Cisneros. Esperánza, a young girl growing up in the Hispanic section of Chicago, learns to make a happy life in the middle of broken-down buildings and personal difficulties. (110 pages)

Me, Too, by Vera and Bill Cleaver. A 12-year-old girl tries to help her twin sister. (158 pages)

Where the Lilies Bloom, by Vera and Bill Cleaver. A young girl keeps her brothers and sisters together after both of their parents die. Set in the Great Smoky Mountains in the American South. (175 pages)

The Chocolate War, by Robert Cormier. A student fights a secret society of other students and becomes a hero in the school. (191 pages)

Children of the River, by Linda Crew. Sundara has fled Cambodia and is now living in Oregon, trying to be a "good Cambodian girl" in America. (213 pages)

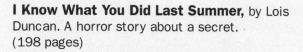

I Know What You Did Last Summer, by Lois Duncan. A horror story about a secret. (198 pages)

Ransom, by Lois Duncan. Five students take a strange and scary bus ride. (172 pages)

The Autobiography of Miss Jane Pittman, by Ernest J. Gaines. The story of an American black woman born during the days of slavery. How she saw black people get freedom. (245 pages)

Julie of the Wolves, by Jean Craighead George. Julie, an Eskimo girl, is to be married at the age of 13. She runs away, makes friends with a wolf pack, and survives. (170 pages)

The Miracle Worker, by William Gibson. A play about Annie Sullivan and how she helped a blind girl named Helen Keller. (122 pages)

Morning Is a Long Time Coming, by Bette Greene. A young American finds adventure and love in Paris after World War II. (261 pages)

Summer of My German Soldier, by Bette Green. A friendship between a young Jewish girl and a German prisoner in America. (199 pages)

The Drowning of Stephen Jones, by Bette Green. Carla's boyfriend Stephen makes her part of a hate campaign against a gay couple. She does not know what to think. Then Stephen drowns himself. (217 pages)

The Friends, by Rosa Guy. A family moves to the United States from the West Indies. This story tells about the love and friendship they find. (185 pages)

Ruby, by Rosa Guy. The problems of an 18-year-old girl as she tries to become a woman. (186 pages)

Zed, by Rosemary Harris. A young boy tells the story of his experience as a hostage of political terrorists. (185 pages)

The Old Man and the Sea, by Ernest Hemingway. A lonely old fisherman struggles to catch a big fish. Then he has to fight off the sharks who want to eat it. A young boy is with him. (140 pages)

Jazz Country, by Nat Hentoff. Life in New York City is tough for a young musician. (146 pages)

This School Is Driving Me Crazy, by Nat Hentoff. More about life in New York City. (154 pages)

Rumblefish, by S. E. Hinton. Rusty wants to be tough, like his older brother, but he gets into trouble. (122 pages)

Night Shift, by Stephen King. Twenty horror stories to make you afraid of the dark. A best-seller! (326 pages)

I Want to Keep My Baby, by Joanna Lee. A 15-year-old girl is going to have a baby. (166 pages)

Very Far Away from Anywhere Else, by Ursula K. LeGuin. A young man wants to become a scientist, but his parents want him to be like everyone else. (87 pages)

The Lion, the Witch, and the Wardrobe, by C. S. Lewis. Three children climb into a wardrobe and find a strange new world when they go through the back of it. For readers who like fantasy. (154 pages)

The Contender, by Robert Lipsyte. Alfred, a high-school dropout, wants to be a champion boxer. Then he learns a valuable lesson. (167 pages)

A Summer to Die, by Lois Lowry. The story of a young girl whose sister dies of leukemia. (120 pages)

Anne of Green Gables, by Lucy Maud Montgomery. The beloved classic story of a red-haired, lively orphan girl who steals people's hearts. (310 pages)

The Dog Who Wouldn't Be, by Farley Mowat. A funny story about an unusual dog. (195 pages)

The Boat Who Wouldn't Float, by Farley Mowat. Another funny story by a very amusing writer. (241 pages)

Edgar Allen, by John Neufeld. A white American family adopts a black child. (128 pages)

Lisa, Bright and Dark, by John Neufeld. A 16-year-old girl knows she is losing her mind. But no one believes her except her three good friends, who help her. (143 pages)

The Black Pearl, by Scott O'Dell. Ramon wants to find the "Pearl of Heaven" in order to show how good a diver he is. Ramon finds the pearl, but he learns an important lesson. (140 pages)

Animal Farm, by George Orwell. The animals are not happy on the farm. So they take over from the humans. Is their life any better? Read and find out! (132 pages)

The Light in the Forest, by Conrad Richter. A white boy is raised by Indians in Pennsylvania. This book tells about early life in the United States. (117 pages)

Shane, by Jack Schaefer. A stranger helps a family in the American West. He teaches a young boy courage and self-respect. (119 pages)

My Name Is Davy—I'm an Alcoholic, by Anne Snyder. A lonely high-school student drinks too much. (128 pages)

The Pearl, by John Steinbeck. A poor fisherman finds a big pearl and hopes to get rich by selling it. Can a pearl bring happiness to his family? (118 pages)

Sons from Afar, by Cynthia Voigt. Two brothers are very different from each other, but both wish they could find their father. (263 pages)

Wrestling Sturbridge, by Rick Wallace. A young wrestler in a small town wants to be the champion. (134 pages)

A Boat to Nowhere, by Maureen Crane Wartski. Kien is a young Vietnamese boy who is trying to escape from the government. This is his story. (191 pages)

My Brother, My Sister, and I, by Yoko Kawashima Watkins. A family struggles in poverty in war-torn Japan. Then the brother is accused of murder! (233 pages)

Charlotte's Web, by E. B. White. Written for children, this book is popular with all ages. It tells a story of love and loyalty that everyone can understand. (184 pages)

Nonfiction

Go Ask Alice, by Anonymous. The true story of a 15-year-old girl who became addicted to drugs. She tells how and why it happened. (188 pages)

New Burlington: The Life and Death of an American Village, by John Baskin. A village is moved to make way for a new lake. The people from the village tell their own stories. (259 pages)

Cheaper by the Dozen, by Frank B. Gilbreth and Ernestine Gilbreth Carey. Life in a very large family, with 12 children and two very special parents. (237 pages)

The Upstairs Room, by Johanna Reiss. How two Jewish sisters lived with a Christian family during World War II in Holland. (196 pages)

Almost Lost, by Beatrice Sparks. The true story of an anonymous teenager's life on the streets of a big city. (239 pages)

It Happened to Nancy, by Beatrice Sparks. A true story from Nancy's diary. She thought she had found love, but instead she found AIDS. (238 pages)

Stephen Hawking: A Life in Science, by M. White and J. Gribbin. Stephen Hawking is an English scientist. Most other scientists think he is the smartest man alive. He has a serious illness, but he is still working on new ideas. (304 pages)

Writing about your pleasure reading book

➤ *Write a letter to a friend about your book. Here is an outline of a letter. Copying from this form, write the letter on a separate piece of paper.*

_____
(date)

Dear _____,

    I just finished reading a book called _____

_____. It was written by _____

_____. It is _____ pages long.

    This book is about _____

_____

_____

_____.

    The book is _____ to read. The best part is

_____

_____.

I think you would _____ this book because _____

_____

_____.

                                  Sincerely,

                                  _____

Some words to use in writing about the book:

interesting/not interesting	sad/happy	action
exciting/boring	difficult/easy	fiction/nonfiction
long/short	people	imaginary/real life

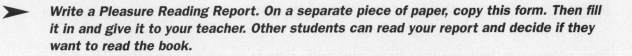

➤ *Write a Pleasure Reading Report. On a separate piece of paper, copy this form. Then fill it in and give it to your teacher. Other students can read your report and decide if they want to read the book.*

PLEASURE READING REPORT

Title of book: _____

Author: _____

Number of pages? _____   Date published? _____

Fiction or nonfiction? _____

What is this book about? _____

_____

_____

What is the best part? _____

_____

_____

Would you tell a friend to read this book? _____

Why? _____

_____

_____

_____

_____

Fill in this information about yourself:

Name _____   Date _____

Native language _____   Age _____

Gender _____   Profession _____

This book is _____ easy _____ just right _____ difficult

Using your pleasure reading book to figure out your reading rate

You can use your pleasure reading book to practice reading faster. But first you must find out how fast you read.

➤ *Read this page from a book called* **Murder in the Language Lab.**

Before you start to read, write the starting time: _____ min. _____ sec.

Murder in the Language Lab   11

Against one wall there was a large machine. The sides of the machine were made of black metal. The bottom half of it looked like a large typewriter. The top part of the machine was like a television set.

5   The man walked over to the tree. He looked up at the hole in the roof.

The man called out, "Sally! Come down, Sally!"

After a short time, a face appeared in the opening. The face had small, bright eyes. The mouth was very wide, and
10 the nose was flat. There were very big ears. The face was covered with short brown hair. It was the face of a chimpanzee.

The animal's lips opened, showing yellow teeth. It looked like a smile. The chimpanzee made a happy sound.

15   "Come down here, Sally," the man said again.

Sally climbed down the tree very quickly. With her long arms, it was easy for her to climb up or down very fast. Sally looked at the man and smiled again.

"Do you want a banana, Sally?" the man asked.

20   Sally made another happy sound. She ran across the room to the machine. She stood in front of the machine. It looked like she was thinking very hard. She was studying the part that was like a typewriter. There were many more keys than are usually found on a typewriter. Also,
25 instead of letters there were little pictures or symbols on the keys. There were circles and squares in different colors, and many other symbols as well.

Sally looked at the keys with their symbols. She put out her finger and pressed several keys. When she pressed
30 a key, that symbol appeared on the television part of the machine. At the same time, words in English appeared above the symbols. Sally finished pressing the keys. She looked at the symbols on the television.

Write the time you finished reading: _____ min. _____ sec.

➤ *Look at the next page and read the directions carefully.*

➤ **To figure out your reading rate:**

1. Count the number of words in three lines. There are 30 words in three lines on this page of *Murder in the Language Lab.*

2. Divide the number of words by three. Then you will know the average number of words in a line.

    30 ÷ 3 = 10 words in one line.

3. Count the lines on the page. On this page of *Murder in the Language Lab,* there are 33 lines.

4. (number of × (average number of = number of words
    lines)   words in one line)   on a page.

    33   ×   10   =   330.

    Now you know that there are about 350 words on each page in this book. You can find out how many words you can read in one minute.

5. How many minutes did you take to read the page of *Murder in the Language Lab?* _____ minutes

    330 words on a page ÷ _____ minutes = _____ words per minute.

    For example, if you read the page in 5 minutes,

    330 words on a page ÷ 5 minutes = 66 words per minute.

➤ **Next, you will learn how to figure out your reading rate for your own book.**

Figure out your reading rate for your own book

➤ **You can use your own book to learn to read faster. About once a week, check your pleasure reading rate. Just remember to time yourself when you read.**

READING RATE

Book Title _____

1. Find a full page in your book.

2. Count the number of words in three lines: _____ words.

3. Divide that number by three to get the average number of words in one line: _____ words.

4. Count the lines on one page: _____ lines.

5. _____ × _____ = _____.
      (number of lines)   (average words in one line)   (words on a page)

   Now that you know how many words there are on one page in your book, you can figure out your reading rate (words per minute).

6. Open your book and mark the page you are on. Before you start to read, write the starting time here: _____ min. _____ sec.

   When you stop reading, write finishing time: _____ min. _____ sec.

7. How many minutes did you read? Finishing time minus starting time equals reading time. _____ min. _____ sec.

8. How many pages did you read? _____

9. How many words did you read? _____

   _____ × _____ = _____.
      (number of pages)   (number of words on a page)   (number of words read)

10. To find your reading rate, divide the number of words by the number of minutes.

    _____ words ÷ _____ minutes = _____ words per minute.

➤ **Now turn to page 269 and mark your reading rate on the Reading for Pleasure Progress Chart. Write today's date at the bottom of the chart. Remember, check your pleasure reading rate about once a week, not more often.**

Reading sprints

Reading quickly is important in reading for pleasure. When you read very slowly, you cannot follow the story. You get bored and you want to stop reading.

You can improve your reading speed by doing reading sprints. Runners often use sprints to learn to run faster. Reading sprints can help you read your book faster. You will enjoy it more.

Use your pleasure reading book for these reading sprints.

READING SPRINTS

Title of your book: _____

1. Find out how many pages you can read normally in five minutes. Write the number of pages here. (If you read only part of a page, include that amount.) _____

2. From where you just finished reading, count ahead that number of pages. (For example, if you read one and a half pages in five minutes, count ahead one and a half pages.) Mark the place in the margin with a pencil.

3. Try to read those next pages in only *four* minutes. If you cannot do it the first time, try again. (Use new pages.) Make your eyes move faster across the page. You may need to try several times.

4. Now try to read that same number of pages in *three* minutes. Count the number of pages again, and mark the place. Again, try until you can do it.

5. Finally, try to read the same number of pages in *two* minutes. You may be able to get only a few words. This does not matter. You are not reading for comprehension. The important thing is to make your eyes move more quickly and get *something* from the text.

6. Now you are ready to read "normally" again. Read for five minutes. Don't push yourself, but don't relax too much either!

   How many pages did you read? _____

   Compare that with your first reading. Is it the same?

Repeat these reading sprints regularly. They will help you read your pleasure reading book quickly. And you will build up speed in all of your other reading, too. Reading faster will become easier, and your comprehension will improve.

Part Two

Reading
Comprehension
Skills

Reading Comprehension Skills

In each unit of Part Two, you will work on a different reading skill. The first exercises in each unit may be easy, but then the exercises become more difficult. Do the exercises in order, and do not skip any.

Read the directions before you begin to work. In some of the exercises, you must work with another student. Be sure to do that. You will improve your English that way.

The Answer Key for all units begins on page 275.

Scanning

What is scanning?

Scanning is very fast reading. When you scan, you skip over many words. You look for some information as quickly as you can.

Scanning is especially important for improving your reading. Many students try to read every word when they read, so they read very slowly. You often do not need to read every word. If you learn to scan, you can learn to read and understand faster.

You usually scan:

    a table of contents in a magazine
      or a book,
    an index in a textbook,
    a timetable,
    the ads in a newspaper,
    a list of movies in the newspaper,
    a telephone book,
    the pages of a dictionary.

You usually do not scan:

    a mystery story,
    a textbook for an important course,
    important papers from a lawyer,
    a map for finding your way home,
    a question on a test,
    a poem.

EXAMPLE

Your friend made a list of things you need to buy for school. Did he remember to include a *dictionary?*

pen	paper
notebook	dictionary
eraser	pencil sharpener
pencils	glue
pencil case	assignment book

How many words did you read? You did not need to read all the words to find "dictionary." The other words were not important to you.

In this unit, you will practice scanning. Do not try to read every word. Scan to find the answers to the questions. Work fast.

Scanning a table of contents

On the facing page is the table of contents of *Sanctuary* magazine. The table of contents is always at the front of a magazine or a book. It tells you what you can find in each chapter or part.

➤ *Read each question and then scan the table of contents to find the answers.*
Work as fast as you can.

1. How many Features are there in the magazine? _____

2. What is the title of the article on noise pollution?

   _____

3. On what page can you read about Long Lake? _____

4. How many departments are there in the magazine? _____

5. Does this magazine have any poetry? On what page? _____

6. On what page can you read about birds? _____

7. Does this magazine have an editor? What is his or her name?

   _____

8. On what page can you read about freshwater ponds? _____

9. What is the title of the article by Betsy Colburn?

   _____

10. On what page is the article by Deborah Knight? _____

➤ *Now you write a question about this table of contents.*

_____

_____

➤ *Ask another student to scan the table of contents for the answer to your question.*

SANCTUARY

July/August 1996
Volume 35 Number 6

Departments

18 News

21 Notes From the Field

22 Advocacy

23 About Birds

25 Sanctuary Events

29 Curious Naturalist

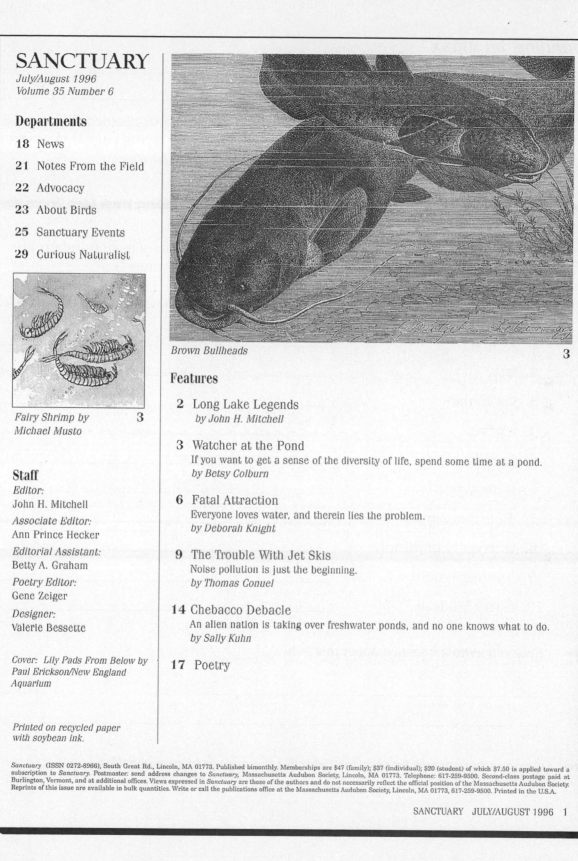

Brown Bullheads   3

Fairy Shrimp by   3
Michael Musto

Staff

Editor:
John H. Mitchell

Associate Editor:
Ann Prince Hecker

Editorial Assistant:
Betty A. Graham

Poetry Editor:
Gene Zeiger

Designer:
Valerie Bessette

*Cover: Lily Pads From Below by
Paul Erickson/New England
Aquarium*

*Printed on recycled paper
with soybean ink.*

Features

Sanctuary (ISSN 0272-8966), South Great Rd., Lincoln, MA 01773. Published bimonthly. Memberships are $47 (family); $37 (individual); $20 (student) of which $7.50 is applied toward a subscription to *Sanctuary*. Postmaster: send address changes to *Sanctuary*, Massachusetts Audubon Society, Lincoln, MA 01773. Telephone: 617-259-9500. Second-class postage paid at Burlington, Vermont, and at additional offices. Views expressed in *Sanctuary* are those of the authors and do not necessarily reflect the official position of the Massachusetts Audubon Society. Reprints of this issue are available in bulk quantities. Write or call the publications office at the Massachusetts Audubon Society, Lincoln, MA 01773, 617-259-9500. Printed in the U.S.A.

Scanning an index

<u>**Exercise 2**</u>

An index is usually at the back of a book. It is in alphabetical order. You can use an index to find information quickly. The index on the facing page is taken from a book titled *The Theater Arts and the Teaching of Second Languages*.

➤ *Scan the index to locate the page numbers for the entries below. Work fast. Try to do this exercise in two minutes or less.*

On what page(s) can you read about the following (if many page numbers are listed, write down the first two or three and "and many more").

Page(s)

1. TOEFL _____

2. taste _____

3. vocabulary _____

4. writing _____

5. sound _____

6. stereotype _____

7. *Time* magazine _____

8. University of Illinois _____

9. Andrew Wright _____

10. Garry Trudeau _____

➤ *Now you write a question about this index.*

_____

_____

➤ *Ask another student to scan the index for the answer to your question.*

Scanning a timetable

Exercise 3

When you travel, you often need to scan a timetable. On the facing page, you will find a timetable for taking a ferry from Seattle, Washington, to Victoria, British Columbia. (A ferry is a big ship that carries people, cars, bicycles, buses, and trucks.)

➤ *Scan the timetable to answer these questions. Work fast!*

1. What time(s) does the ferry depart from Seattle? _____

2. What time(s) does the ferry depart from Victoria? _____

3. Can you take the ferry on a Wednesday in March or April? _____

4. During which months are there two ferry trips every day?

   _____

5. During which months are there ferry trips only on the weekends?

   _____

6. How much is a round-trip ticket for a student? _____

7. How much would a father and two little children pay for round-trip tickets?

   _____

8. What is the latest time that you can take a ferry from Victoria to Seattle in

   July? _____

9. How long does the ferry take to travel from Seattle to Victoria?

   _____

10. Can you take a ferry from Victoria at 4:20 P.M. in October? _____

➤ *Now you write a question about this timetable.*

   _____

   _____

➤ *Ask another student to scan the timetable for the answer to your question.*

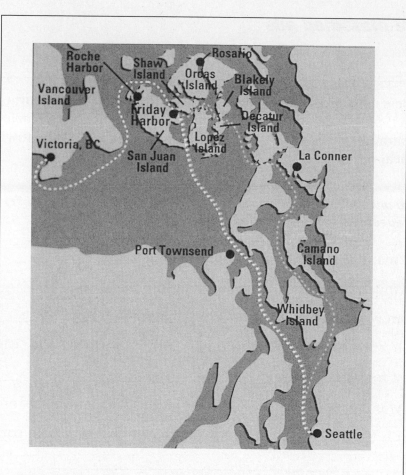

Timetable and Fares
for the San Juan Victoria Express
Seattle, Wash.–Victoria, BC

Scheduled Departures and Arrivals

	Depart Seattle	Arrive Victoria	Depart Victoria	Arrive Seattle
Feb. 9–April 30 (Weekends Only)	7:00 A.M.	12:20 P.M.	2:00 P.M.	7:20 P.M.
May 1–June 29 (Daily)	7:00 A.M.	12:20 P.M.	2:00 P.M.	7:20 P.M.
June 30–Sept. 14 (Daily)	7:00 A.M.	12:20 P.M.	2:00 P.M.	7:20 P.M.
	11:00 A.M.	3:20 P.M.	4:20 P.M.	9:40 P.M.
Sept. 15–Sept. 30 (Daily)	7:00 A.M.	12:20 P.M.	2:00 P.M.	7:20 P.M.
Oct. 1–Oct. 15 (Weekends Only)	7:00 A.M.	12:20 P.M.	2:00 P.M.	7:20 P.M.

Fares

	Adults	Seniors & Students	Children
One way	$30	$27	$16
Round trip	$45	$39	$24

Call for more information: 1-800-023-0230
Call for reservations: 1-206-002-4343

Reading Comprehension Skills

Scanning the classified ads

Exercise 4

Newspapers usually have a part called "classified ads." In this part of the newspaper, people can find things to buy, sell, or rent. On the facing page are some ads for apartments (apts.) near Boston. The names of the towns are in alphabetical order.

➤ *Read each question and then scan the ads for the answer. Work fast! Try to answer all of the questions in three minutes.*

1. How many apartments are for rent in Malden? _____

2. How much is the cheapest apartment in Brockton? _____

3. Whom would you call about an apartment in Canton? _____

4. If you want to live in Brighton near public transportation, which apartment is best for you? _____

5. Can you have a cat at the Lakeside Village apartment in Easton? _____

6. What is the phone number for the apartment in Lynn with parking?

   _____

7. If you want a three-bedroom (3 bdrm.) apartment, where could you find one? (Name at least three towns.) _____

8. What is the phone number for the Essex Realty Company?

   _____

9. Where is the apartment with the highest rent? _____

10. Where is the apartment with the lowest rent? _____

11. What is the rent for a studio in Brighton? _____

12. What is the rent for a one-bedroom (1 bdrm.) apartment near Boston

    University? _____

28

➤ *Now you write a question about these ads.*

_____

_____

➤ *Ask another student to scan the ads for the answer to your question.*

CLASSIFIED ADS

BRIGHTON, 2 bdrm., full kitchen, dining area, $660. Call 876-5522.

BRIGHTON, Sunny studio, fresh paint, laundry. $550. Downtown Real Estate Company. 521-0021.

BRIGHTON, near Boston Univ. Studio. $525; Move in 9/1. 341-8003.

BRIGHTON, Near transportation. Extra large. Studio. Clean. Good owner. $590 with heat. Call 741-8800.

BRIGHTON, New, 1 bdrm. in house, dishwasher, garden. $650. Real Estate Company. 452-0667.

BRIGHTON, Cozy 1 bdrm. with new kitchen & bath. Laundry. Parking. Near Boston Unlv. $565. Call 962-5431.

BRIGHTON, 3 bdrm. in house, new kitchen, tile bath, lg BR's. $995, no heat. Real Estate Company. 286-3152.

BROCKTON, Oak Park. Many large new apts. w/dishwasher, heat, carpeting, balcony, walk-in closet, pool, sauna, clubhouse, tennis court. Convenient to public transpt. & shop'g. 1 bdrm. $675, 2 bdrms. $735-$780. Equal Housing Opportunity. ESSEX REALTY 598-8440.

BROCKTON, Oak Green Apts. near Stoughton. New apts. w/dishwasher, carpeting, parking & pool. Studio $610, 1 bdrm. $670, 2 bdrms. $760. Rent includes heat. Equal Housing Opportunity. ESSEX REALTY 598-8440.

BROOKLINE. 6 rooms, 3 bdrm., new kitchen and bath. Porch, parking. $995 no heat. Collins Real Estate Company. 776-1461.

BROOKLINE VILLAGE, 2 bdrm. in 3-family house. New kitchen. $825, no heat. Village Real Estate Company. 542-3200.

BURLINGTON, Ideal locale, neighboring mall and major routes, large 1 & 2 bdrm. apts. Tennis, pool & more. Model open Mon.-Fri. 9-5, Sat. & Sun. 10-4. SIR WINDSOR APTS. 756-6422.

CAMBRIDGE, 2 bdrm. luxury apt. in new brick building. w/carpeting, tile bath, all electric kit., balcony & assigned prkg. $825. with heat. Call Bonnie 355-4400 or 626-8181.

CAMBRIDGE, Shepard St., large 4 rms.-1 bdrm., large closets, porch. With heat, prkg, no fee. $884. 5/1. 341-8003.

CANTON, 2 bdrm., eat-in kitchen, sunny, garden, near shops & transportation. $775. May 1. Call Susan 792-5670 or Mrs. Young 265-4147.

CHARLESTOWN, Bunker Hill St. near city pool, 1 bdrm. with heat. $525. 256-8622, after 5pm.

CHELMSFORD, Lowell line, nr. Rtes 3 & 128. Large 2 bdrm. $470 incl. heat, air conditioning. 745-5420.

CHELSEA, Luxury 1 & 2 bdrm. apts.-near subway, deck, with heat. $490-$550. 465-2881.

CONCORD, 3 bdrm. townhouse, pool, tennis, near river. $1050 with heat. 532-4591, after 7 pm.

DORCHESTER, At Ashmont. Studios $310. 1 bdrm. $335-$400. with heat $500. 983-4257.

DORCHESTER, So. Boston. New 1 & 2 bdrm. apts. $360-$375. 983-7330.

EASTON. Lakeside Village. Unique 1 & 2 bdrm. spacious townhouses. Just 30 minutes from Boston, convenient bus service available. Spectacular sports complex, private backyard. Small pets allowed & owner managed. Reasonable. 832-1186.

EASTON, 1 & 2 bdrm. condos avail. Pool & tennis courts. Some with garages. Starting at $475 mo. Some include utilities. KINGSLEY PROPERTIES. 832-9501.

EAST BOSTON, 2 bdrm. condo, deck, overlooking harbor & skyline, all new, with laundry, carpeting, and dishwasher. $800 mo. Call Ed 754-0432.

EAST BOSTON, 6 modern rooms, 2nd floor. Call 755-6016.

LYNN, Newly painted studio & 2 bdrm. apts. ocean views. Rents from $350 with heat, hot water, and new kitchens & baths. 654-9876.

LYNN, Nahant line, steps to ocean, studio. $275. with parking. NSP R.E. 954-4121.

LYNN, Ultra-modern ocean front 1 bdrm. apt., including new kitchen & bathrm., carpets, many extras. $675. 955-8653.

LYNN, Steps from beach. Completely new 1 bdrm. apt. $400. Studios $295. with heat. HALL R.E. 954-2025.

MALDEN, Huxley Estates. Beautiful 1 1/2 bdrm., new kitchen, air-conditioned, heated, with parking, pool, walk to subway. No pets please. Avail. 6/1. 644-2281. M-F 9-5, Sun 1-5.

MALDEN, Very clean 4 rooms, 1 bdrm., $436 no heat. Baldwin R.E. 644-7562.

MATTAPAN, Modern 2 bdrm., a/c, $575 no heat. 288-5001.

NEEDHAM, modern apts. 1 & 2 bdrm. Rents $595 to $925 + heat. Call 453-2986. Mon-Fri 9-5.

NEWTON, Luxury 1 bdrm., $650 with pool, tennis, parking, heat, near subway. No pets. Rental fee - $200. For Info, 256-5488.

NEWTON, Large. sunny 2 rm. apt, new kitchen & bath. Air conditioned. $425. R.E. 256-9753.

Scanning a newspaper story

Exercise 5

  Scan the news story below to find the answers to these questions. Work fast.

1. How many stores were damaged in the fire? _____

2. In which store did the fire (blaze) start? _____

3. What time did the fire start? _____

4. Where is the shopping center? _____

➤ *Now you write a question about this news article.*

_____

_____

➤ *Ask another student to scan the article for the answer to your question.*

THE NEW YORK TIMES

14 Yonkers Stores Damaged by Fire

Special to The New York Times

YONKERS, Nov. 12—A four-alarm fire damaged 14 stores today in the Cross County Shopping Center, the largest shopping center in Westchester County.

Fire investigators said the blaze apparently started in a pile of cardboard cartons at the rear of a shoe store and spread through a utilities duct above the 13 other stores. The fire started at 4:40 P.M. and was declared under control at 6:14 P.M. The center is on the Cross County Parkway at the Gov. Thomas E. Dewey Thruway.

Two firefighters were treated at the scene for minor cuts. Lieut. John Carey of the Yonkers Arson Squad said the cause of the fire was under investigation.

Exercise 6

➤ *Scan the news story below to find the answers to these questions. Work fast.*

1. How many people died in the typhoon (storm)? _____

2. On what day did the typhoon begin? _____

3. How many people lost their homes (were homeless)? _____

4. What is the name of the island that was hit the worst? _____

5. What is the name of the typhoon? _____

6. How many people are missing? _____

➤ *Now you write a question about this news article.*

_____

_____

➤ *Ask another student to scan the article for the answer to your question.*

THE NEW YORK TIMES

Philippines Sends Aid for Typhoon Damage

MANILA, Nov. 10 (AP)—The Philippine Air Force ferried medical teams and relief supplies today to provinces ravaged by Typhoon Agnes. The authorities said 515 people had died in the typhoon and more than 400 were missing.

An Air Force spokesman said more than 163 tons of food, medicine and clothing had been sent to the Visayan region, 300 miles south of Manila, and more aid was on the way.

The typhoon hit the region Monday. The spokesman said helicopters were rescuing people stranded by floods that remained chest-deep today in some areas of Panay Island, which appeared to have been hit the worst. Most of the fatalities and missing were on the island, where 445,000 people were homeless.

The Philippine National Red Cross reported that 90 percent of the 86,000 houses in Capiz Province on Panay were destroyed. Many of the dead were children who drowned as 30-foot waves smashed into coastal villages.

Scanning two news stories for information

Exercise 7

➤ *Scan the two news stories on the next page to answer these questions. Work fast.*

1. How many passengers and crew members were on the train? _____

2. On what date did this happen? _____

3. Where was the train when it derailed (went off the track)?

_____

4. Where was the train coming from? _____

5. How many persons were injured seriously? _____

6. What is the name of the Senator who visited the crash?

_____

7. Where has train travel stopped because of the accident?

_____

8. What could have caused this accident? _____

➤ *Now you write a question about these news articles.*

_____

_____

Several cars of a derailed train headed to Boston lie in the remote marshes of Secaucus, N.J., yesterday.

> *Ask another student to scan the articles for the answer to your question.*

THE NEW YORK GLOBE

Amtrak Derailment Near Secaucus Injures 35

by Richard L. O'Brien

NEW YORK, Nov. 23—An Amtrak fast-mail train carrying 108 passengers and crew members derailed as it was nearing New York at 6:33 A.M. on Saturday. The train was speeding across the Hackensack River Bridge when it left the track, almost hit a train headed in the opposite direction, and then fell 30 feet down an embankment into a marsh.

Amtrak announced that no one was killed. But 35 persons were injured, including two who were injured seriously. Dozens of other passengers were badly shaken up in the crash. The two train locomotives were hurled nose down into the muddy marsh of an empty New Jersey meadow.

The Hackensack River Bridge is a swing bridge. It is the type that opens to allow tall boats to pass through. Senator Frank Lautenberg, a member of the Transportation Appropriations subcommittee in the Senate, went to the accident scene and talked to railroad officials. He was informed that a boat had passed through the bridge just two hours earlier. It was speculated that the bridge may not have closed completely after the boat went through, and a gap in the track may have caused the crash.

THE BOSTON TIMES

Boston-Bound Train Derails, 34 Hurt

by Madelyn Burton

New York, Nov. 23—An Amtrak train headed for Boston derailed just south of New York City yesterday, falling into a muddy marsh and injuring 34 people, none of them seriously. The train was a passenger and mail train en route from Washington, D.C., to Boston.

Railroad officials described the wreck as one of the worst in recent memory in this part of the country, called the Northeast Corridor. The accident stopped all train travel between New York and Newark. The tracks to and from New York to Boston, however, were still open and in use.

According to Amtrak officials, 15 crew members and 17 passengers suffered only minor injuries. Most were treated and released from hospitals in the area. Two crew members, however, stayed in the hospital overnight.

Scanning a newspaper ad

Exercise 8

➤ *Scan the ads below to find the answers to these questions. Work fast.*

1. Which computer has the lowest price? _____

2. What is the price of the computer that comes with a monitor, or screen?

   _____

3. What is the name of the computer store? _____

4. How many computer courses can you take at DSI? _____

5. Which computer runs Softwind programs? _____

6. What is the price of the Horatio Plus? _____

➤ *Now you write a question about these ads.*

   _____

   _____

➤ *Ask another student to scan the ads for the answer to your question.*

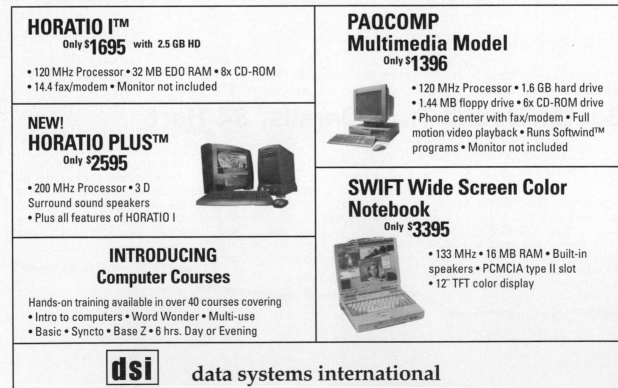

HORATIO I™
Only $**1695**   with 2.5 GB HD

• 120 MHz Processor • 32 MB EDO RAM • 8x CD-ROM
• 14.4 fax/modem • Monitor not included

NEW!
HORATIO PLUS™
Only $**2595**

• 200 MHz Processor • 3 D
Surround sound speakers
• Plus all features of HORATIO I

INTRODUCING
Computer Courses

Hands-on training available in over 40 courses covering
• Intro to computers • Word Wonder • Multi-use
• Basic • Syncto • Base Z • 6 hrs. Day or Evening

PAQCOMP
Multimedia Model
Only $**1396**

• 120 MHz Processor • 1.6 GB hard drive
• 1.44 MB floppy drive • 6x CD-ROM drive
• Phone center with fax/modem • Full
motion video playback • Runs Softwind™
programs • Monitor not included

SWIFT Wide Screen Color
Notebook
Only $**3395**

• 133 MHz • 16 MB RAM • Built-in
speakers • PCMCIA type II slot
• 12" TFT color display

dsi data systems international

250 West 17th Street, New Winchester, NY 10211 505-526-0008 M-F 9-5 SAT 10-6

Previewing
and Predicting

What do you usually do when you get a letter?

A.

```
Main Street Bank
12 Main Street
Memphis, TN 38194
```

```
                    MEMPHIS
                    AUG 26'97      ≡0.32≡
                      TN        U. S. POSTAGE
                              PB METER
                              123456789
```

```
          Ms. Grace Tanaka
          6324 Beacon St.
          Tampa, Florida 32800
```

B.

```
G. Stein
6 Oak St.
Kingsport, TN 37660
```

```
          Grace Tanaka
          6324 Beacon St.
          Tampa, FL. 32800
```

You look at the kind and size of the envelope. You look at the writing and the return address. You look at the date in the postmark. If it is from another country, you look at the stamp.

This is called **previewing.** When you preview, you look for information. Then you can make guesses about what is in the letter. When you make guesses like this, you are **predicting.**

Previewing and predicting help you read faster and understand better. This is because you are already thinking about what you will read. You should *always* preview and predict before you read!

EXAMPLE

➤ *Make some predictions about the letters.*

Letter A

1. Is it a personal letter or a business letter? _____

2. Who is it from? _____

3. Where is it from? _____

4. Do you think it will be an interesting letter? _____

   Why or why not? _____

Letter B

1. Is it a personal letter or a business letter? _____

2. Who is it from? _____

3. Where is it from? _____

4. Do you think it will be an interesting letter? _____

   Why or why not? _____

Exercise 1

Here is a picture of the place where you are going on vacation.

Get away from the crowd!

➤ **Make predictions about your vacation.**

1. What will you do during the day? _____

_____

2. What will you do in the evening? _____

3. What will you eat? _____

4. What will you wear? _____

5. What will you buy? _____

6. How will you feel when you come home? _____

Exercise 2

Here is a picture of the place where your friend is going on vacation.

Chicago: Where it all happens.

➤ *Make predictions about your friend's vacation.*

1. What will she do during the day? _____

   _____

2. What will she do in the evening? _____

3. What will she wear? _____

4. What will she eat? _____

5. What will she buy? _____

6. How will she feel when she comes home? _____

Exercise 3

➤ *The pictures below illustrate stories. Match the pictures with the titles of the stories.*

Picture   **Title of story**

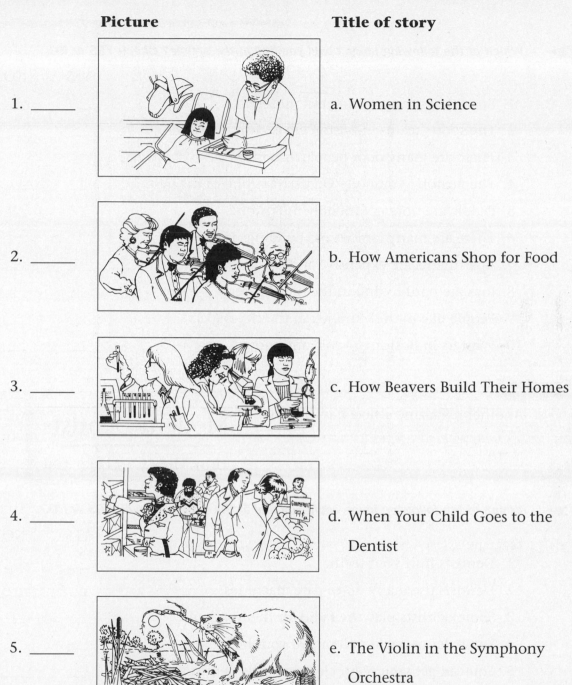

1. _____   a. Women in Science

2. _____   b. How Americans Shop for Food

3. _____   c. How Beavers Build Their Homes

4. _____   d. When Your Child Goes to the
                                  Dentist

5. _____   e. The Violin in the Symphony
                                  Orchestra

Exercise 4

A magazine article has this title:

> **BOSTON: A GOOD PLACE TO LIVE**

➤ *Which of the following ideas could you find in the article? Check YES or NO.*

		YES	NO
1.	Boston has many wonderful museums.	✓	
2.	The sports teams in Boston are exciting to watch.		
3.	There are many poor people in Boston.		
4.	The Boston Symphony Orchestra is one of the best.		
5.	People are not very friendly in Boston.		
6.	There are many famous old buildings in Boston.	✓	
7.	Apartments are expensive and hard to find.		
8.	Jobs are hard to find in the Boston area.		
9.	People like to walk and jog in the city parks.		
10.	Winters in Boston are cold and snowy.	✓	

Exercise 5

Another magazine article has this title:

> **Modern Dentists**
>
> How They Can Help You

➤ *Which of the following ideas could you find in the article? Check YES or NO.*

		YES	NO
1.	Dentists hurt your teeth.		
2.	Dentists use many up-to-date machines.		
3.	Some dentists play the radio for their patients.	✓	
4.	Some dentists will pull out all your teeth.		
5.	You can get your teeth cleaned at the dentist's office.	✓	
6.	The dentist may x-ray your teeth.		
7.	A visit to the dentist is very expensive.		
8.	The dentist tells you how to take care of your teeth.	✓	
9.	Some dentists become very rich.		
10.	Modern dentists must study for many years.		

Exercise 6

➤ *Predict what will come next in each story. Circle the letter of the sentence that could be next.*

EXAMPLE

Yesterday, there was a big snowstorm in Detroit. Many schools were closed, and people had to stay home from work.

   a. It was a warm, sunny day and the beaches were crowded.
   b. It was very cold, but the snow on the trees looked beautiful.
   c. Only one inch of snow fell in the downtown area.

The correct answer is choice b.
Choice a is not correct. People don't go to beaches when there is snow!
Choice c is not correct. In a big snowstorm, many inches of snow fall.

1. There were many good shows on TV last night. The Smith family stayed home.
   a. They turned off the TV and went to bed early.
   b. The only interesting show was about traveling by bicycle.
   c. They saw a play, a music show, and the news.

2. John and Alice Babson are not happy with the school in their town.
   a. Their children love to go to school.
   b. The classrooms are too crowded.
   c. It is a beautiful building.

3. Many young people move to New York after college.
   a. New York is a dangerous city.
   b. It's difficult to find jobs in New York.
   c. There are lots of interesting things to do in New York.

4. Fly Happy Time Airlines! Take an exciting trip to Holiday Island!
   a. This trip is very expensive.
   b. Holiday Island has warm, sunny weather.
   c. Happy Times Airlines is never on time.

5. Alex had trouble falling asleep last night. He was awake until 3:00 A.M.
   a. This morning, he feels tired.
   b. This morning, he feels rested and ready to work.
   c. This morning, he is hungry.

6. The roads were covered with ice and were dangerous today.
   a. Sam drove home quickly.
   b. Sam took a long time to drive home.
   c. Sam enjoyed driving home.

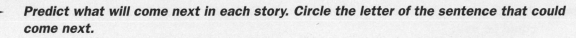

Exercise 7

➤ *Predict what will come next in each story. Circle the letter of the sentence that could come next.*

1. Tomiko got a cat last week. It's a pretty little cat, and it follows her everywhere.
   a. Tomiko can never find the cat.
   b. It even goes out for walks with her in the park.
   c. Tomiko's father doesn't like cats.

2. Sergio likes to listen to classical music in the evenings.
   a. Sometimes he falls asleep while he is listening.
   b. He works hard all morning and afternoon.
   c. His favorite kinds of music are pop and country.

3. Miriam and her brother, Peter, both go to dance classes.
   a. Peter likes to be different from his sister.
   b. Peter doesn't like dancing.
   c. Peter likes to do the same things as his sister.

4. My clock doesn't work very well. It's always a little slow.
   a. I'm often late for work.
   b. It's black with white numbers.
   c. It helps me get to work on time.

5. Rudy went to China last month. He didn't know how to speak Chinese.
   a. He didn't know any Japanese or Korean.
   b. Some Chinese people visited Jorge in Dallas, Texas.
   c. But a lot of Chinese people spoke English.

6. The weatherman on TV predicted cold weather on Saturday.
   a. I like to watch the weather report on TV.
   b. You don't have to bring any warm clothes this weekend.
   c. You should bring some warm clothes this weekend.

7. On Sundays, Gina's grandmother often cooks a big meal.
   a. Gina doesn't like cooking very much.
   b. She invites Gina and all her cousins for dinner.
   c. Gina doesn't see her grandmother very often.

8. Daren wants to go to Europe next summer.
   a. He says he is not interested in European history.
   b. In college, he is studying African history.
   c. He is saving money to pay for the plane ticket.

Exercise 8

Previewing:

➤ *In this short passage, you can see only the parts to preview. Read these parts. Then make predictions about the parts you cannot see.*

Big Dreams for Blanca

Blanca Garcia lives and works in Oakland, California, but she was born in Ecuador. Her family came to the United States from Ecuador ten years ago. Blanca is now 19 years old. She has two sisters, Clara, 16, and xxxxxxxxxxxxxxxxxxxx xxxxxxxxxxxxxxxxxxxxxxxxxxxxxxxxxxxxxxxxxxxxxxxxxxxxxxxxxxxxxxxxxxxxxx.

Blanca finished high school last year, and now she works in xxxxxxxxxxx xxxxxxxxxxxxxxxxxxxxxxxxxxxxxxxxxxxxxxxxxxxxxxxxxxxxxxxxxxxxxxxxxxxxxx xxxxxxxxxxxxxxxxxxxxxxxxxxxxxxxxxxxxxxxxxxxxxxxxxxxxxxxxxxxxxxxxxxxxxx xxxxxxxxxxxxxxxxxxxxxxxxxxx.

When she has enough money, she wants to go to college. She xxxxxxxxxxxxx xxxxxxxxxxxxxxxxxxxxxxxxxxxxxxxxxxxxxxxxxxxxxxxxxxxxxxxxxxxxxxxxxxxxxx xxxxxxxxxxxxxxxxxxxxxxxxxxxxxx.

Blanca also wants to have her own children. She has a xxxxxxxxxxxxxxxxx xxxxxxxxxxxxxxxxxxxxxxxxxxxxxxxxxxxxxxxxxxxxxxxxxxxxxxxxxxxxxxxxxxxxxx xxxxxxxxxxxxxxxxxxxxx wants just two children. She says having both a large family and a job would be too much work!

Predictions:

1. What is the rest of the first paragraph about?

   _____

2. What is paragraph 2 about?

   _____

3. What is paragraph 3 about?

   _____

4. What is the rest of the last paragraph about?

   _____

➤ *Now turn the page and read the whole passage. How good were your predictions?*

Big Dreams for Blanca

Blanca Garcia lives and works in Oakland, California, but she was born in Ecuador. Her family came to the United States from Ecuador ten years ago. Blanca is now 19 years old. She has two sisters, Clara, 16, and Alba, 14, and a brother, Miguel, 10. Her father works in a restaurant and her mother works in a hospital.

Blanca finished high school last year, and now she works in a factory. The factory makes children's clothes. Blanca starts work early in the morning. Often she has to work extra hours in the afternoon. She doesn't really like the work, but she wants to save some money.

When she has enough money, she wants to go to college. She would like to be a nurse someday. She likes helping people, especially children. She hopes that she can work in a hospital for children.

Blanca also wants to have her own children. She has a boyfriend, but she doesn't want to get married now. She wants to go to college first. Then she would like to have a family. She wants just two children. She says having both a large family and a job would be too much work!

Guidelines for Previewing Short Passages

1. Read the title.

2. Look at the pictures (if there are any).

3. Read the first few sentences in the first paragraph.

4. Read the first line of the other paragraphs.

5. Read the last sentence of the last paragraph.

6. Watch for names, dates, and numbers.

Exercise 9

Previewing:

➤ *In this passage, read only the underlined parts. You have 30 seconds. Then make predictions about the parts you did not read.*

<u>Do Pigeons Take the Train?</u>

<u>Pigeons are smart birds. They are good at finding places. They can find their way home from many miles away. Scientists are not sure how pigeons know their way, but they do. They almost never get lost.</u>

<u>Can pigeons find their way under the ground?</u> Some passengers say that they see pigeons on the Underground trains. Rachel Robson says she saw a pigeon at Paddington Station. It got on the train and then got off again at the next stop.

<u>Some train lines are especially popular with pigeons.</u> They are often seen on the Northern and Picadilly lines. Lorna Read also sees pigeons at the Paddington Station. Once, a passenger tried to get a pigeon off the train. The pigeon flew back in just before the doors closed. It seemed all upset—like a person who doesn't want to miss the train.

<u>Why do pigeons get on the trains?</u> Some people say that the pigeons are not looking for food. They say the pigeons want to save time. London is a big city. The pigeons get tired of flying and they do what people do. They take the train. <u>What do the scientists think of this? They say they must have some more information—but anything is possible with pigeons!</u>

Predictions:

Talk about the passage with another student. Without looking back, can you say what it is about? When you agree, go back and read the passage again. How good were your predictions?

Exercise 10

Previewing:

➤ **In this passage, you must decide what parts to preview. Read only those parts.**
<u>**Do not read the whole passage!**</u> **You have 30 seconds. Then make predictions**
about the parts you did not read.

Thomas and the Gorillas

It was a hot summer day in Chicago. The Kemper family decided it was a
good day to go to the Brookfield Zoo. Janet and Kevin Kemper had two children:
Thomas, 3, and Sally, 6 months. Thomas loved going to the zoo. He liked
watching all the animals, but he especially loved the gorillas.

The Kempers went straight to the gorilla exhibit. There were six adult gorillas
and a three-month-old baby gorilla. In the Brookfield Zoo, the animals are not in
cages. They are in large areas dug out of the ground. These areas have fences
around them so the animals cannot get out and people cannot fall in.

But three-year-old boys are good climbers. While the Kempers were watching
the gorillas, little Sally started to cry. Kevin took her from Janet, and Janet looked
in her bag for a bottle of juice. In those few seconds, Thomas climbed up the
fence.

A woman saw him and shouted, "Stop him!" A tall man reached up to get
him, but it was too late. Thomas fell down the other side of the fence. He fell 18
feet onto the hard concrete floor. He lay very still, with blood on his head. Janet
and Kevin shouted for help. People crowded around the fence, and someone ran
to get a zoo worker.

But before the zoo worker arrived, a gorilla went over to Thomas. It was Binti
Jua, an eight-year-old mother gorilla. She had her baby gorilla on her back. With
one "arm" she picked up the little boy. She carried him carefully over to a door,
walking on three legs. There she put Thomas down so a zoo worker could get
him.

Janet and Kevin ran to the door, too. Thomas was badly hurt and had to go to
the hospital, but after a few days he was better. The story was on the evening
news in Chicago. Some people cheered and others cried when they heard it. But
many of them thought about that mother gorilla and asked themselves, "What is
she doing in a zoo? What is the difference between a gorilla and me?"

Predictions:
Talk about the passage with another student. Can you say what it is about? When
you agree, go back and read the passage again. How good were your predictions?

Building a Powerful Vocabulary

Building a powerful vocabulary means more than learning new words. It means learning new ways to think about words. In this unit you will learn some thinking skills that will help you guess the meaning of unknown words. Then you will learn how to use synonyms and pronouns to understand what you read.

Using the context to guess unknown words

What is the context?

The **context** is the sentence or sentences around a word. You can often guess the meaning of words you do not know by using the context. Use the context to guess which word belongs in each blank in the passage below.

EXAMPLE

➤ *First read the whole passage. Then go back and choose a word to write in each space. Show your work to another student. Do the two of you agree on the answers?*

Last week was Henry's birthday. He was 21 years old. His girlfriend bought

him a new _____. His brother and _____ gave him a
                (1)   (2)

party. Henry's mother made a special chocolate birthday _____, and
                                                       (3)

all of Henry's good friends came to his _____. They danced all
                                         (4)

_____. Henry really enjoyed his birthday.
      (5)

watch	cake	night	house	sister

➤ *Now check your answers below:*

(1) watch   (2) sister   (3) cake   (4) house   (5) night

Exercise 1

 First read the whole passage. Then go back and choose a word to write in each space. Show your work to another student. Do the two of you agree on the answers?

The Story of Helen Keller (1)

Helen Keller was a famous writer and speaker. She was born in 1880 and she died in 1968. She wrote _____ and articles about education
(1)
and politics. She _____ to every part of the world. But the
(2)
surprising fact about Helen Keller _____ this: She could not
(3)
see and she could _____ hear. In those days, blind and deaf
(4)
people _____ very closed and sad lives. But not Helen Keller. She
(5)
was a very special _____ .
(6)

person	books	traveled	was	not	had

Helen Keller

Exercise 2

➤ *First read the whole passage. Then go back and choose a word to write in each space. Show your work to another student. Do the two of you agree on the answers?*

The Story of Helen Keller (2)

Helen Keller _____ not always blind and deaf. She was all right
    (1)

_____ she was born on June 27, 1880. But she _____
  (2)   (3)

very sick the next year. After _____, she was not the same. Her
                                           (4)

_____ loved her and they tried to _____ care of her. But
  (5)   (6)

it was _____ easy. Her parents could not show _____
        (7)   (8)

what to do.

By the time Helen was six _____ old, her parents were
                                  (9)

very unhappy. _____ knew that Helen was very smart.
               (10)

_____ they could not teach her. They did _____ know
  (11)   (12)

what to do. But they knew they had to do _____.
                                             (13)

Often, Helen was not a nice child to be near. She did not know how to

_____ at the table. She made strange _____ like a bird.
  (14)   (15)

She sometimes hit _____ mother or her father. She often
                         (16)

_____ around the room and hurt herself.
  (17)

When Helen was seven, her parents decided _____ find help for
                                          (18)

her. They wrote to Michael Anagnos, a _____ in Boston. They asked
                                      (19)

him to _____ a teacher for Helen. He _____ to them
          (20)   (21)

and said: "I know _____ good teacher for Helen. Her name
                     (22)

_____ Annie Sullivan. I will send her to you."
  (23)

her	to	teacher	ran	find	wrote	a	But
when	that	take	became	her	years	was	noises
is	parents	not	They	not	something	eat	

Exercise 3

➤ *First read the whole passage. Then go back and choose a word to write in each space. Show your work to another student. Do the two of you agree on the answers?*

The Story of Helen Keller (3)

The Kellers were very pleased. They _____ (1) a good teacher for Helen. Then _____ (2) could learn and they could all _____ (3) happy. The teacher could show Helen _____ (4) to do. She could teach Helen _____ (5) read and to talk.

Annie Sullivan finally came to the Keller _____ (6). She came by train from Boston. Helen's _____ (7) and father tried to tell Helen _____ (8) Annie was her friend. They could _____ (9) make her understand.

_____ (10) was hard to know what Helen _____ (11). She could not see and she _____ (12) not hear. So she could not _____ (13) the world. No one knew how _____ (14) tell her things. And she could _____ (15) tell things to anyone else.

Annie began to _____ (16) care of Helen. She tried to _____ (17) her. She showed Helen the names _____ (18) things. She wrote the words on _____ (19) hands. But Helen did not understand. _____ (20) began to feel hopeless.

Annie	take	could	that	what	be	mother
thought	not	Helen's	of	to	It	to
home	she	teach	know	not	wanted	

Exercise 4

➤ *In this exercise, you must think of the missing words. First read the whole passage. Then go back and write a word in each space. Show your work to another student. Do the two of you agree on the answers?*

The Story of Helen Keller (4)

One day, Annie was trying to teach Helen. They went for a walk, and

_____ came to a well. Helen was _____ warm and
          (1)   (2)

thirsty. Annie put Helen's hand _____ the water. She took a
                                          (3)

_____ and gave Helen a drink. Helen _____ glad to
          (4)   (5)

have a cool drink.

_____ Annie took Helen's hand. She used her _____
          (6)   (7)

to write "W A T E R" on Helen's _____. Suddenly, Helen understood!
                                          (8)

She knew that _____ was telling her something. The feeling
                    (9)

_____ her hand was the name for _____! Helen was
          (10)   (11)

very happy. She _____ excited. Now she could find out the
                          (12)

_____ of everything.
          (13)

The next year, Annie Sullivan took Helen _____ Boston. They
                                                     (14)

stayed with Michael Anagnos. _____ went to a special school. She
                                          (15)

_____ how to speak and how to "listen" _____ her
          (16)   (17)

hands. She learned to read _____ with her fingers. Then she was
                                    (18)

_____ to go to another school, _____ New York. Annie
          (19)   (20)

and Helen went to New York, _____ Helen went to the Gilman
                                      (21)

School.

Exercise 5

➤ *In this exercise, you must think of the missing words. First read the whole passage.*
Then go back and write a word in each space. Show your work to another student.
Do the two of you agree on the answers?

The Story of Helen Keller (5)

Soon Helen was 19 years old. _____ was time for her to go
(1)

_____ college. She took an examination for Radcliffe, a famous
(2)

_____ in Massachusetts. Helen was a _____ student.
(3) (4)

She passed the examination. She _____ to Radcliffe, and she
(5)

_____ in 1904.
(6)

Annie and Helen stayed _____. Helen wrote a book about
(7)

_____ life. It was called *The Story of My Life*. She _____
(8) (9)

wrote many other books. Some of _____ books became movies.
(10)

Annie _____ Helen traveled to England, Scotland, Greece,
(11)

and other _____. Helen visited almost every part of the
(12)

_____. She tried to help other _____ people. She also
(13) (14)

tried to _____ poor people and she tried to _____ wars.
(15) (16)

Helen _____ that her life was happy because _____
(17) (18)

Annie Sullivan. She loved Annie, and _____ wrote a book about
(19)

her called *Teacher*. _____ is the name that Helen used for
(20)

_____ all of her life. Helen Keller died in June 1968.
(21)

Guessing meaning from context

When you want to understand a new word, use the context. It can tell you a lot about a new word. It can tell you what kind of word it is—noun, verb, adjective, adverb, etc. It can also give you some idea of the meaning of the word. Then you do not have to stop and look in a dictionary. You can read much more quickly this way and you can understand better.

When you do the following exercises, you should work alone. Do not use a dictionary, and do not ask other students or the teacher about the words. Try to guess the answers from the context. When you finish the exercises, check your answers in the Answer Key or a dictionary.

EXAMPLE

➤ *Read the sentences below and guess the meaning of "glue." Write the meaning in English. It does not have to be exact. A general meaning is okay.*

I can't find the glue. Do you know where it is? I used it yesterday to put together a broken cup. Now I need to fix this broken toy. I can't do it without the glue.

What is "glue"?

_____

➤ *Now check your answer:*

"Glue" is something we use to put together or fix broken things.

Exercise 6

➤ *In the following sentences there is a word you probably do not know. Use the context to guess the general meaning of the word. Write the general meaning in English.*

1. The kettle was always on the stove. Now Polly filled it with water and turned on the stove. She wanted to make some tea.

   What is a "kettle"?

   _____

2. Marjorie liked to knit a lot. She knitted warm wool sweaters for her children. She knitted socks and hats, too.

   What does "knit" mean?

   _____

3. A lot of Greek art shows <u>nude</u> men and women. The Greeks believed that the human body was beautiful. They wanted to show the human body in their art.

   What does "nude" mean?

   _____

4. That's not true! You're a liar. You didn't see a fish in the swimming pool. It's not possible! There aren't any fish in the swimming pool!

   What is a "liar"?

   _____

5. George was standing by the closed door. He was very tired, so he started to <u>lean</u> against the door. Suddenly, the door opened and George almost fell into Lily's arms.

   What does "lean" mean?

   _____

6. That poor horse is lame. Last year he stepped in a hole and broke his leg. Now he is better, but he still can't run.

   What is a "lame" horse?

   _____

➤ *Now check the meanings of the words in a dictionary.*

Exercise 7

➤ *For each item, guess the general meaning of the word from the context. Write the general meaning in English.*

1. When the war started, many people left Rwanda. They lived in big refugee camps in Zaire and Burundi. Life was hard for the refugees in these camps.

   What is a "refugee"?

   _____

2. I bought a new stamp for my brother. In his free time, he likes to collect stamps. He has stamps from all over the world.

   What does "collect" mean?

   _____

3. Mr. Hudson's secretary was a very thorough person. He always did his work carefully, and he never forgot anything.

   What is a "thorough" person?

   _____

4. Don't eat that bread! It's old and stale. We'll give it to the birds. Here's some fresh bread for our sandwiches.

   What is "stale" bread?

   _____

5. Timmy's clothes were full of purple stains. It happened every time he drank grape juice. Some juice always fell on his shirt and pants.

   What is a "stain"?

   _____

6. Mrs. Sweeny was ready to retire from her job. She was 65 years old, she was tired of working, and she wanted to have more time at home.

   What does "retire" mean?

   _____

➤ *Now check the meanings of the words in a dictionary.*

Exercise 8

➤ *For each item, guess the general meaning of the word from the context. Write the general meaning in English.*

1. George often boasts about how well he can play tennis. He says he can beat any of us! He thinks he's the best tennis player in town!

   What does "boast" mean?

   _____

2. I sat down on the grass to rest. Then I felt something on my leg. It was a little black ant. There were many more of them near my foot. I jumped up quickly.

   What is an "ant"?

   _____

3. Jimmy's medicine had a nasty taste. He took it the first time, but he didn't want to take it again. His mother had to put some sugar in it.

   What is a "nasty" taste?

   _____

4. You can get to Jarrod's Island by small boat taxis or by ferry. The ferry can also carry cars. In good weather, it takes about half an hour.

   What is a "ferry"?

   _____

5. One stormy night a fishing boat crashed into some rocks. All the people on the boat perished. No one ever found their bodies.

   What does "perish" mean?

   _____

6. Miriam was enthusiastic about dancing. She loved her dance classes, and she told everyone she wanted to be a dancer.

   What does "enthusiastic" mean?

   _____

➤ *Now check the meanings of the words in a dictionary.*

Exercise 9

 For each item, guess the general meaning of the word from the context. Write the general meaning in English.

1. Sir Cavendish stood with his head held high. The King was very angry. "Why are you on your feet?" he shouted. "You must get down on your knees before the King!"

   What does "knees" mean?

   _____

2. My mother was an absentminded person. She was always thinking about something else, so she often forgot things. One day, she went to work with her slippers on!

   What is an "absentminded" person?

   _____

3. We brought our boat into the harbor just before the storm started. It was a small harbor, and it was crowded with other boats. But it was safe from the strong winds.

   What is a "harbor"?

   _____

4. The exam had a few difficult parts. But on the whole, it was not hard and almost all the students did well.

   What does "on the whole" mean?

   _____

5. The tall woman caught Sally by her arm. Sally tried to get away, but the woman had a strong grip and held onto her arm.

   What does "grip" mean?

   _____

6. Look at all the rust on your bicycle! I think you left it outside in the rain. Now you should clean and oil it.

   What is "rust"?

   _____

Now check the meanings of the words in a dictionary.

Exercise 10

➤ *In this passage the underlined words may be new to you. Read the whole passage. Use the context to guess the meaning of the words you do not know. Do not use a dictionary and do not ask anyone about the words.*

Ballooning

The first kind of air <u>transportation</u> was not a plane. It was a <u>balloon</u>. People traveled by balloon 100 years before there were planes or jet <u>aircraft</u>. Those early days of ballooning were exciting, but they were also dangerous. Sometimes the balloons fell suddenly. Sometimes they burned. However, the danger did not stop
5 the <u>balloonists</u>.

The first real balloon flight was in France in 1783. Two Frenchmen, the Montgolfier brothers, made a balloon. They filled a very large paper bag with hot air. Hot air is lighter than cold air, so it goes up. The Montgolfiers' hot air balloon went up 1,000 feet in the sky.

10 Later that same year, two other Frenchmen <u>ascended</u> in a basket under a balloon. They built a fire under the balloon to make the air hot. This made the balloon stay up in the air for a few hours. But their balloon was tied to the ground. So it could not go anywhere.

The first free balloon flight was in December, 1783. The balloon flew for 25
15 minutes over Paris. It traveled about 5 1/2 miles. Flying a balloon is not like flying a plane. The balloon has no engine and therefore no power of its own. The wind directs the balloon. It goes where the wind blows. The <u>pilot</u> can <u>control</u> only the <u>altitude</u> of the balloon. He or she can raise and lower the balloon to find the right wind direction. That is how a good pilot controls where the
20 balloon goes.

Soon balloonists tried longer flights. A <u>major</u> event in the history of ballooning was the first long flight over water. In 1785, an American and a Frenchman flew over the English Channel. They left England on a cold, clear January day. After about an hour, their balloon began to <u>descend</u> toward the
25 water. They threw out some <u>equipment</u> and food to make the balloon lighter. The balloon continued to fall, so they threw out almost everything in the basket—even some of their clothes. Finally, after about three hours, they landed in France, cold but safe.

During the nineteenth century, ballooning became a popular sport. There
30 were balloon races in Europe. Balloons were also used by scientists to study the air and by armies in wartime. After the airplane was <u>invented</u>, people lost interest in balloons. Planes were much faster and easier to control. But some people today still like to go up in balloons. High up in the balloon basket, they find quiet. They have a wonderful view of the world below.

➤ **A. Now you can check the meanings of the underlined words in the passage. The underlined words are in Column 1. The meanings are in Column 2. Write the letter of the best meaning after each word. You may look back at the passage. Work with another student.**

Column 1

1. transportation _____
2. balloon _____
3. aircraft _____
4. balloonist _____
5. ascend _____
6. pilot _____
7. control _____
8. altitude _____
9. major _____
10. descend _____
11. equipment _____
12. invent _____

Column 2

a. important
b. distance above the earth
c. way of traveling
d. a vehicle for traveling by air
e. go down
f. person who flies a plane or balloon
g. special things you need to do something
h. someone who travels in a balloon
i. go up
j. make for the first time
k. a bag full of air
l. make something do what you want it to do

➤ **B. Circle the best ending to complete each of the following sentences about the passage. You may look back at the passage.**

1. The first kind of air travel was in
   a. a jet plane.
   b. an aircraft.
   c. a balloon.
   d. a ship.

2. Many early balloonists lived in
   a. England.
   b. the United States.
   c. Italy.
   d. France.

3. The balloon rises if the air inside gets
   a. colder.
   b. hotter.
   c. out.
   d. descended.

4. One way to control a balloon is to
   a. use the engine.
   b. find the right wind direction.
   c. ask the pilot.
   d. not change altitude.

5. People stopped using balloons for air travel because
   a. balloons are dangerous.
   b. balloons are not comfortable.
   c. it is not fun
   d. planes are easier to control.

Exercise 11

➤ *Read the whole passage. Use the context to guess the meaning of the underlined words you do not know. Do not use a dictionary and do not ask anyone about the words.*

The Story of Photography

In 1826, a Frenchman named Niepce needed pictures for his business. But he was not a good artist. So he invented a very simple camera. He put it in a window of his house and took a picture of his yard. That was the first photograph.

The next important date in the history of photography was 1837. That year,
5 Daguerre, another Frenchman, took a picture of his <u>studio</u>. He used a new kind of camera and a different <u>process</u>. In his pictures, you could see everything clearly, even the smallest <u>details</u>. This kind of photograph was called a *daguerreotype*.

Soon, other people began to use Daguerre's process. Travelers brought back daguerreotypes from all around the world. People photographed famous
10 buildings, cities, and mountains.

In about 1840, the process was <u>improved</u>. Then photographers could take pictures of people and moving things. The process was not simple. The photographers had to carry lots of film and processing equipment. But this did not stop the photographers, especially in the United States. After 1840,
15 daguerreotype artists were popular in most cities.

Matthew Brady was one well-known American photographer. He took many <u>portraits</u> of famous people. The portraits were unusual because they were lifelike and full of <u>personality</u>. Brady was also the first person to take pictures of a war. His 1862 Civil War pictures showed dead soldiers and <u>ruined</u> cities. They made
20 the war seem more real and more terrible.

In the 1880s, new inventions began to change photography. Photographers could buy film ready-made in rolls. So they did not have to make the film themselves. Also, they did not have to process the film <u>immediately</u>. They could bring it back to their studios and <u>develop</u> it later. They did not have to carry lots
25 of equipment. And finally, the invention of the small handheld camera made photography less expensive.

With the small camera, anyone could be a photographer. People began to use cameras just for fun. They took pictures of their families, friends, and favorite places. They called these pictures "snapshots."
30 <u>Documentary</u> photographs became popular in newspapers in the 1890s. Soon magazines and books also used them. These pictures showed true events and people. They were much more real than drawings.

Some people also began to think of photography as a <u>form</u> of art. They thought that photography could do more than show the real world. It could also
35 show ideas and feelings, like other art forms.

A. The underlined words from the passage are in Column 1. The meanings are in Column 2. Write the letter of the best meaning after each word. You may look back at the passage. Work with another student.

Column 1	Column 2
1. studio ___f___	a. a way of doing something
2. process ___a___	b. what makes people who they are
3. details ___i___	c. completely fallen down, useless
4. improve ___H___	d. showing how things really are
5. portraits ___j___	e. kind or type
6. personality ___b___	f. a place for artists and photographers to work
7. ruined ___c___	g. change film into photographs
8. immediately ___k___	h. make better
9. develop ___g___	i. small, important parts
10. documentary ___d___	j. pictures of people
11. form ___e___	k. without waiting, right away

B. Circle the best ending to complete each of the following sentences about the passage. You may look back at the passage.

1. The first photograph was taken with
   a. a small handheld camera.
   b. a daguerreotype.
   c. a very simple camera.
   d. new film.

2. The story of photography
   a. began in the sixteenth century.
   b. began in France.
   c. is unknown.
   d. began in the United States.

3. Matthew Brady was well known for
   a. inventing daguerreotypes.
   b. taking pictures of French cities.
   c. portraits and war photographs.
   d. the small handheld camera.

4. The new inventions in photography made it possible for
   a. Brady to take pictures of the Civil War.
   b. anyone to be a photographer.
   c. only rich people to take pictures.
   d. people to use daguerreotypes.

5. Photography can also be an art form, because photographers can
   a. take photographs to show the real world.
   b. make documentaries.
   c. show ideas and feelings in photographs.
   d. copy old pictures.

Using pronouns and synonyms

Writers do not use the same word many times. That would be boring for the reader. So writers often use other words that mean the same thing, like pronouns or synonyms. These small words help tie ideas together when you read.

Pronouns

Sometimes **pronouns** are used instead of nouns. They are small words, but they are very important when you are reading. You will understand more of what you read if you pay attention to pronouns.

Some pronouns

I	we	you	he	she	it	they
him	her	them	that	this	these	those

In the following examples, the pronouns are underlined:

EXAMPLE A

Mary Simms lives in New York City. <u>She</u> has an apartment near Central Park. Mary jogs in the park. <u>She</u> thinks that jogging is good for <u>her</u>. So <u>she</u> jogs three times a week.

All the underlined pronouns take the place of the noun "Mary Simms." The noun "Mary Simms" is called the **referent,** because the pronouns refer back to it.

EXAMPLE B

Jogging is good for your health for a few reasons. <u>It</u> is especially good for your heart. If you do <u>it</u> a few days a week, your heart will be stronger. <u>It</u> is also good for your legs. And many people believe <u>it</u> is good for your mind.

All of the underlined pronouns take the place of the noun "jogging." "Jogging" is the referent.

EXAMPLE C

Swimming and bicycling are also popular sports. People like <u>them</u> because <u>they</u> are easy to do. Yet <u>these</u> are sports which help people make their hearts and lungs stronger. <u>They</u> are also good because <u>they</u> are not dangerous, and people can enjoy <u>them</u> with friends.

All of the underlined pronouns take the place of the phrase "swimming and bicycling." "Swimming and bicycling" is the referent.

Exercise 12

➤ *In each of the following sentences, the pronoun is underlined. Circle the referent.*

1. Running is not a new sport. People were doing <u>it</u> hundreds of years ago.

2. Runners know that a good diet is important. <u>They</u> eat healthy foods, especially before a race.

3. During a race, people along the road give water to the runners. <u>This</u> helps keep the runners from becoming too thirsty.

4. In Kenya and other parts of Africa, running is part of everyday life. <u>It</u> is a usual way for people to travel.

5. Many Africans are good runners. <u>They</u> often win marathons and races in the Olympics.

6. In some races, the winners get large amounts of money. <u>That</u> is a good reason to try to win.

Exercise 13

In this passage, the pronouns are underlined. Write the pronouns and their referents on the lines below.

The Boston Marathon

Every year, in the middle of April, thousands of people go to Boston. <u>They</u> go to run the Boston Marathon. <u>This</u> is one of the oldest road races in the United States. <u>It</u> began in 1897.

Each year, more runners join the Boston Marathon. <u>They</u> come from every
5 part of the world. In 1996, 38,708 runners from almost every country in the world ran in the Marathon. About 35,810 of <u>them</u> finished <u>it</u>.

The Boston race is 26.2 miles, or 42 kilometers. <u>It</u> starts in Hopkinton, Massachusetts, and ends in the center of Boston. The runners go through 13 more towns during the race. Crowds of people watch <u>them</u> as <u>they</u> go through
10 the towns. The people cheer for <u>them</u> and hand <u>them</u> water.

Pronouns	Referents
_____	_____
_____	_____
_____	_____
_____	_____
_____	_____
_____	_____
_____	_____
_____	_____
_____	_____
_____	_____

Exercise 14

➤ *In this passage, the pronouns are underlined. Write the pronouns and their referents on the lines below.*

Jogging

Jogging is a popular activity in New York City. In the winter, the weather is too cold for <u>it</u>. But in the spring, <u>it</u> is warmer, and many New Yorkers go out to jog in Central Park. <u>This</u> is a good place to run.

Other New Yorkers also like to go to Central Park. Many of <u>them</u> go there with
5 their dogs. Dogs can run in the park. Sometimes the dogs run after the joggers.
<u>They</u> may try to bite <u>them</u>. So the joggers sometimes kick the dogs or throw stones at <u>them</u>. The dog owners do not understand. <u>They</u> wonder why the joggers do not like dogs. The park police are trying to solve the problem. <u>They</u> want all of the people to use the park in peace.

Pronouns   *Referents*

_____   _____

_____   _____

_____   _____

_____   _____

_____   _____

_____   _____

_____   _____

_____   _____

Exercise 15

➤ *There are 18 pronouns in this passage. Write them and their referents below.*

Joggers and Dogs in Central Park

Mary Simms and Jim Fuller went jogging in Central Park last Saturday. They ran into a problem: a large white dog. It ran after them and tried to bite their legs.

They were scared and did not know what to do. Mary picked up a big stick
5 and showed it to the dog. She wanted to scare it away, but the dog just barked at her. Then Jim threw a large rock at the animal. It hit the dog on the head.

The dog's owner was angry. "Stop hurting my dog!" she shouted. "It will not hurt you. It is just a puppy."

Then she took a large stick and tried to hit Mary and Jim.
10 Just then, a park police officer came along the path. He saw them fighting. "This is terrible!" he said. "Stop fighting!"

Pronouns   Referents

_____   _____

_____   _____

_____   _____

_____   _____

_____   _____

_____   _____

_____   _____

_____   _____

_____   _____

_____   _____

_____   _____

_____   _____

_____   _____

_____   _____

_____   _____

_____   _____

More about pronouns

Sometimes pronouns can take the place of a group of words.

EXAMPLE

The city park police officer often meets dangerous people. Some people go to the park to steal. Other people are there to sell drugs. Sometimes people start serious gunfights in the park. The park police officer may meet any of <u>these</u> in the park.

Pronoun　　　　　*Referent*

these　　　　　　　people who steal, sell drugs, or start gunfights

Exercise 16

　The pronouns in these passages are underlined. Circle the referents.

1. Two Frenchmen went up in a basket under a balloon. <u>They</u> built a fire to make the air hot. <u>This</u> made the balloon stay up in the air.

2. The pilot of a balloon can control its altitude. <u>He</u> or <u>she</u> can raise and lower the balloon to find the right wind direction. <u>That</u> is how a good pilot can control where the balloon goes.

3. Early photographers had to carry film and heavy equipment everywhere <u>they</u> went. But <u>this</u> did not stop them.

4. Helen Keller was deaf and blind. <u>She</u> could not speak until <u>she</u> was seven years old. <u>That</u> did not stop her. <u>She</u> became a famous writer and teacher.

5. A tornado is a dangerous storm. <u>It</u> brings strong winds, and <u>it</u> travels very fast. The strong winds can turn over cars, destroy houses, and kill people. And <u>this</u> happens in just a few minutes.

6. Tornadoes blow dust and dirt into the air. <u>They</u> make a cone shape in the sky. When people see <u>this</u>, <u>they</u> get ready for the storm.

7. When tornadoes touch the ground, <u>they</u> move along at about 35 to 45 kilometers per hour. No one knows which way <u>they</u> will go.

8. In a small town, a tornado can destroy an entire street of homes and stores. Many families lose their homes. The government tries to help <u>them</u> when <u>this</u> happens.

9. Tornadoes are common in Kansas, Arkansas, Nebraska, Iowa, and Missouri. People in <u>those</u> states worry when <u>they</u> see a cone-shaped cloud in the sky. <u>It</u> tells <u>them</u> a tornado is coming.

10. The wind of a tornado is strong. No one knows exactly how fast <u>it</u> is in the center. The wind always breaks the machines used to measure <u>it</u>!

Synonyms: General and specific

Synonyms are different words or phrases that refer to the same idea. They are another way for an author to tie ideas together. You can understand more if you pay attention to these words. Read the following sentences:

> The Pope visited Colombia, Peru, and Mexico last year. Crowds of Catholics greeted him in <u>these countries</u>. It was his first visit to <u>that part of the world</u>.

"These countries" is a synonym for Colombia, Peru, and Mexico. "That part of the world" is another synonym for Colombia, Peru, and Mexico.

1. **Specific:** "Colombia, Peru, and Mexico"
2. **Less specific:** "these countries"
3. **General:** "that part of the world"

Exercise 17

➤ *Put the following synonyms in order from specific to general. Write "1" above the most specific word. Write "2" above the less specific word. Write "3" above the most general word.*

EXAMPLE

2   1   3
company, IBM Corporation, organization

1. music, rock music, twentieth-century music

2. Japanese mountain, Mount Fuji, mountain

3. problems, water pollution problems, pollution problems

4. pine tree, evergreen tree, tree

5. musicians, Sting, popular musicians

6. Nicaragua, country, Central American country

7. man, Dr. Diamond, dentist

8. place, Boston, city

9. The *New York Times,* newspaper, reading material

10. group, Diamond family, people

11. storm, tornado, windstorm

12. president, person, political leader

13. shirt, white shirt, clothing

14. flute, musical instrument, wind instrument

15. jet plane, Boeing 737, air transportation

Exercise 18

➤ *In each passage, there is a word underlined. Find and circle the synonym(s) for it in the passage.*

EXAMPLE   Liz and Jeff moved to <u>Paris</u> last month. They like the (city) very much.

1. Chrys was born in London, but she lives in <u>Glasgow</u> now. She has learned to love Scotland. It is her new homeland.

2. Hiroko plays the <u>violin</u> in the Boston Symphony Orchestra. The sound of this stringed instrument is very special.

3. The president of the city council gave a long speech. As the <u>leader</u>, she has to plan many new projects.

4. The <u>tornado</u> hit a small town in Kansas. The storm swept down the main street. The terrible winds caused five stores to fall down.

5. Lemons, limes, and oranges are all delicious to eat. These <u>citrus fruits</u> are also healthy for you. They are a good source of vitamin C.

6. Many Americans skip <u>breakfast</u>. They say they do not have time for food in the morning. This is a mistake. The human body needs that meal.

7. Joanne's big car uses a lot of <u>gasoline</u>. She has to stop often to fill the tank with fuel.

8. We saw a lion with three little cubs at the wild animal park. The <u>cats</u> were lying on the rocks in the warm afternoon sun. We were happy to see such wonderful animals in such a nice place.

9. In some countries, the <u>winter</u> is long and cold. It is not a popular season. Some people are so unhappy at that time of the year that they get sick.

10. Astronauts all have one problem: They get <u>motion sickness</u>. This illness makes it difficult to do their work. Doctors and scientists are working on this problem.

Learning to Look for the Topic

What is a topic?

A **topic** is a word or phrase (a few words) which tells what something is about. For example, a friend may ask you, "What is this book about?" Your friend doesn't want to know everything about the book. He or she just wants to know the topic.

In this unit, you will learn to look for the topic when you read. The topic is the key to understanding what you read. It also helps you remember. A good reader always asks, "What is this about? What is the topic?"

 In the groups of words below, one of the words is the topic for all the other words. Circle the topic and write it on the line.

EXAMPLE A

Sometimes the topic is the name of a group of things.

 Which word is the topic?

| football | baseball | tennis | (sports) | skiing |

The topic is __sports__. (The other words are names of sports.)

| red | purple | color | green | yellow | blue |

The topic is __collor__.

EXAMPLE B

Sometimes the topic is the name of something with many parts.

➤ *Which word is the topic?*

France	Germany	Italy	(Europe)	Belgium	Austria

The topic is _Europe_ . (The other words are parts of Europe.)

nose	ears	eyes	mouth	head	chin

The topic is _____ .

➤ *Work with another student on the exercises in Unit Four. Ask each other, "What is this about? What is the topic?"*

Finding the topic

Exercise 1

➤ *Circle the topic in each group of words. Some of the topics are names of groups of things. Other topics are the names of things with many parts. Do not use the dictionary. If you do not know the meaning of a word, try to guess it. Work with another student.*

1. | mother | sister | uncle | grandmother | aunt | family |
   |--------|--------|-------|-------------|------|--------|
   | | | father | grandfather | | |

2. | nine | sixteen | number | four | seventy-seven |
   |------|---------|--------|------|---------------|
   | | fifteen | eighty | thirty-two | |

3. | dog | cat | elephant | lion | animal | horse | camel | mouse |
   |-----|-----|----------|------|--------|-------|-------|-------|

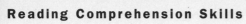

4. | bedroom | bathroom | house | diningroom | kitchen |
   | cellar | hall | livingroom |

5. | table | chairs | refrigerator | oven | microwave |
   | kitchen | stove | sink |

6. | New York | Paris | Rome | Moscow | Tokyo |
   | Beijing | Los Angeles | City |

7. | bread | fruit | milk | butter | food |
   | cheese | meat | vegetables |

8. | music | food | people | party | laughing |
   | dancing | games | singing |

9. | table | furniture | chair | chest | bed |
   | bookcase | desk | sofa |

10. | shirt | skirt | suit | clothes | sweater |
    | dress | pants | blouse |

Exercise 2

➤ *Circle the topic in each group of words. Some of the topics are names of groups of things. Other topics are the names of things with many parts. Do not use the dictionary. If you do not know the meaning of a word, try to guess it. Work with another student.*

1.   milk   cola   coffee   drink   cocoa
     orange juice   water   tea

2.   dollar   quarter   half-dollar   nickel   money
     penny   dime   silver dollar

3.   subway   metro   bus   airplane   train
     travel   boat   ship

4.   wheels   engine   windows   seats   doors
     car   brakes   tires

5.   river   lake   water   ocean   sea
     well   pond   swimming pool

6.   teacher   students   books   classroom   pens
     notebooks   pencils   desks

7.   doctor   nurse   hospital   beds   patients
     x-rays   medicine   lab

8.	happy	sad	<u>feeling</u>	angry	nervous
		proud	excited	bored	

9.	diskette	keyboard	hard drive	monitor	<u>computer</u>
		mouse	software	modem	

10.	oxygen	nitrogen	helium	argon	neon
		hydrogen	gas	radon	

Working with topics

Exercise 3

➤ *Think of words for these topics. Write the words on the lines below. Then talk to another student about his or her words. Are they the same as yours?*

1. TOPIC: Good foods in my country

_____

_____

_____

_____

_____

2. TOPIC: Important places in my country or city

_____

_____

_____

_____

_____

3. TOPIC: Reasons for learning English

_____

_____

_____

_____

_____

4. TOPIC: _____

(Now you write the topic.)

_____

_____

_____

_____

_____

Writing the topic

Exercise 4

➤ *Read all the words in each group. What is the topic? Write it on the line. Work with another student.*

EXAMPLE

| knife | fork | spoon | cup | bowl | glass | dish | chopsticks |

TOPIC: _Things for eating_

1.

| Venezuela | Mongolia | Mexico | China | Canada | Germany |

TOPIC: _____

2. | hospital | factory | library | school | hotel | bank |

TOPIC: _____

3. | table of contents | index | title page | chapters | cover | pages |

TOPIC: _____

4. | French | Greek | Japanese | English | Arabic | Chinese |

TOPIC: _____

5. | physics | chemistry | astronomy | biology |
   | geology | biochemistry |

TOPIC: _____

6. | cheese | milk | ice cream | butter | cream | yogurt |

TOPIC: _____

7. | morning | afternoon | noon | midnight | dusk | evening |

TOPIC: _____

8. | gymnastics | swimming | soccer | running |
   | diving | horseback riding |

TOPIC: _____

Exercise 5

➤ *Read all the words in each group. What is the topic? Write it on the line. Work with another student.*

1. | Amazon   Ganges   Danube   Tigris   Nile   Yangtze |

TOPIC: _____

2. | doctor   orderly   lab technician   nurse   receptionist   patient |

TOPIC: _____

3. | yen   deutschmark   dollar   franc   lira   ruble |

TOPIC: _____

4. | bridge   road   highway   street   turnpike   avenue |

TOPIC: _____

5. | Colorado   New Mexico   California   Massachusetts
                    Iowa   Florida |

TOPIC: _____

6. | homesickness   joy   anger   sadness   pride   fear |

TOPIC: _____

7.

| Kennedy | Truman | Reagan | Carter | Bush | Lincoln |

TOPIC: _____

8.

| war | hunger | sickness | many poor people | few jobs |
no money for school

TOPIC: _____

Exercise 6

➤ *Read the words in each group. One word does not belong with the others. Cross out the word that does not belong. Then write the topic on the line. Work with another student.*

EXAMPLE

| bicycle | motorcycle | car | ~~ship~~ | van | bus | truck |

TOPIC: _Ways to travel on land_____

1.

| Boston | New York | Chicago | Paris | San Francisco | Los Angeles |

TOPIC: _____

2.

| teacher | chalk | students | books | ice cream | pens |

TOPIC: _____

3. | hat | gloves | bathing suit | scarf | mittens | jacket |

TOPIC: _____

4. | February | April | March | June | January | Tuesday |

TOPIC: _____

5. | ice cream | cake | carrots | pie | cookies | candy |

TOPIC: _____

6. | sailor | scientist | secretary | husband | doctor | taxi driver |

TOPIC: _____

7. | box | bag | pocket | table | back pack | basket |

TOPIC: _____

8. | roof | wall | tree | window | door | floor |

TOPIC: _____

Finding two topics

Exercise 7

➤ *You can divide each group of words into two topics. Write the two topics. Then write the words under the topics. Work with another student.*

EXAMPLE

ladder	concert	opera	movie	stairs	TV
	elevator	play	movie escalator		

Topic A   <u>Ways to go up</u>

      <u>ladder</u>

      <u>elevator</u>

      <u>stairs</u>

      <u>escalator</u>

Topic B   <u>Things to watch for fun</u>

      <u>movie</u>

      <u>play</u>

      <u>opera</u>

      <u>TV</u>

      <u>concert</u>

1.

Zimbabwe	Buddhist	Ethiopia	Catholic	Muslim	Jew
Nigeria	Christian	Zambia	Kenya		

Topic A _____

_____

_____

_____

_____

Topic B _____

_____

_____

_____

_____

2.

dog	ocean	lake	elephant	horse	cow	camel
	river	stream	canal	sea	cat	

Topic A _____   Topic B _____

_____   _____

_____   _____

_____   _____

_____   _____

_____   _____

3.

California	Australia	Arizona	Ireland	Washington	Oregon
	Scotland	England	Nevada	Canada	

Topic A _____   Topic B _____

_____   _____

_____   _____

_____   _____

_____   _____

(continued on the next page)

4.

hour	bang	boom	tick	minute	thud	roar	month
	day	screech	year	century			

Topic A _____   Topic B _____

_____   _____

_____   _____

_____   _____

_____   _____

_____   _____

_____   _____

5.

cold	windy	snow	mountain	ice	hill	river	sleet
		valley	lake				

Topic A _____   Topic B _____

_____   _____

_____   _____

_____   _____

_____   _____

_____   _____

Exercise 8

➤ *You can divide each group of words into two topics. Write the two topics. Then write the words under the topics. Work with another student.*

1.

chair	table	book	bookcase	magazine	newspaper
	bed	desk	letter	map	

Topic A _____   Topic B _____

_____   _____

_____   _____

_____   _____

_____   _____

2.

rain	clouds	sun	stars	snow	hail	moon	thunder
		planet	comet				

Topic A _____   Topic B _____

_____   _____

_____   _____

_____   _____

_____   _____

(continued on the next page)

3.

| chest | arm | penicillin | leg | aspirin | quinine |
| antihistamine | | tetracycline | | hip | neck |

Topic A _____   Topic B _____

_____   _____

_____   _____

_____   _____

_____   _____

_____   _____

4.

| cotton | nucleus | wool | nylon | neutron | proton |
| | | electron | linen | | |

Topic A _____   Topic B _____

_____   _____

_____   _____

_____   _____

_____   _____

5.

| jazz | classical | drum | accordion | folk | trumpet | clarinet |
| | | rock | blues | piano | | |

Topic A _____   Topic B _____

_____   _____

_____   _____

_____   _____

_____   _____

Understanding Paragraphs

What is a paragraph?

A **paragraph** is a group of sentences. All the sentences in a paragraph are about one topic.

   In this unit, you will first learn how to find the topic of a paragraph. Then you will learn how to find the main idea of a paragraph. The topic and the main idea are important. They help you to understand meaning quickly, and they help you remember what you read.

Exercise 1

➤   *Read each group of sentences and decide whether all the sentences in the group are about one topic. Is the group of sentences a paragraph? Check Yes or No.*

1.   Paragraph?   Yes____ No____

It is easy to make a good cup of tea.
The first people to grow coffee beans lived in the Middle East.
Most of the oranges for juice grow in Florida.
That is how people in other parts of the world learned about rice.
Cover the pot and wait a few minutes.

2.   Paragraph?   Yes____ No____

A doctor's job is not easy.
Doctors often spend many hours with patients.
There are usually more patients waiting.
So doctors do not have much free time during the day.
They often have to work all night in the hospital, too.

3.   Paragraph?   Yes____   No____

In the United States, sports stars make a lot of money.

It is not unusual for a basketball player to get $6 million a year.

Some baseball players are also paid millions of dollars.

These sports stars also get extra money from sporting equipment companies.

For example, sneaker manufacturers pay sports stars to wear the sneakers they
    make.

4.   Paragraph?   Yes____   No____

In some countries, students can go to college for free.

It is often difficult to get a good job in a small town.

The populations of most countries are growing quickly.

Many families have five or six children.

In the winter, there is always a lot of snow in Maine.

Choosing the best topic

A good reader always asks, "What is this paragraph about? What is the topic?"

EXAMPLE

➤ *Read this paragraph. Ask yourself, "What is it about?"*

Mexico City is a popular place for tourists. Every year thousands of people go
to Mexico City. They visit the old and beautiful buildings. In Mexico City's
museums, they learn about the history of Mexico. In the restaurants, they enjoy
the spicy and delicious Mexican food.

➤ *What is the topic? Circle it. Then write "too specific" or "too general" after the other
two topics.*

    a. Mexican food   _____*too specific*_____

    b. Mexico   _____*too general*_____

    c. (Mexico City)   _____

The best choice is c, Mexico City. It tells what the paragraph is about.

Choice a is too specific. Only one sentence is about food.

Choice b is too general. The paragraph is not about all of Mexico. It is only about
Mexico City.

Exercise 2

➤   *Read each paragraph. Ask yourself, "What is this about?" Circle the topic. Then write "too specific" or "too general" after the other two topics. Work with another student.*

More about Mexico City

1.   Mexico City is growing quickly. In 1970, the city had about 9 million people. Now it has over 17 million. All these people are causing problems for the city. There are not enough jobs. Also, there is not enough housing. Large families have to live together in small homes. Many homes do not have water. They also do not have bathrooms or electricity. The Mexican government is worried about all these problems. It is working hard to make life better in the city.

   a. Mexican government   _____

   b. Large cities   _____

   c. Mexico City's problems _____

2.   Why is Mexico City growing so fast? Where are all these people coming from? They are coming to the city from the country. Life is hard on the farms in Mexico. Most people on farms have to live a very simple life. They have no extra money for modern things. People think life in the city must be better. So they leave their farms and move to Mexico City.

   a. Why people are moving to Mexico City   _____

   b. How Mexicans live in the country   _____

   c. Life in Mexico today   _____

3.   All around the world, large cities have the same problems. One of them is air pollution. Mexico City has bad air. It is dirty and unhealthy. Cars are one reason for the dirty air. Many Mexicans now own their own cars and drive in the city. The factories in the area also cause air pollution. These factories put a lot of smoke into the air. It is not easy to clean up the air in a large city. The government has to make new laws, and everyone has to help.

   a. Air pollution   _____

   b. Mexico City's air pollution   _____

   c. How factories cause air pollution _____

Exercise 3

➤ *Read each paragraph. Ask yourself, "What is this about?" Circle the topic. Then write "too specific" or "too general" after the other two topics. Work with another student.*

TV in the United States

1. In the United States, there are many ads on TV about kinds of soap. The ads show soap for washing clothes. They also show soap specially for washing dishes. Some ads show soap only for washing floors. Other ads are about soap for washing cars. TV ads show soap for washing people, too. Often the ads tell about special soap for washing your hair. Other soap is just for taking care of little babies. American TV seems very interested in cleaning!

   a. Soap in the United States _____

   b. Soap for washing in the house _____

   c. Ads for soap on American TV _____

2. The evening news on TV is popular with many people in the United States. They like to find out what is happening. On TV they can see real people and places. They believe it is easier than reading the newspaper. Many people think TV makes the news seem more real. They also think the news on TV is more interesting. The TV news reporters sometimes tell funny stories and even tell jokes. This makes the news about wars and crime seem less terrible.

   a. News programs have funny stories _____

   b. Americans like TV news _____

   c. TV news _____

3. In the United States there are two kinds of TV stations. One kind is commercial, and the other kind is public. Most of the TV stations in the United States are commercial. That is, they are businesses, and they show ads to make money. Public TV stations are not businesses and do not show any ads. They get money from the government and from some large companies. They also get some money from the people who watch their programs.

   a. The two kinds of TV stations in the United States _____

   b. Public TV stations _____

   c. TV in the United States _____

Exercise 4

➤ *Read each paragraph. Ask yourself, "What is it about?" Circle the topic. Then write "too specific" or "too general" after the other topics. Work with another student.*

Forests

1.   Some of the largest trees in the world are in California. These are called *redwood trees*. Redwood National Park is a large forest of redwood trees. Visitors in the park can walk and drive through the forest to look at the trees. Some redwoods are hundreds of years old. They are very tall and are very wide at the bottom. One tree has a large hole at the bottom of it. The hole is so big you can drive a car through it.

   a. Parks in California   _____

   b. Redwood trees in California   _____

   c. The age of redwoods   _____

2.   In many hilly areas of Scotland, there once were large forests. Over the years, the forests became smaller. People cut down the trees to use the wood for heating or building. They used the land for farming. After a while, the land was not good for farming. It became rocky because the earth was washed away by the rain. There were no trees to hold the earth in place. Now the Scottish government is planting new trees. These new forests look nice and green. They also will help improve the earth for the future.

   a. The land in Scotland   _____

   b. How trees hold earth in place   _____

   c. Forests in Scotland   _____

3.   Large forests are important to us in many ways. They give us wood for building and heating. They are a home for many kinds of plants and animals. For many city people, forests are a place to go for a vacation. There they can learn about nature, breathe fresh air, and sleep in a quiet place. There is one more reason why forests are important for everyone. The leaves on trees help clean the air. Dirty air is a serious problem in many parts of the world. Without our forests this problem might be even worse.

   a. The importance of forests   _____

   b. Taking vacations in forests   _____

   c. Large forests   _____

Thinking of the topic

In Exercises 5 through 8, the topic is not given. Read each paragraph and ask yourself, "What is this about? What is the topic?" Work with another student.

EXAMPLE

➤ *What is the topic of this paragraph? Think carefully. The topic should not be too specific or too general. Write the topic below the paragraph.*

Fog is really a cloud near the ground. Both fog and clouds are made of many little drops of water. These drops stay in the air because they are so small. You cannot see each drop, but fog can make it hard to see other things. It can be dangerous if you are driving, for example. Sometimes where there is a lot of fog you cannot see the road. Sailors also have trouble when there is fog. Boats may get lost and hit rocks or beaches in the fog.

Topic: _____

The topic of this paragraph is "Fog" or "How fog causes problems."
"Driving in fog" is too specific.
"Weather problems" is too general.

Exercise 5

➤ *Read each paragraph. Working with another student, decide on the topic. Be sure your topic is not too general or too specific. Write the topic below the paragraph.*

Some Facts about Weather

1.   When there is a heavy rainstorm, you sometimes see lightning, which is a bright flash of light in the sky. In the past, people thought lightning came from an angry god. In the 1700s Benjamin Franklin found out that lightning was electricity. Storms with lightning really are electrical storms. Scientists today still do not know everything about lightning, however. They do not know exactly what it comes from, and they never know where and how it will hit the earth.

Topic: _____

2.   All clouds are made of many little drops of water. But not all clouds are alike. There are three kinds of clouds. Cirrus clouds are one kind. These are made of ice drops. They look soft and light. Cumulus clouds are another kind of cloud. They are large and deep and flat on the bottom. We usually see cumulus clouds on warm summer days. Finally, there are stratus clouds, which cover the whole sky. These clouds make the sky gray and the sun does not shine at all.

Topic: _____

Exercise 6

➤   *Read each paragraph. Working with another student, decide on the best topic. Be sure your topic is not too general or too specific. Write the topic below the paragraph.*

The Use of Water

1.   In the United States, drinking water comes from a few different places. Many cities get their drinking water from special lakes called *reservoirs*. Other cities get their water from lakes and rivers. For example, the drinking water for New Orleans comes from the Mississippi River. In some areas, people get their water from the mountains. The water from mountain snow is delicious and clean. In other areas, people dig deep holes in the ground for water. These holes are called *wells*. Outside of cities, most people get their water this way.

   Topic: _____

2.   Many American scientists are worried about the drinking water in the United States. They think that soon there may be no more clean drinking water. Dirt, salt, and chemicals from factories can get into the water, making it unsafe to drink. This is already true in some places. One example is a small town in Massachusetts. Many children in this town became sick because of chemicals in the water. Another place with water problems is California. The water near old Air Force airports is not safe to drink. Many other cities and towns have water problems, too.

   Topic: _____

3.   It is important to use water carefully. Here are some ways you can use less water. First, be sure to turn off faucets tightly. They should not drip in the bathroom or kitchen sink. Second, do not keep the water running for a long time. Turn it off while you are doing something else. For example, it should be off while you are shaving or brushing your teeth. It should also be off while you are washing the dishes. Finally, in the summer you should water your garden in the evening. That way you will not lose a lot of water. During the day the sun dries up the earth too quickly.

   Topic: _____

Exercise 7

➤ *Read each paragraph. Working with another student, decide on the best topic. Be sure your topic is not too general or too specific. Write the topic below the paragraph.*

Galileo Galilei

1.　Galileo Galilei was one of the first modern scientists. He was born in Pisa, Italy, in 1564. At first he studied philosophy, but later he studied mathematics and astronomy. He was interested in the way the earth and other planets move around the sun. He found out several important facts about our world. He also started a new way of working in science. Before Galileo, scientists did not do experiments. They just guessed about how something happened. Galileo was different. He did not just make guesses. He did experiments and watched to see what happened.

Topic: _____

2.　Galileo is famous for his study of how things fall. He was the first person to do experiments about this problem. Before, people thought that heavy things always fell faster than light things. He found out that this was not true. He took a heavy ball and a light ball and he dropped them both from a high place. They fell at the same speed. This meant that weight is not important. This is the law of falling bodies. It is an important law for understanding our world.

Topic: _____

3.　The life of a scientist was not always easy in the 1500s. For example, Galileo got into trouble because of his scientific ideas. His ideas were not the same as the religious ideas at the time. Many religious people did not agree with him. During his whole life he had to worry about this. He even went to prison for a while. But no one could stop him from thinking. He continued to look for scientific answers to his questions about the world.

Topic: _____

Exercise 8

➤ *This exercise is a bit different! In each paragraph, one sentence does not belong with the others. Cross out that sentence. Then write the topic below the paragraph.*

Popular Drinks

1.   It is easy to make a good cup of tea. Just follow these steps. First, boil some water. Next put some hot water in the teapot to warm it. ~~In some countries, people drink tea with every meal.~~ Pour the water out of the pot and put in some tea leaves. You will need one teaspoon of tea leaves for each cup of tea you want. Then pour the boiling water into the teapot. Cover the pot and wait a few minutes. Then the tea will be ready to drink.

Topic: _____ How to make tea _____

2.   The first people to grow coffee beans lived in the Middle East. The Persians, Arabs, and Turks were drinking coffee many hundreds of years ago. Then, in the 1600s, Europeans learned about coffee and quickly came to like it. They also liked other foods from the Middle East. Soon there were coffeehouses in many European cities. Europeans took coffee with them when they traveled to new countries. That is how people in other parts of the world learned about coffee. Now coffee is popular in North and South America, in Africa, and in parts of Asia.

Topic: _____

3.   In the United States orange juice is one of the most popular cold drinks. Most of the oranges for juice grow in Florida. In many homes around the country, orange juice is always served at breakfast. It is also a favorite snack at any time of the day. Another good snack is apple juice. When there is bad weather in Florida, the whole country knows about it. Bad weather in Florida means fewer oranges. That means more expensive orange juice!

Topic: _____

Algonquin College
Language Institute
1385 Woodroffe Avenue, Room B442
OTTAWA, ON K2G 1V8

Main ideas of paragraphs

The main idea of a paragraph tells you more about the topic. It tells you the writer's *idea* about the topic. The main idea is important. There can be many paragraphs about the same topic, but they do not all have the same main idea.

EXAMPLE A

In this example, the topic is *elephants*. Here are three main idea statements about elephants. You can think of many more.

1. Elephants live in Africa and Asia.
2. Elephants are killed for their ivory tusks.
3. Elephants can cause serious problems for farmers.

EXAMPLE B

In this example, the topic is *supermarkets*.

➤ *Write three different main-idea statements about supermarkets. Then show your statements to another student. Are they the same as yours?*

1. _____

2. _____

3. _____

EXAMPLE C

In this paragraph, the topic is *bicycles*. What is the author's main idea about bicycles?

    Bicycles are popular today in many countries. Many people use bicycles for exercise, but exercise is only one of the reasons why bicycles are popular. Another reason is money. Bicycles are not expensive to buy. They do not need gas to make them go. They are easy and cheap to fix. In cities, many people like bicycles better than cars. With a bicycle, they never have to wait in traffic. They also do not have to find a place to park. Finally, bicycles do not cause any pollution!

➤ *Complete the best main-idea statement and circle the letter in front of it.*

    a. _____ do not cause pollution.

    b. _____ are better than cars.

    (c.)_____Bicycles_____ are popular today for many reasons.

The best choice is c, "Bicycles are popular today for many reasons." This is the writer's main idea about bicycles. All the information in the paragraph is about this idea.

Choice a is not correct because it is too specific. It is only one part of the paragraph.

Choice b is not correct because the paragraph does not say bicycles are better than cars. It says that some people like bicycles better than cars.

Choosing the best main-idea statement

Exercise 9

➤ *In this exercise, the topic of each paragraph is the same: clothes. Read each paragraph and ask yourself, "What is the main idea about clothes in this paragraph?" Complete the best main-idea statement and circle the letter in front of it. Show your work to another student. Do the two of you agree on the main idea?*

Some Ideas about Clothes

1.   Clothes can tell a lot about a person. Some people like very colorful clothes. They want everyone to look at them. They want to be the center of things. Other people like to wear nice clothes, but their clothes are not colorful or fancy. They do not like people to look at them. There are also some people who wear the same thing all the time. They do not care if anyone looks at them or not. They do not care what anyone thinks about them.

   a. _____ are colorful.

   (b.) _____ can tell a lot about a person.

   c. _____ always look nice on some people.

2.   It is important to bring the right clothes when you travel. If you are traveling to a cold country, you should bring warm clothes. Be sure you have a hat and gloves, too. If you are going to a hot country, you need different clothes. You do not want heavy or dark clothes. In hot weather, light clothes are best. If you are going to a city, you may need some nice clothes. You may want to go to a special restaurant or a concert. It is different if you are traveling by bicycle in the country. Then you will want comfortable clothes. One rule is the same for all travelers, however. Do not bring too many clothes!

   a. _____ for warm weather are light.

   (b.) _____ have to be chosen carefully when you travel.

   c. _____ can be heavy.

3.   Today's clothes are different from the clothes of the 1800s. One difference is the way they look. For example, in the 1800s all women wore dresses with long skirts. Today women do not always wear dresses with long skirts. Sometimes they wear short skirts, and sometimes they wear pants. Another difference between the 1800s and today is the cloth. In the 1800s, clothes were made only from natural kinds of cloth, such as cotton, wool, silk, and linen. Today, there are many kinds of manmade cloth, such as nylon, rayon, and polyester. A lot of clothes are made from these kinds of cloth.

   a. _____ of the 1800s were beautiful.

   b. _____ are made of manmade cloth.

   (c.) _____ today are different from the clothes of the 1800s.

Exercise 10

 Read each paragraph. Ask yourself, "What is the topic? What is the main idea?" Complete the best main-idea statement and circle the letter in front of it. Work with another student.

Chemistry in the Past

1. Chemistry is an old science. People were always interested in chemicals. People who worked on chemicals before the 1700s are called *alchemists*. They did not study chemistry like modern chemists. Their kind of chemistry was called *alchemy*. They had some strange ideas. For example, they believed they could make gold by mixing together the right things. For hundreds of years alchemists tried to do this. Of course, no one ever made gold this way.

    a. _____ never made gold.

    b. _____ lived before the 1700s.

    c. _____ studied chemicals in strange ways.

2. Robert Boyle (1627–1691) is sometimes called the "father of chemistry." He started out as an alchemist, but he began to think in a different way. For example, alchemists thought that everything was made of four things—earth, air, fire, and water—but Boyle found that things are made up of many different elements. In fact, he wrote a definition for what an element is. He said that an element is something that cannot be broken into smaller parts. Boyle's work marked the end of alchemy as a science.

    a. _____ helped build the science of alchemy.

    b. _____ said everything is made of four elements.

    c. _____ helped to start the science of chemistry.

3. Antoine Lavoisier (1743–1794) is important in the history of modern chemistry. In about 1776, he began to use a new way to study chemicals. Before Lavoisier, scientists just looked at something and thought about it. Lavoisier did experiments. He studied the size and weight of many different things. He found out something important. He found out that nothing really goes away. It just changes into something else. For example, when water boils, it becomes steam. This was an important idea for the future of chemistry.

    a. _____ learned an important fact by doing experiments.

    b. _____ studied the size and weight of water.

    c. _____ lived in the 1700s.

Exercise 11

➤ *Read each paragraph. Ask yourself, "What is the topic? What is the writer's idea about the topic?" Choose the best main-idea statement by circling the letter in front of it. Work with another student.*

Pets

1.   Cats and dogs are both popular pets. Cat owners think that cats are nicer pets in some ways. Cats are cleaner, first of all. They keep themselves clean, and they do not make the house dirty. Cats are also quieter than dogs. They usually do not make a lot of noise. Cats are safer, too. Dogs sometimes bite people, but cats almost never do. Finally, cats are easier to take care of. You do not have to spend much time with a cat. In fact, many cats prefer to be alone.

   a. Some people prefer cats as pets.

   b. Cats do not make a lot of noise.

   c. Cats are nicer than dogs in some ways.

2.   Many children want to have a pet. Some parents may not like the idea of a dog or a cat in the house, but pets can be good for children. A pet is fun for a child to play with. This can be especially important if there is only one child. Also, children can learn a lot from a pet. They can learn about animals and the natural world. Children also learn about taking care of something. They cannot forget about their pet. This is an important lesson for all children.

   a. Children usually want a dog or a cat.

   b. Pets may be good for children.

   c. Parents sometimes do not like pets.

3.   Most Americans think of cats as pets, but not all cats are pets. Some cats can help people, and other cats can be a problem. For example, on farms and in old houses, cats can help. They kill small animals such as rats or mice. Some people do not want cats around, however. They like to watch birds in their yards. Cats may kill the birds or scare them away. Cats can also be a problem in cities. In Rome, for example, thousands of cats live in the streets and old buildings. They make a lot of noise, and they are dirty and dangerous.

   a. Cats can be a problem.

   b. Most Americans think of cats as pets.

   c. Cats are not just pets.

Exercise 12

➤ *Read each paragraph. Ask yourself, "What is the topic? What is the writer's idea about the topic?" Choose the best main-idea statement by circling the letter in front of it. Work with another student.*

What Science Tells Us about the Earth

1.   The earth is always changing. One way it changes is by erosion. Some erosion is caused by the weather. For example, the wind causes erosion. In a desert, the wind blows the sand around. Rain also causes erosion. It washes away earth and even changes the shape of some rocks. Another kind of erosion is caused by rivers. When a river goes through a mountain, it cuts into the mountain. After a long time, the mountain is lower and the land is flatter.

   a. Rain causes erosion.

   b. Mountains change after a long time.

   c. Erosion changes the earth.

2.   Mt. Vesuvius in Italy and Mt. St. Helens in the United States are both famous mountains. They are both volcanoes. A volcano is a mountain that is open at the top. Smoke and hot air come out of the hole. Sometimes very hot rock also comes out of the hole. That can mean trouble for people nearby. This is what happened with Mt. Vesuvius and Mt. St. Helens. Hot rock poured out of Mt. Vesuvius and covered the town of Pompeii in 79 A.D. Everyone in the town was killed. The Mt. St. Helens volcano did not kill many people, because there were no cities close to the mountain. However, the hot rock killed a large part of the forest on the mountain, and a lot of dust fell on cities many miles away.

   a. Volcanoes can be dangerous.

   b. Two volcanoes that caused trouble.

   c. A volcano is a mountain with a hole at the top.

3.   Scientists may know a lot about the outside of the earth, but they still are not sure about the inside. For example, they understand how mountains are made and what a volcano is, but they do not know when a volcano will send hot rock into the air. Scientists also are not sure about how the earth was made. They have many different ideas about this. There are still many difficult questions for scientists who study the earth.

   a. Scientists have different ideas about how the earth was made.

   b. Scientists now know a lot about the earth.

   c. Scientists still have many questions about the earth.

Exercise 13

➤ *Read each paragraph. Ask yourself, "What is the topic? What is the writer's idea about the topic?" Then write a main-idea statement. Show your work to another student. Do the two of you agree on the main idea?*

Classified Ads in the Newspaper

1.   Not all newspaper ads are for selling things. Some ads are about people. The "Help Wanted" ads give information about jobs. All kinds of jobs are found in this part of the newspaper. There are ads for secretaries and electricians, doctors and professors. Another kind of ad about people is the "Personal" ad. These ads are not about work. They are written by people who are looking for friends. Sometimes these people are even looking for husbands and wives. Newspaper ads are a good way to get people together.

Main idea: _____

_____

2.   We can learn a lot about a country from the Personal ads. These ads tell us about people and their problems. One example of this is from Spain. One small town in Spain had 42 men and not many women living in it. The men wanted to find wives, so they put a Personal ad in a city newspaper. Some women living in the city were not happy living alone and answered the ad by telephone. They wanted to find out more about the town and the men. The women did not go to live in the town, however. They did not really want to work on farms. They did not really want to marry small-town men. So the men did not find wives, and the women are still alone. Not all men and women in Spain are like these people, but this ad may tell us something about larger problems in Spain.

Main idea: _____

_____

3.   Personal ads are usually written for good reasons. Most of the people who write them really do want a friend. Sometimes though, people write personal ads for other reasons. They may write the ad as a joke. This is not a nice thing to do. The people who answer the ads may be unhappy. They may need a friend very much. Some of the people who write the ads can cause worse problems. They may want to hurt someone. So, if you answer a Personal ad, you should be careful. The ad may not mean what it says.

Main idea: _____

_____

Exercise 14

➤ *Read each paragraph. Ask yourself, "What is the topic? What is the writer's idea about the topic?" Then write a main-idea statement. Show your work to another student. Do the two of you agree on the main idea?*

The Great Depression

1.   Black Thursday is a famous day in U.S. history. It was October 24, 1929, the beginning of the Great Depression. Before that day, business in America was growing fast. Between 1914 and 1929, it grew about 62 percent. On Black Thursday everything changed. That day, American business suddenly stopped growing. In fact, many businesses stopped completely. The next few years of American history are called the Great Depression. These were terrible years for business and for the people. Five thousand banks and 85,000 businesses failed. Many people lost all their money. About 12 million Americans lost their jobs.

Main idea: _____

_____

2.   The Great Depression of the early 1930s surprised many people. They did not think American business could have such terrible problems. For a long time, they did not believe the problems were serious. Many businessmen hoped for better times soon. Even President Hoover did not think the Depression was serious. He told Americans in 1930 that the problems were already going away. This was not true. Millions of Americans did not have jobs. Many of these people did not have homes or food. Life was hard for many Americans, and it did not get easier for many years.

Main idea: _____

_____

3.   The Great Depression finally ended for several reasons. One reason was that a new government with new ideas was in place. In 1932, Franklin D. Roosevelt became president of the United States. He made many changes in the laws to help people. New laws helped American banks and businesses. Other laws gave people jobs and housing. Roosevelt's government was only one reason for the end of the Depression, however. The other reason was World War II. In the late 1930s, the United States began to get ready for the war. New factories were built for war planes and ships. That meant more jobs. These jobs gave many people a chance to change their lives.

Main idea: _____

_____

Finding the Pattern of Organization

 Study these pictures for 60 seconds. Your teacher will time you. After 60 seconds, turn the page.

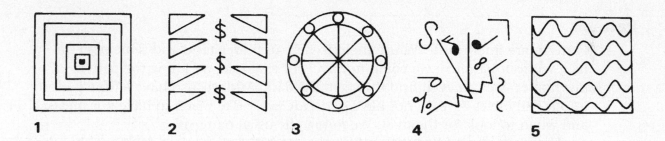

1   2   3   4   5

➤ *Try to remember the pictures. Draw them here. Do not look back.*

➤ *Now look back and check your drawings.*

Which picture was the most difficult to remember? _____

Why? _____

Pictures 1, 2, 3, and 5 were easy because they have a pattern. Picture 4 does not have a pattern, so it is more difficult to remember.

Patterns

Patterns are important. We use them to help us understand and remember. In fact, without patterns, we could not live! For example, we know the pattern of our home—we can even find things in the dark. And we also have a time pattern in our daily lives—we do not have to decide every day when to have our meals and when to look for the mail. We follow the usual patterns.

The night sky is filled with millions of stars. People noticed long ago that they could see patterns in the stars. For thousands of years, travelers and sailors used those star patterns to find their way.

In languages there are patterns, too, but each language has different patterns. To read well in English, you must be able to find the patterns used in English. They will help you understand and remember what you read.

In this unit, you will learn about four patterns.

1. **Listing**

   The writer gives a list of examples or reasons.

   Ways to travel:

   plane, train, bus, ship, bicycle

2. **Time order**

   The writer gives information in time order.

   Wars in American history:

   1776—American Revolution
   1812—War of 1812
   1861—Civil War
   1914—World War I

3. Cause and effect

The writer shows how one thing causes another.

Big snowstorm *(cause)* -----➤ School is closed. *(effect)*

4. Comparison

The writer shows how two things are alike and how they are different.

TV NEWS	compared with	THE DAILY NEWSPAPER
sound		no sound
more pictures		fewer pictures
less information		more information
needs electricity		can be read anywhere

The listing pattern

In this pattern, the writer gives a list of details to explain the main idea. The details are usually reasons or examples, and the writer uses a signal word to point out each detail.

Signal Words for the Listing Pattern

first	and	one	some	second	too	other	many
third	also	another		for example		finally	

EXAMPLE A

➤ *Read this paragraph. Find out why diamonds are expensive. Answer the question below.*

Diamonds are expensive for several reasons. <u>First</u>, they are difficult to find. They are found in only a few places in the world. <u>Second</u>, they are useful. People use diamonds to cut other stones. <u>Third</u>, diamonds do not change. They stay the same for millions of years. <u>Finally</u>, diamonds are beautiful.

How many reasons are given? _____

Four reasons are given. The underlined words are the signal words. They show the pattern. So it is easy to find the reasons. There is a signal word for each reason.

Signal Words	*Details (reasons)*
first	difficult to find
second	useful
third	do not change
finally	beautiful

EXAMPLE B

➤ *Read this paragraph. Find out how many different kinds of pollution we know about.*

We know about many different kinds of pollution. <u>One</u> kind is air pollution. This usually is a problem for cities. Water pollution is <u>another</u> problem. It is found in rivers, lakes, and oceans. <u>Also</u>, pollution of the earth is sometimes a problem near farms. <u>Finally</u>, there is noise pollution, especially in crowded cities and near airports.

➤ *Write the signal words*

Signal Words	Details (kinds of pollution)
_____	air pollution
_____	water pollution
_____	pollution of the earth
_____	noise pollution

Exercise 1

➤ *Underline the signal words in each paragraph. Write the topic and the main idea. Then write the signal words and details. The Answer Key is on page 280.*

Some Ideas about Computers (1)

1. Computers are helpful in many ways. First, they are fast. They work with information much more quickly than a person can. Second, computers can work with lots of information at the same time. Third, they keep information for a long time. They do not forget things the way people do. Also, computers are almost always correct. They are not perfect, of course, but they usually do not make mistakes.

Topic: _____

Main idea: _____

_____

Signal Words	Details
_____	_____
_____	_____
_____	_____
_____	_____

2. These days, it is important to know something about computers. There are a number of ways to learn. Some companies have computer classes at work. Also, most universities offer day and night courses in computer science. Another way to learn is from a book. There are many books about computers in bookstores and libraries. Or, you can learn from a friend. After a few hours of practice, you too can work with computers. You may not be an expert, but you can have fun!

Topic: _____

Main idea: _____

_____

Signal Words   *Details*

_____   _____

_____   _____

_____   _____

_____   _____

Exercise 2

➤ *Underline the signal words in each paragraph. Write the topic and the main idea. Then write the signal words and details.*

Some Ideas about Computers (2)

1. Today, computer companies sell many different programs for computers. First, there are programs for doing math problems. Second, there are programs for scientific studies. Third, some programs, called *word processors,* are like fancy typewriters. They are often used by writers and business people. Other programs, called CD-ROMs, are on compact discs (CDs). These programs have movies, books, and even music on them. Finally, there are programs for fun. These include exciting games and puzzles for children and adults.

Topic: _____

Main idea: _____

_____

Signal Words   *Details*

_____   _____

_____   _____

_____   _____

_____   _____

_____   _____

2.   Computer language can be funny at times. For example, we say computers have a "memory." We know they do not really remember or think. But we still say "memory." Also, computer programs have "menus." Of course, we are not talking about restaurants or food. This is a different kind of menu, one for choosing a program or section of the memory. Another example is the "mouse" we use to "talk to" the computer. It is hard not to think about a real mouse when you hear the word. But there are no little gray animals in the machine.

Topic: _____

Main idea: _____

_____

Signal Words   Details

_____   _____

_____   _____

_____   _____

Exercise 3

➤ *Underline the signal words in each paragraph. Write the topic and the main idea. Then write the signal words and details.*

Some Ideas about Computers (3)

1.   Computers come in all shapes and sizes. For example, large companies, universities, and hospitals have very large computers. There are other special computers for factories. These large computers tell the factory machines what to do. Many big buildings have computers to take care of everything. They turn the building's lights on and off. They turn on the heat or the air conditioning. Of course, there are also many small personal computers for use at home or in an office. There are even some computers so tiny you cannot see all their parts. These computers are in telephones, television sets, and cars.

Topic: _____

Main idea: _____

_____

Signal Words   Details

_____   _____

_____   _____

_____   _____

_____   _____

2.   Computers are useful, but they also can cause problems. One kind of problem is with the computer's memory. It is not perfect, so sometimes computers lose important information. Another problem is with the machinery. Computers are machines, and machines can break down. When computers break down, they may erase information, like chalk on a blackboard, or they may stop doing anything at all. There is one other, different kind of problem with computers. Some doctors say they may be bad for your health. They say you should not work with computers all day.

Topic: _____

Main idea: _____

_____

Signal Words   *Details*

_____   _____

_____   _____

_____   _____

Exercise 4

➤   *Underline the signal words in each paragraph. Write the topic and the main idea. Then write the signal words and details.*

Some Ideas about Computers (4)

1.   Today, computers are used in almost every profession. For example, scientists use them. So do mathematicians and economists. And business people use them to make business decisions. Doctors also use computers to help their patients. Computers make work easier for writers, too. Even students now use computers for help with their studies. Finally, some people use computers at home to help them make plans and pay bills.

Topic: _____

Main idea: _____

_____

Signal Words   *Details*

_____   _____

_____   _____

_____   _____

_____   _____

Reading Comprehension Skills

2.   Today, computers usually do not work alone. There are many new programs that let computers "talk" to each other. For example, people can use their computers to work together on a job. Also, the cash registers in big supermarkets are computers. Those computers "tell" the big supermarket office computer about the business. Then the owners of the supermarket can find out what people like to buy. Finally, people use computers to connect to the Internet. The Internet is a giant group of computers, all talking to one another.

Topic: _____

Main idea: _____

_____

Signal Words   *Details*

_____   _____

_____   _____

_____   _____

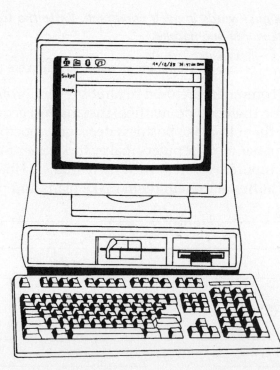

108

The time order pattern

EXAMPLE A

➤ *Read the following time order paragraph. Answer the question below.*

Albert Einstein was born in <u>1879</u> in Ulm, Germany. He graduated from the University of Zurich in Switzerland in <u>1905</u>. In <u>1905</u> he also did some of his most famous work in physics. In <u>1921</u> he won the Nobel Prize for Physics. <u>Between 1919 and 1933</u> he lived in Germany and traveled a lot to talk to other scientists. Then <u>in 1933</u> he had to leave Germany because of Hitler and the Nazi party. He moved to the United States. From <u>1933 until his death</u> he lived in Princeton, New Jersey. He died on <u>April 18, 1955</u>.

What is the topic of this paragraph? _____

The underlined signal words are all dates. Each date points to a major event in the life of Albert Einstein.

➤ *Here are the signal words. Write the events.*

Signal Words	Events
1879	<u>Albert Einstein was born in Ulm, Germany.</u>
1905	_____
1905	_____
1921	_____
1919–1933	_____
1933	_____
1933 until his death	_____
April 18, 1955	_____

EXAMPLE B

The following paragraph is about the same events as Example A, but the signal words are different.

➤ *Read the paragraph.*

Albert Einstein was born near the end of the nineteenth century in Ulm, Germany. He graduated from the University of Zurich in Switzerland at the age of 26. That was also when he did his famous work in physics. Sixteen years later he won the Nobel Prize for Physics. For the next ten years he lived in Germany. He also traveled a lot to talk with other scientists. Then in the early 1930s he had to leave Germany because of Hitler and the Nazi Party. He moved to the United States. From that time until his death he lived in Princeton, New Jersey. He died at the age of 76.

➤ *Here are the signal words. Write the events.*

Signal Words	Events
near the end of the 19th century	_____
at the age of 26	_____
That was also when	_____
Sixteen years later	_____
For the next ten years	_____
in the early 1930s	_____
From that time until his death	_____
at the age of 76	_____

Signal Words for the Time Order Pattern

- Dates
- Other words:

first	next	soon	after	at last	finally
last	later	before	while	then	times

Exercise 5

➤ *Read each paragraph. Look for the signal words and underline them. Then write the topic, the signal words, and the events on the lines below.*

The Vietnam War (1)

1.   The Vietnam War began soon after World War II. At first, in 1946, the war was between the Vietnamese and the French. The government of Vietnam was French. But the Vietnamese people wanted the French to leave so they could have their own government. The Vietnamese fought hard, and slowly they won more and more land. By 1953, the French Army was in trouble. They were not winning the war. French soldiers were dying, and the war was costing a lot of money. So, in 1954, the French Army stopped fighting and left Vietnam. That was the end of the first part of the Vietnam War.

Topic: _____

Signal Words   *Events*

_____   _____

_____   _____

_____   _____

2.   The second part of the Vietnam War began in 1954. After the French Army left, there were two Vietnams: North Vietnam and South Vietnam. There were also two governments. Both governments wanted to be the only government for all of Vietnam. So from 1954 until 1960, the North and the South were fighting all the time. The North Vietnamese slowly grew stronger. By the beginning of 1965, the North Vietnamese were winning the war. But the U.S. government did not want the North Vietnamese to win. So in March 1965, the United States began to help South Vietnam. They sent guns and airplanes to help the South. At first, the United States sent only a few soldiers, but by July 1965, there were about 75,000 American soldiers in Vietnam.

Topic: _____

Signal Words   *Events*

_____   _____

_____   _____

_____   _____

_____   _____

_____   _____

Exercise 6

➤ *Read each paragraph. Look for the signal words and underline them. Then write the topic, the signal words, and the events on the lines below.*

The Vietnam War (2)

1.   In 1965 the Vietnam War became an American war. That year, the United States sent airplanes with bombs over North Vietnam. The North Vietnamese were moving into South Vietnam, and the U.S. government wanted to stop them. More and more bombs were used each year. The bombs killed thousands of North Vietnamese men, women, and children. Thousands more lost their homes and their land. The United States also sent more soldiers every year. By the end of 1967, there were almost 510,000 Americans in Vietnam. However, the North Vietnamese were still winning the war.

Topic: _____

Signal Words	*Events*
_____	_____
_____	_____
_____	_____
_____	_____

2.   In the United States, some people did not want the war. In the early 1960s only a few people felt this way. But by the late 1960s many people believed Americans should not be fighting in Vietnam. Finally, the U.S. government had to listen to these people. In May 1968, the Americans began to talk to North Vietnam about stopping the war. For the next few months, fewer bombs were used against the North. By the end of the year, the bombing stopped. It still took a long time to end the war. American soldiers started to go home in 1970. The last Americans left three years later.

Topic: _____

Signal Words	*Events*
_____	_____
_____	_____
_____	_____
_____	_____
_____	_____
_____	_____

Exercise 7

➤ *Read each paragraph. Look for the signal words and underline them. Then write the topic, the signal words, and the events on the lines below.*

The Story of Anh Nguyen (1)

1. Anh Nguyen is Vietnamese. She was born in 1960 in Hue, a large city in South Vietnam. When she was four years old, her family moved to Saigon. She finished grammar school in 1972, and then she went to high school. The first year of high school was a happy year for Anh. She liked her classes, especially French and English. In the fall, she won a prize for a French paper. That winter she decided she wanted to go to study in France. Anh dreamed about France all year. She studied hard for her French class, and in the spring she did well on her examinations.

Topic: _____

Signal Words   *Events*

_____   _____

_____   _____

_____   _____

_____   _____

_____   _____

2. Anh had to change all her plans because of the war. In 1973, life in Saigon was changing. The American soldiers were leaving. The war did not end after the American soldiers left. However, the South Vietnamese did not have a strong army anymore, and they could not stop the North Vietnamese. In 1974, the North Vietnamese Army moved into Saigon. That was the end of South Vietnam. It was also the end of the old life for Anh. There were troubles that year. Food, clothing, and other things became more expensive. Sometimes the shops were empty. But there were worse troubles. Anh's father was taken away from his family because he once worked for the Americans. She never saw him again.

Topic: _____

Signal Words   *Events*

_____   _____

_____   _____

_____   _____

Exercise 8

> *Read the passage. Look for the signal words and underline them. Then write the topic, the signal words, and the events on the lines below and on the next page.*

The Story of Anh Nguyen (2)

The next few years were unhappy and difficult for Anh. She continued to go to school, but she did not enjoy it anymore. She could not study English or French. After a while she stopped going to school and started working in a factory. Her family needed money, and there were no other jobs. Anh did not like
5 factory work.

At last Anh decided she had to do something. She did not want to work in a factory all her life. She wanted an education. She wanted a more interesting job. So she decided to leave Vietnam and go to the United States. Other Vietnamese people had the same idea. In fact, from 1974 to 1976, hundreds of thousands of
10 Vietnamese left their country.

The day came for Anh to say good-bye to her family. She did not know if she was going to see them again. She walked many miles to a small town by the ocean. She and about 40 other people got into a small boat. They left Vietnam at night.

For several days they sailed with no trouble. Then the wind stopped and the
15 boat stopped moving. They did not have enough food or water. Some people began to get sick. A boat came near them, but it did not stop to help them.

Finally a large Japanese ship came near. It stopped and picked up all the Vietnamese. Almost all of them were very sick, including Anh. The ship took them to a camp in the Philippine Islands. This was a special camp for Vietnamese
20 people. It was crowded in the camp, but Anh felt safe.

Anh had a cousin who lived in the United States. She wrote to him right away and asked if she could stay with him and his family in Boston. He wrote back and said yes. She showed his letter to the U.S. immigration office. She applied for an American visa, but she had to wait many months for it. While she was waiting,
25 she took English classes and studied hard.

Finally, almost one year later, Anh got her visa. A refugee group gave her a plane ticket and some money. She was ready at last to start her new life.

Topic: _____

Signal Words   *Events*

_____   _____

_____   _____

_____   _____

_____   _____

Signal Words   *Events*

_____   _____

_____   _____

_____   _____

_____   _____

_____   _____

_____   _____

_____   _____

Exercise 9

➤ **Read the passage. Look for the signal words and underline them. Then write the topic, the signal words, and the events on the lines below and on the next page.**

The Story of Anh Nguyen (3)

Anh arrived in Boston in December 1979. She had only her suitcase and her English dictionary. The only person she knew in the United States was her cousin Pho. He and his wife To-van were there to meet her at the airport. She was happy to see them!

5 That evening Anh asked Pho and To-van many questions. She wanted to know about Boston and about Americans. She was surprised that To-van often could not answer her questions. To-van's friends were all Vietnamese people. She shopped only at the Vietnamese stores in their neighborhood. She worked at Pho's Vietnamese restaurant nearby. So To-van did not know much about Boston,
10 and she did not speak English well.

That night Anh made a decision before she went to sleep. She decided that she did not want to be like To-van. She wanted to speak English well. She wanted to go to school with Americans, and she wanted to work with them. Of course, she did not want to forget about Vietnam, but she wanted to be part of her new
15 country.

At first, it was not easy. There were many new things in her life. The first winter in Boston seemed very cold to Anh. In January, she started studying at the high school. English was a serious problem. She could not understand her teachers, and they could not understand her. Anh often felt very unhappy and
20 alone. Her old home in Saigon seemed far away, and she missed her family terribly.

By summer, the worst times were over for Anh. Her English was much better, and she began to make some friends at school. For the next two years she studied hard. In math, science, and French she was the best student in her class. She won
25 a prize for a chemistry experiment.

Best of all, at the end of her last year of high school, she won a scholarship to college. The scholarship was important to Anh. She needed the money to go to college. Going to college was the key to success, she knew. Finally Anh had a plan. She planned to study science and computers in college. After college she
30 could get a good job. She could earn money and send it to her mother. Then her mother could come to the United States, too. It seemed a long time to wait. But Anh knew she could do it!

Topic: _____

Signal Words	Events
_____	_____
_____	_____
_____	_____
_____	_____
_____	_____
_____	_____
_____	_____
_____	_____

Exercise 10

➤ *Read the passage. Look for the signal words and underline them. Then write the topic, the signal words, and the events on the lines on the next page.*

The Story of Anh Nguyen (4)

Anh was busy during her college years. Her scholarship paid for her courses and books, but she did not have enough money to live at the college. So Anh lived with To-van and Pho, and she took the bus to classes every day. And she needed money for food, clothing, and other expenses. She went to classes during
5 the week, and on weekends she worked at Pho's restaurant.

After studying for one semester, Anh began to feel lonely at college. She wished she had some Vietnamese friends there. One day, she heard about a new club, the College Vietnamese Club. Through the club, Anh met other students who were working hard. Many of the club members shared a dream. They wished
10 to go back to Vietnam someday, to help their country and see their families.

However, in the 1980s, the U.S. government was still unfriendly to Vietnam. Some American soldiers were still in the country, and the Vietnamese government did not tell the U.S. government where they were. So the U.S. government did not allow its citizens to do business in Vietnam. In fact, they
15 could not even travel there for a visit.

In 1988, Anh graduated from college with a degree in computer science. She found a job with a big bank in New York, and she began to plan to send for her mother. That was not easy. Life in New York was very expensive. Anh had many expenses: She had to buy a car and she had to pay rent. She needed to find a
20 better job.

In 1990, Anh became a U.S. citizen. She also went back to school for a master's degree in business administration (MBA). The MBA would help her get a better job. She hoped that after that she would be able to go back to Vietnam to look for her mother.
25 The U.S. government changed some laws about communication with Vietnam in 1992. It allowed American companies to do business in Vietnam and American citizens to visit Vietnam. Many young Vietnamese in the United States (like Anh) began thinking about going back home. They loved the United States, but they felt homesick. They wanted to help build up their home country.
30 In June 1994, Anh traveled to Vietnam. She wanted to see the "new" Vietnam with her own eyes. As she boarded the plane at JFK Airport in New York, she had many questions. Would her mother look the same? Would Vietnam be a good place to live? Would it be a good place for Anh to work? Would she want to return to the United States? Only time would tell.

Topic: _____

Signal Words   *Events*

_____   _____

_____   _____

_____   _____

_____   _____

_____   _____

_____   _____

_____   _____

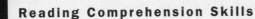

The cause-and-effect pattern

EXAMPLE A

Shoes with high heels *can cause* foot problems.

(Cause) -------------------► (Effect)

What is the cause of foot problems? _____Shoes with high heels_____

What is the effect of shoes with high heels? _____Foot problems_____

What are the signal words? _____can cause_____

EXAMPLE B

Some ear problems *are caused by* noise pollution.

(Effect) ◄--------------------- (Cause)

What is the cause of some ear problems? _____Noise pollution_____

What is the effect of noise pollution? _____Some ear problems_____

What are the signal words? _____are caused by_____

Exercise 11

➤ *Under each sentence, write* **C** *under the cause and* **E** *under the effect. Draw an arrow (--------►) from the cause to the effect. Then underline the signal word(s).*

1. Exercise <u>can make you</u> thirsty.

   C -------------------► E

2. Many car accidents happen because of ice and snow on the road.

3. Bad food and not enough sleep are two reasons for bad health.

4. Doctors tell us that smoking cigarettes often leads to cancer.

5. Some people become nervous because of drinking coffee.

6. Many fires in homes are due to careless smokers.

7. Heart disease is sometimes the result of eating too much.

8. Bright sunlight can cause your eyes to hurt.

9. High insurance costs are one result of car accidents.

10. Serious family problems can cause illness.

Exercise 12

➤ *Under each sentence, write* **C** *under the cause and* **E** *under the effect. Draw an arrow (-------➤) from the cause to the effect. Then underline the signal word(s).*

1. Sam won a prize because he had the highest score.

2. Some students go to college in order to play football.

3. Reading for pleasure can result in a larger vocabulary.

4. Helen found a job quickly because of her English skills.

5. As a result of your phone call, I could not go back to sleep.

6. The students made too much noise, so he called the police.

7. She received an award because of her computer program.

8. Eating too much chocolate can result in weight gain.

9. Doctors say that good health comes from regular exercise.

10. The team needs a new coach because they lost all their games.

Signal Words for the Cause-and-Effect Pattern

If the arrow goes **C** --------➤ **E**, use these signal words:

so	can make	is a cause of
leads to	stops	results in
causes	makes	had an effect on
can help	effects	is the reason for

If the arrow goes **E** ◄-------- **C**, use these signal words:

is the effect of	the effect of	are caused by
because of	is caused by	is the reason for
is due to	results from	because

Finding causes and effects in paragraphs

EXAMPLE A

Sometimes one cause has many effects.

➤ *In this paragraph look for the effects of a cold winter in Florida. The signal words are underlined.*

A cold winter <u>causes</u> serious problems on Florida farms. The farmers there grow a lot of oranges. Very cold weather <u>can cause</u> orange trees to die. Cold weather also <u>results in</u> fewer tourists. There are many hotels and vacation places in Florida. These places are in trouble if there are fewer tourists. Finally, very cold weather <u>can cause</u> health problems. Many people do not have heating in their homes, so they become ill from the cold.

Main idea: _____ A cold winter causes serious problems in Florida. _____

Causes	Signal Words	Effects
cold weather	causes	problems
	can cause	orange trees to die
	results in	fewer tourists
	can cause	health problems

EXAMPLE B

Sometimes, one effect has many causes.

➤ *In this paragraph look for the causes of car accidents. The signal words are underlined.*

There are many different causes for car accidents in the United States. Sometimes accidents <u>are caused by</u> bad weather. Ice or snow can make roads dangerous. Accidents also can <u>result from</u> problems with the car. Even a small problem like a flat tire can be serious. Bad roads are another <u>cause of</u> accidents. Some accidents happen <u>because</u> the driver falls asleep. Finally, some accidents <u>are caused by</u> drinking too much alcohol. In fact, this is one of the most important causes of accidents.

Main idea: _____ Car accidents have many causes in the United States. _____

Causes	Signal Words	Effects
bad weather	are caused by	car accidents
car problems	result from	
bad roads	cause of	
driver falls asleep	because	
drinking alcohol	are caused by	

Exercise 13

➤ *Read each paragraph. Underline the signal words. Write the causes and the effects on the lines below. Then write the main idea of the paragraph.*

Effects of Drugs on Your Body

1.   Most people do not think of coffee as a drug. In fact, it is a drug, and it has important effects on your body. Some of the effects are good and some are not. Coffee can help you stay awake while you are driving or working. However, it can also keep you awake at night when you want to sleep. Coffee makes some people feel more alive so they can work better. Other people feel too nervous when they drink coffee. After a large meal, coffee can help your stomach. But too much coffee can cause a stomachache.

Main idea: _____

_____

Causes   *Effects*

_____   _____

_____   _____

_____   _____

_____   _____

_____   _____

2.   Aspirin is a simple drug. It has many useful effects. It can stop a headache or an earache. It helps take away pain in the fingers or knees. Aspirin can stop a fever if you have the flu, and it can make you feel better if you have a cold. Some doctors believe that aspirin also can result in a healthy heart. They say that some people should take an aspirin every day. For those people, aspirin may stop heart disease.

Main idea: _____

_____

Causes   *Effects*

_____   _____

_____   _____

_____   _____

_____   _____

Exercise 14

➤ *Read each paragraph. Underline the signal words. Write the causes and the effects on the lines below. Then write the main idea of the paragraph.*

The Problem of Being Fat

1. Scientists and doctors say that more than half of all Americans are too fat. Why is this? One cause is the kind of food Americans eat. Many Americans like "fast foods." These foods often are full of fat and sugar. Another cause is the way Americans eat. Their little snacks between regular meals add extra fat to the body. A third cause is too little exercise. Many Americans like to drive everywhere and do not walk anywhere. In their homes, they lie on the couch and watch TV. They do not even get up to change channels—they use the remote control.

Main idea: _____

_____

Causes   *Effects*

_____   _____

_____   _____

_____   _____

2. If you are too fat, you may soon have serious problems with your health. A group of doctors wrote a report about some of the effects of too much fat. One important effect is stress on the heart. If you are fat, your heart has to work harder. This may lead to a heart attack or to other heart problems. Extra fat can also change the amount of sugar in your blood. This can cause serious diseases, such as diabetes. High blood pressure is another possible result of being fat. Even cancer can sometimes be a result. More studies are needed about all these problems, but one thing is clear: Extra fat may make your life shorter.

Main idea: _____

_____

Causes   *Effects*

_____   _____

_____   _____

_____   _____

_____   _____

Exercise 15

➤ *Read each paragraph. Underline the signal words. Write the causes and the effects on the lines below. Then write the main idea of the paragraph.*

Causes of Illness

1. Some people become unhappy and ill every winter. In the past, doctors didn't know why. But now they have some new ideas about this. Winter really does cause health problems for these people, but the cause is not the cold weather. The problems are the result of the short and cloudy days. On these winter days, people don't get enough light. This may lead to unhappiness and illness.

    Main idea: _____

    _____

    Causes   *Effects*

    _____   _____

    _____   _____

    _____   _____

2. In the United States, many of the poor city children have health problems. Some of the children are ill because of their diet. They do not get enough food, or they do not get healthy food. Their poor health is also caused by bad housing. Many children live in poor apartments which have no heat in the winter and little fresh air in the summer. Some of the children have poor health because they do not receive good medical care. Many poor children do not see a doctor for checkups or for shots to keep them healthy.

    Main idea: _____

    _____

    Causes   *Effects*

    _____   _____

    _____   _____

    _____   _____

The comparison pattern

EXAMPLE A

➤ *Compare an apple and an orange.*

How are they alike?
Both are kinds of fruit.
Both are round.
Both have skins.
Both taste good.

How are they different?
They are *different* colors.
They taste *different*.
Oranges grow in *warm* places. Apples grow in *cool* places.
Sometimes oranges *do not have* seeds. Apples always *have* seeds.

EXAMPLE B

➤ *Compare the United States and Canada.*

How are they alike?
Both are in North America.
Both have many people from around the world.
Both are large countries.
Both have land on the Atlantic and the Pacific oceans.
Both countries were once part of the British Empire.

How are they different?
Canada has two official languages, *but* the United States has no official language.
The United States has *more* people *than* Canada.
Canada has *more* land *than* the United States.
Canada is a *younger* nation *than* the United States.

➤ *Compare your country and the United States.*

How are they alike?

How are they different?

Both _____   _____

Both _____   _____

Both _____   _____

Signal Words for the Comparison Pattern

Words That Show Likeness	Words That Show Difference
alike	different
similar	unlike
same	more than
also	less than
both	but
and also	however

EXAMPLE C

This paragraph tells how two fruits are alike. It does not tell any differences.

➤ *Underline the signal words. Answer the question below.*

Lemons and limes are similar kinds of fruit. Both are grown in warm places. Both have hard skins and soft insides. People do not usually eat whole lemons and limes. That is because both of these fruits have a very sour taste. The two are often used in desserts and main dishes. People make juice from lemons and also from limes. Finally, both fruits have a lot of vitamin C in them.

What is this paragraph comparing? _____

Signal Words	*Likenesses*
Both	are grown in warm places
Both	have hard skins and soft insides
both of	have a sour taste
The two	are used in cooking
and also	people make juice from them
both	have a lot of vitamin C

EXAMPLE D

This paragraph tells some differences between lemons and limes.

➤ *Underline the signal words. Answer the question below.*

Lemons and limes are both citrus fruits, but they are quite different. First of all, the color is different. Lemons are yellow. Limes are green. The taste is different, too. Also, lemons are grown all over the world, but limes are grown in only a few places. This is because lemons are an old kind of fruit, but limes are new. They are really a special kind of lemon. Scientists made them from lemons only about 50 years ago.

What is this paragraph comparing? _____

Signal Words	*Differences*
different	color
different	taste
but	where they are grown
but	lemons are old; limes are new

Exercise 16

> *Read each paragraph and underline the signal words. Answer the question following the paragraph. Then write the main idea and the likenesses, differences, or both on the lines below.*

1.   Peter and Joe are roommates in Chicago. They both like to cook good meals and have dinner parties, but they have different ideas about what to cook. Peter likes to cook simple food. His favorite foods are steak, potatoes, and apple pie. But Joe prefers special dishes from far-away places. He likes to cook Indian curries and to prepare Japanese sushi. No matter who's cooking, dinner at Peter and Joe's apartment is always delicious.

What is the paragraph comparing? _____

Main idea: _____

_____

Differences   *Likenesses*

_____   _____

_____   _____

2.   Shopping for food in the United States today is not the same as it used to be. In the past, every neighborhood had a little food market. Now every neighborhood has a big supermarket. These are very different places. The old markets were usually small and friendly. People from the neighborhood often stopped there to hear the news or to talk. However, this is not true in today's supermarkets. Supermarkets are usually large and not very friendly. They are not good places for meeting friends or talking. Many people in supermarkets seem to be tired and in a hurry. Often they are not very polite.

What is this paragraph comparing? _____

Main idea: _____

_____

Differences   *Likenesses*

_____   _____

_____   _____

_____   _____

_____   _____

_____   _____

Reading Comprehension Skills

Exercise 17

➤ *Read each paragraph and underline the signal words. Answer the question following the paragraph. Then write the main idea and the likenesses, differences, or both on the lines below.*

1.　　The food in India is similar to the food in China. First of all, in both countries, rice is an important food: It is served at almost every meal in India and China. Both Indian and Chinese dishes can be spicy. They are also alike because they both use many different vegetables. In both countries, meat is not always the most important part of the meal. Finally, both countries include many different kinds of cooking. In India and China, each part of the country has its own favorite kinds of food and way of cooking.

What is this paragraph comparing? _____

Main idea: _____

_____

Likenesses

_____

_____

_____

_____

_____

2.　　People used to have very different ways of eating in Europe. Now everyone uses forks, knives, and spoons. But a thousand years ago, no one used forks at the table. They used only spoons and knives. Today most Europeans do not eat with their fingers. But back then many people picked up their food in their hands. In those days most people did not use glasses for drinking. Instead they drank from bowls or large wooden cups.

What is this paragraph comparing? _____

Main idea: _____

_____

Differences

_____

_____

_____

_____

_____

127

Reading Comprehension Skills

Exercise 18

➤ *Read each paragraph and underline the signal words. Answer the question following the paragraph. Then write the main idea and the differences.*

1.   If you travel around Europe, you will find many differences in how doctors work. For example, English doctors are quick to give strong antibiotics for colds, but German doctors usually are not. The Germans, on the other hand, give medicine for low blood pressure, but the English do not think low blood pressure is a problem. German doctors seem very concerned about heart problems. They give six times as many heart drugs as English doctors do. Patients in the two countries are different, too. The English are more likely to accept their doctors' orders without question. The Germans, however, are likely to ask their doctors to explain their treatment.

What is this paragraph comparing? _____

Main idea: _____

_____

Differences: _____

_____

_____

_____

2.   French ideas about medicine are also different from English ideas about medicine. In France, doctors often give strong medicine to move blood to the brain. However, doctors in England do not think that is helpful. French doctors often worry about a patient's liver and diet. But English doctors do not. And French doctors take stomach illnesses very seriously. They often give their patients magnesium, calcium, and vitamin D. But in England, doctors often think such stomach problems are "just nerves." French doctors are usually interested in trying out a variety of new treatments. English doctors, however, first wait to see if the new treatments really work.

What is this paragraph comparing? _____

Main idea: _____

_____

Differences: _____

_____

_____

_____

Exercise 19

➤ *Read each paragraph and underline the signal words. Answer the question following the paragraph. Then write the main idea and the likenesses, differences, or both.*

1.　　Poland and Italy may seem like very different countries, and, of course, they are different in some ways. Poland is in the north of Europe, but Italy is in the south. Poland has a much colder winter than Italy. However, there are also similarities. In both countries, the most important religion is Catholicism. Also, in both Italy and Poland, the history of their country is very important to the people. Finally, both the Italians and the Polish are famous for their friendliness and good spirit.

What is this paragraph comparing? _____

Main idea: _____

_____

Differences　　　　　　　　　　　　　　　*Likenesses*

_____　　　　　_____

_____　　　　　_____

_____　　　　　_____

_____　　　　　_____

2.　　The way people pay for health care is very different in Canada and in the U.S. In Canada, everyone has a chance to have health care. People pay a tax to the government, and the government pays most of the doctor, dentist, and hospital bills. In the U.S., on the other hand, some people pay insurance companies, and the insurance companies pay doctor, dentist, and hospital bills. But in the U.S., unlike Canada, many poor people cannot pay insurance companies. So they have very little health care.

What is this paragraph comparing? _____

Main idea: _____

_____

Differences: _____

_____

_____

_____

_____

_____

Using all four patterns

<u>**Exercise 20**</u>

➤ *In each of the following paragraphs, there is a different pattern and a missing sentence. Working with another student, decide what the pattern is and which sentence fits best. The patterns and missing sentences (plus one extra) are listed below. After each paragraph, write the letter of the pattern and the letter of the missing sentence.*

Linda's New House

1. The kitchen in Linda's new house had many problems. The first problem was the sink. The water did not go down the drain. Finally, there was also a problem with the refrigerator. Water came pouring out and it made a terrible mess.

    Pattern _____L_____   Sentence _____d_____

2. Linda had a terrible time in her new house last week. On Monday, the sink was not draining well. She had to call the repair company. Next, on Wednesday, the stove broke. The repair person had to come back to her house. The repair person spent many hours working in Linda's house that week.

    Pattern _____TO_____   Sentence _____b_____

3. Linda thought the problem with the stove was serious, but then she found out that the refrigerator problem was worse. The stove was not easy to fix, but the refrigerator was even more difficult. It was also much more expensive to fix the refrigerator.

    Pattern _____   Sentence _____

4. Linda had a difficult week because of all the problems in her house. She could not cook any food, because the stove did not work. Then, all her food spoiled because her refrigerator broke. She had to throw it all away. Linda was upset. She almost decided to sell her new house.

    Pattern _____CE_____   Sentence _____

Patterns:
L—listing   **TO**—time order   **CE**—cause and effect   **C**—comparison

Missing Sentences:
a. The refrigerator problem was also much messier than the stove problem.
b. Then, on Friday, the refrigerator made a terrible mess.
c. Linda decided to buy a new stove and a new refrigerator.
d. Another problem was with the stove. It did not get very hot.
e. She could not wash her dishes because of the broken sink.

Exercise 21

> *In each of the following paragraphs, there is a different pattern and a missing sentence. Working with another student, decide what the pattern is and which sentence fits best. The patterns and missing sentences (plus one extra) are listed below. After each paragraph, write the letter of the pattern and the letter of the missing sentence.*

William Shakespeare

1.   Shakespeare was born in Stratford-on-Avon on April 16, 1564. For a few years he studied at a school near home. He moved to London when he was still young. By the age of 35, he was already a well-known writer.

   Pattern _____   *Sentence* _____

2.   Two great writers were born in England in 1564. One was William Shakespeare. The other was Christopher Marlowe. Shakespeare lived until the age of 52, but Marlowe died suddenly when he was only 29. Both were famous in their time, and both are still loved today.

   Pattern _____   *Sentence* _____

3.   Many people ask why Shakespeare was so great. He was a genius, of course. He had many ideas about life, and he had a wonderful way with words. Shakespeare was also great because he lived at the right time. The English, in those days, were interested in new ideas. They loved plays and poetry.

   Pattern _____   *Sentence* _____

4.   Shakespeare wrote plays, but they were not all alike. He wrote three kinds of plays. One kind was the history play. Another kind was the tragedy, such as "Macbeth."

   Pattern _____   *Sentence* _____

Patterns:
L—listing   TO—time order   CE—cause and effect   C—comparison

Missing Sentences:
a. At the age of 18, he married Ann Hathaway.
b. He also wrote many comedies, such as "A Midsummer Night's Dream."
c. Shakespeare wrote many plays and some poetry. But Marlowe finished only four plays.
d. A genius like Shakespeare had a chance to use his great mind.
e. Some people think Shakespeare's plays were written by someone else.

Exercise 22

➤ *In each of the following paragraphs, there is a different pattern and a missing sentence. Working with another student, decide what the pattern is and which sentence fits best. The patterns and missing sentences (plus one extra) are listed below. After each paragraph, write the letter of the pattern and the letter of the missing sentence.*

Let's Go to the Zoo

1.   Zoos in the United States are changing. The old zoos had lots of cages. Even large animals were kept in big cages. Often, the cages had nothing in them except an animal, and the animal was sad looking. Many animals live together in these cages, and the cages are not empty. They are full of trees, flowers, rocks, and water. They are like pieces of real country, not like cages at all.

Pattern _____   *Sentence* _____

2.   These new zoos teach people a lot about animals. They show people how the animals really live. They also show the way they have families and how the mothers take care of the babies. And they show how many kinds of animals form groups and live together. In addition, the animals in the new zoos do not look sad. Are they really happy? They cannot tell us, of course, but they look healthier.

Pattern _____   *Sentence* _____

3.   Zoo workers say that some animals change when they come to the new cages. For example, a gorilla named Timmy lived at the Cleveland Metroparks Zoo. As a young gorilla, he lived in a small cage in a dark building. Then he was moved to the Bronx Zoo, to a large cage outside. He just sat on some rocks. He didn't like walking on the grass. That soon changed, though. He started to move around a lot, and he did many things he never did back in his old cage. In fact, after only a few months, he became a father!

Pattern _____   *Sentence* _____

Patterns:

L—listing   **TO**—time order   **CE**—cause and effect   **C**—comparison

Missing Sentences:

a. You see the way they eat and sleep.

b. Soon many other countries will have new zoos, too.

c. The new zoos still have cages, but they are very big.

d. For the first few days, he never moved.

Making Inferences

Writers in English often do not explain everything to the reader. For example, sometimes they may not state the topic or tell the reader the time or place of a story. Often the reader has to guess these things. This is called **making inferences.**

Making inferences is a necessary reading skill. It helps you understand ideas, even when you do not know all the words. Good readers make inferences all the time as they read.

Making inferences from conversations

In the following exercises, you will find part of a conversation. Read through the conversation quickly and make some inferences about the people who are talking. What are they talking about? Where are they? Work with another student.

EXAMPLE

➤ *Read the conversation and answer the questions below.*

A: Look at the long line! Do you think we'll get in?

B: I think so. Some of these people already have tickets.

A: How much are the tickets?

B: Only $4.50 for the first show. I'll pay.

A: Thanks. I'll buy some popcorn.

1. What are these people talking about?   <u>*going to a movie*</u>

2. Where are they? <u>*in front of the movie theater*</u>

3. Which words helped you guess the topic?   <u>*line, get in, tickets, show, popcorn*</u>

Exercise 1

➤ *Read the conversation and answer the questions below.*

A: Was it a girl or a boy?

B: A girl. She's eight pounds and very healthy!

A: When will they come home from the hospital?

B: I'm going to bring them home tomorrow.

A: Well, congratulations! What a nice change for the neighborhood!

1. What are these people talking about? _____

2. Where are they? _____

3. Which words helped you guess the topic? _____

_____

Exercise 2

➤ *Read the conversation and answer the questions below.*

A: I like the color.

B: So do I. Red is my favorite color.

A: How many miles does it have on it?

B: Only 30,000. They told me it belonged to an old man. He didn't use it much.

A: What's the price?

B: It's really cheap.

A: And the engine?

B: It's almost new.

A: Then I think you should get it.

1. What are these people talking about? _____

2. Where are they? _____

➤ *Underline the words that helped you guess the topic.*

Exercise 3

➤ *Read the conversation and answer the questions below.*

A: Do you think Mom and Dad will be late?

B: No. Swiss Air is usually on time.

A: But it's raining so hard, and there's a lot of wind.

B: There's no message on the announcement board, and they didn't say anything to us at the airline counter. They always make an announcement if the flight is late.

A: Well, I hope you're right. I hate waiting around in these places!

1. What are these people talking about? _____

2. Where are they? _____

➤ *Underline the words that helped you guess the topic.*

Exercise 4

Read the conversation and answer the questions below.

A: When did this happen?

B: Yesterday. I was playing soccer and I fell down.

A: Can you move it at all?

B: Only a little.

A: Can you walk on it?

B: No. It hurts too much.

A: I think we'll have to take an X-ray.

B: Will I be able to play in the game tomorrow?

A: I'm afraid not.

1. What are these people talking about? _____

2. Where are they? _____

Exercise 5

➤ *Read the conversation and answer the questions below.*

A: Well, what do you think?

B: The color is perfect on you.

A: What about the style?

B: It's a very popular style.

A: How does it look on me?

B: It looks great on you. It looks great on everybody.

A: You don't think I look funny in it?

B: Not at all. You look very nice.

1. What are these people talking about? _____

2. Where are they? _____

Exercise 6

➤ *Read the conversation and answer the questions below.*

A: Did you understand everything today?

B: No. I'm so confused!

A: So am I.

B: She doesn't explain things very well!

A: I know. And now we're going to have a test!

B: Maybe we should go to the language lab this afternoon.

A: Good idea. I need more practice.

1. What are these people talking about? _____

2. Where are they? _____

Exercise 7

➤ *Read the conversation and answer the questions below.*

A: Where to?

B: The airport.

A: Okay. How much time do you have?

B: About an hour.

A: I don't know . . . there's a lot of traffic now.

B: I can't miss this flight!

A: Well, I'll do my best.

B: Oh! Look out!

A: Listen, lady. Do you want to catch your flight?

B: I sure do.

A: Then close your eyes and keep quiet. And I'll get you there on time.

1. What are these people talking about? _____

2. Where are they? _____

Exercise 8

➤ *Read the conversation and answer the questions below.*

A: I can't believe that this is my last day here.

B: You're leaving us today?

A: Yes. I'm so nervous about this.

B: I'm sure it will be fine.

A: I don't know. It will be so different.

B: I thought you wanted a change.

A: Yes, I did. And I wanted more pay. But now I'm not sure it was the right thing to do.

B: Stop worrying. Everything will be fine.

1. What are these people talking about? _____

2. Where are they? _____

Exercise 9

▶ *Read the conversation and answer the questions below.*

A: This is one of the reasons I hate working in a big city.

B: I know. Every day, it's the same thing.

A: This is terrible! We may be here all night! I hope we don't run out of gas.

B: No, I think there's enough.

A: Let's turn on the radio. Maybe there's some good music.

B: Sorry, the radio's not working.

A: I think I'll take the train tomorrow!

1. What are these people talking about? _____

2. Where are they? _____

Exercise 10

▶ *Read the conversation and answer the question below.*

A: Excuse me. Do you have the time?

B: Nine o'clock.

A: Already! Are you sure?

B: Of course.

A: Then where's the number 13 bus?

B: The number 13? It's probably downtown by now.

A: What do you mean?

B: It came twenty minutes ago. It always comes at twenty minutes before the hour.

A: So the next bus comes at nine forty?

B: No. There is no next bus.

A: That was the last one!

B: Yeah. After nine o'clock there aren't any more buses.

A: Then what are you doing here?

B: I'm waiting for a taxi.

1. What are these people talking about? _____

2. Where are they? _____

Making inferences from stories

Now you will make inferences from some parts of stories. Read the passages quickly and try to answer the questions. Do not stop for new words. Try to guess their meanings. If you cannot guess, skip the word and continue reading.

Exercise 11

➤ *Read this passage from "Project Omega," a story by Elaine O'Reilly. Try to infer the answers to the questions below. Underline the words or phrases that helped you. Work with another student.*

"My name's Julia Baker. You saved my life."

"Oh, I do that kind of thing when I get the chance," laughed the young man. "I'm Edward West."

"Well, how can I thank you, Edward? Why don't you come in and have some
5 coffee? I think I need a cup too, after that."

They went into the apartment. Clara brought them two cups of coffee—very good Italian coffee.

"The elevator," Julia said. "It wasn't there."

"I know."

10 "But you were there. Was that by chance?"

Edward looked at her. She saw that he was thinking.

"Yes," he said slowly. "I think it was."

"I think they broke the elevator door."

"Yes. That's clear."

15 "You don't think it was an accident?"

"No, I don't think so."

Julia drank the hot, sweet, black coffee. When she put the cup down, she began to cry. For the first time in her eighteen years of life, she knew she needed a friend. She knew it because she was with this young man—this young man
20 with the clear, friendly eyes.

"It's all right," he said. "You're safe now."

"No, I'm not," Julia answered. "I'm in terrible danger." And she told him the story—every part of it, from her father's disappearance to Miss Harper's telephone call. She told him about Project Omega.

1. What kind of story is this passage from? _____

2. When does this story take place? _____

3. Where are these people? _____

4. What happened before this passage in the story? _____

_____

5. What do you think will happen after this? _____

_____

139

Exercise 12

➤ *Read this passage from "Girl against the Jungle," by Monica Vincent. Try to infer the answers to the questions below. Underline the words or phrases that helped you. Work with another student.*

I woke up very late the next morning. The sun was high in the sky, so I got up quickly and started to walk along the bank of the stream. I still followed the rules carefully. First I poked my stick into the undergrowth. Then I took a step or two. I watched for snakes and spiders. I listened for the sounds of danger. I listened to
5 the birds. My mother knew all about birds.

"The birds can tell you about the jungle," she told me. "Listen to them."

She taught me a lot about birds, so I recognised the terrible cries in the sky. I recognised the big, black wings and the ugly bare heads. I knew those sharp, hungry beaks. King vultures! The biggest vultures in the world. They don't kill.
10 They only watch and wait. They fly over the jungle and look for dead bodies. The sky was black with their wings. They flew down between the trees. There was food on the ground—dead flesh. It was the passengers from the plane. I didn't see the bodies, but I knew. The vultures told me.

I didn't feel sad. I didn't feel afraid. I still didn't feel any pain. I walked
15 through the jungle but I walked slowly. Very slowly.

I passed some pieces of the plane. I saw the number clearly on one piece of metal: OBR 941. I saw other passengers' cases. I could smell dead bodies. I could hear the hungry vultures. But I couldn't hear people's voices. I couldn't see any people. I was afraid. "Are all the other passengers dead?" I thought. "Am I alone
20 in the jungle?"

1. What kind of story is this passage from? _____

2. When does this take place? _____

3. Where is the girl in the story? _____

4. What happened before this passage in the story? _____

_____

5. What do you think will happen after this? _____

_____

Exercise 13

➤ *Read this passage from "Sarah, Plain and Tall," by Patricia MacLachlan. Try to infer the answers to the questions below. Underline the words or phrases that helped you. Work with another student.*

"You don't sing anymore," he said. He said it harshly. Not because he meant to, but because he had been thinking of it for so long. "Why?" he asked more gently.

Slowly, Papa straightened up. There was a long silence, and the dogs looked
5 up, wondering at it.

"I've forgotten the old songs," said Papa quietly. He sat down. "But maybe there's a way to remember them." He looked at us.

"How?" asked Caleb eagerly.

Papa leaned back in the chair. "I've placed an advertisement in the
10 newspapers. For help."

"You mean a housekeeper?" I asked, surprised.

Caleb and I looked at each other and burst out laughing, remembering Hilly, our housekeeper. She was round and slow and shuffling. She snored in a high whistle at night, like a teakettle, and let the fire go out.
15 "No," said Papa slowly. "Not a housekeeper." He paused. "A wife."

Caleb stared at Papa. "A wife? You mean a mother?"

Nick slid his face onto Papa's lap and Papa stroked his ears.

"That, too," said Papa. "Like Maggie."

Matthew, our neighbor to the south, had written to ask for a wife and mother
20 for his children. And Maggie had come from Tennessee. Her hair was the color of turnips and she laughed.

Papa reached into his pocket and unfolded a letter written on white paper. "And I have received an answer."

1. What kind of story is this passage from? _____

2. When does this story take place? _____

3. Who are the people in the passage? _____

_____

4. Where do they live? _____

5. What happened before this in the story? _____

_____

6. What do you think will happen after this? _____

_____

Exercise 14

➤ *Read this passage from "Snow Treasure," by Marie McSwigan. Try to infer the answers to the questions below. Underline the words or phrases that helped you. Work with another student.*

Near the cliff Peter could see the bulky figure of the Commandant, the head of the German forces at Riswyk. He was picking his way up the valley.

Peter and Lovisa continued playing in the snow. Peter had begun a snowman and Lovisa was making hers a fancy hat.

5 They wanted to get up and start for home, but they didn't dare move. They felt they would be less noticed if they stayed where they were.

The Commandant came puffing along. He seemed to have trouble lifting his feet in the deep snow. In his hand he carried a light little cane, a swagger stick.

He plodded along until he came to the children. When he got there he
10 stopped in his tracks.

"If he'd only go on," Peter growled to himself. But he didn't dare look up to see. His hands were busy with the snow. His head was hot and his mouth was dry and there was a buzzing in his ears.

What would happen now? What if the Commandant found the bricks buried
15 under the snowmen? Why there were more than a million kroner right here at their feet!

"We're searching for a German infantryman," the Commandant announced to the children. "Have any of you seen a man in the woods?"

Of course, there was no answer. He turned aside to whisper a few words to
20 Lieutenant Sit-Down. Then he spoke to the children in a loud voice:

"I said we are looking for a German infantryman. It's very important for you children to tell if you've seen one on this part of the coast. There's a severe penalty attached if anyone has seen him and has not reported it."

Still the children said nothing.

25 "I've a good mind to give you children a lesson in manners," his voice was angry. "When you're spoken to, it's only right that you should answer. Has no one taught you that? Now then. Yes or no? Have you seen a German infantry soldier in this fiord?"

The children acted as if they had not heard him. Lovisa sat back on her heels
30 to admire her handiwork. But Peter, for all he tried to be cool, felt a terrible thumping in his chest. His cheeks must be as red as rowanberries. For if any snowman were to be knocked down—

The Commandant strode across the snow and stood above Lovisa.

"Little girl, tell me, did you or did you not see a German infantryman?" he
35 screamed in anger. "Answer me."

Lovisa only turned her big blue eyes up at him. Not so much as a nod did she give him.

"Don't you know I can make you talk? Don't you realize that we Germans can make anyone do our will? We've only to command to be obeyed."

40   Peter remembered the pact they had made the day they had started their
undertaking. They had sworn on the sword that they wouldn't give information
about what they were doing. Of course, this wasn't the same. But even so, they
weren't to talk to the Germans for fear they would say something to make them
suspicious. But there was no need to worry about Lovisa. Pledge or not, she
45 wouldn't talk.

1. What kind of story is this passage from? _____

2. When does the story take place? _____

3. Who are the people in the passage? _____

   _____

4. Where are they? _____

5. What are the children doing? _____

6. What does Peter think about the Commandant? _____

   _____

7. Why does the Commandant get angry? _____

   _____

8. Why don't the children answer the Commandant? _____

   _____

9. What do you think will happen after this? _____

   _____

Skimming

Speed is often important when you are reading. You may have a lot to read but not much time. For this kind of reading you usually do not want to know and remember everything. You only want to find out something about the book or article. You can do this by **skimming.**

You may want to skim:

- newspaper or magazine articles.
- book covers in a bookstore (so you can find out if you want to buy the book).
- library books (so you can find out if they have the information you need).
- mystery, detective, or other novels.

Skimming for point of view

Skimming is helpful when you want to find out quickly about the writer. You may want to find out what the writer thinks about something. This is the writer's **point of view.**

When you want to know the writer's point of view, you do not need to read everything. You need to read only a few important words.

EXAMPLE A

➤ *Read this paragraph quickly. Answer the following question by putting a checkmark (✓) beside the answer.*

Dogs are often a problem at home. Many dogs are noisy and dirty. They may even be dangerous for small children.

Is this writer for or against dogs at home?

For _____   Against __✓__

You do not need to read all the sentences to learn this. You only have to read the words "problem," "noisy," "dirty," and "dangerous." From those words you can tell the writer's point of view. This writer is against dogs at home.

EXAMPLE B

➤ *Read this paragraph quickly. Answer the following question by putting a checkmark (✓) beside the answer.*

An apartment looks much nicer with some plants. The green leaves make it seem cooler in summer. The flowers give it a happy feeling.

Is this writer for or against plants in an apartment?

For _____   *Against* _____

How do you know this? List the keywords: _____

_____

Exercise 1

➤ *Read these paragraphs quickly. Ask yourself, "Is the writer for or against the idea?" Put a checkmark (✓) beside the answer. You should finish the page in less than 60 seconds.*

1. Candy is not good for your teeth. It is especially bad for children's teeth. If children eat a lot of candy, they will have problems later.

    For _____   *Against* _____

2. Large cars can cause problems. They are more difficult to park than small cars. They also use more gas.

    For _____   *Against* _____

3. In San Francisco, the air is always a comfortable temperature. It is never too hot or too cold. It is perfect weather all year.

    For _____   *Against* _____

4. Some people take many vitamin pills every day. These people believe lots of vitamin pills are good for their health. But they are wrong. Too many vitamin pills can hurt your health.

    For _____   *Against* _____

5. There is something sad about animals in the zoos. They never really look happy. Maybe they are thinking about their real home. Maybe they do not like people looking at them all the time.

    For _____   *Against* _____

6. Computers are helpful for all kinds of work. They are usually quicker and more correct than people.

    For _____   *Against* _____

7.   Computers may cause serious problems in our world. Now it is possible to keep a lot of information on a computer. The people who have that information may be dangerous.

     For _____   *Against* _____

8.   "A spoonful of sugar helps the medicine go down." This is from a popular song, but it is often true. Sometimes there are good reasons to give children sugar or candy.

     For _____   *Against* _____

Exercise 2

➤ **Read these paragraphs quickly. Ask yourself, "Is the writer for or against the idea?" Put a checkmark (✓) beside the answer. You should finish the page in less than 60 seconds.**

1.   Many people believe that meat is an important food to eat. This is not true. You do not need to eat meat at all. In fact, you may be more healthy if you do not eat meat.

     For _____   *Against* _____

2.   Travel is not always fun. Often there are problems with transportation, language, or hotels. It is also very tiring to travel, and you can easily get sick.

     For _____   *Against* _____

3.   Today it is better not to have a camera when you travel. A camera is heavy and difficult to carry. It is also not necessary. You can buy good picture postcards almost everywhere.

     For _____   *Against* _____

4.   A bicycle is the best way to see a country. It does not need gas. It is not expensive. Also, you get some exercise at the same time you are traveling.

     For _____   *Against* _____

5.   Bicycles can be dangerous. You can hurt yourself by falling off a bicycle. You can also get seriously hurt if you are hit by a car.

     For _____   *Against* _____

6.   Everyone should learn another language. Knowing a second language is useful these days. It also may teach you something about other people and places.

     For _____   *Against* _____

7.   It is not easy to move to another country. There may be problems with language or culture. It may be difficult to find a job or a place to live. In another country, you do not have family or friends to help.

For _____   Against _____

8.   Music often makes you feel better about life. It can make you happy if you are sad. It can make you relax when you are tense.

For _____   Against _____

Skimming for pattern of organization

Sometimes you need to find out quickly how a book or article is organized. You want to know its pattern. You do not need to know the details for this. You do not need to read all the words. You have to read only the signal words. They will tell you the pattern.

EXAMPLE A

➤ *What is the pattern of organization for this paragraph? Put a checkmark (✓) beside the best answer.*

A whale eats a lot of ocean food every day. That is *because* it is a very large animal.

Listing _____   Time order _____   Cause/effect __✓__   Comparison _____

The signal word is "because." The pattern is cause and effect.

EXAMPLE B

➤ *What is the pattern of organization for this paragraph? Put a checkmark (✓) beside the best answer.*

This book has a lot of information about Poland. First it tells about the history. It also explains how to travel around the country. Finally, it lists some interesting places to visit.

Listing _____   Time order _____   Cause/effect _____   Comparison _____

Exercise 3

➤ *Read the following paragraphs quickly. Read only to find the pattern of organization. Put a checkmark beside the best answer. Try to finish the exercise in less than 60 seconds.*

1.   A parakeet is a small bird that lives in tropical forests. The parrot is similar to a parakeet, but it is larger. Both birds sometimes can learn how to say words.

   Listing _____   Time order _____   Cause/effect _____   Comparison _____

2.   Some kinds of birds cannot fly. The penguin is one of these birds. It lives mostly in the very cold Antarctic climate. Another kind of bird that cannot fly is the ostrich. It lives in Africa.

   Listing _____   Time order _____   Cause/effect _____   Comparison _____

3.   Lisa plans to travel in Europe this summer. In June, she will visit Sicily. In July, she will bicycle in northern Italy. In August, she will travel through France. By September, she hopes to be in Paris.

   Listing _____   Time order _____   Cause/effect _____   Comparison _____

4.   Headaches are often the result of psychological causes. For example, worrying about something can cause a headache.

   Listing _____   Time order _____   Cause/effect _____   Comparison _____

5.   The clambake is a popular New England dinner. It usually includes many different kinds of seafood. Clams are the most common kind of seafood at a clambake. There may also be lobster and mussels.

   Listing _____   Time order _____   Cause/effect _____   Comparison _____

6.   Some people do not like to use computers for writing. They prefer to use typewriters. They know computers are faster and more accurate, but they feel more comfortable with typewriters.

   Listing _____   Time order _____   Cause/effect _____   Comparison _____

7.   Gold was first found in California in about 1840. The next ten years in American history are called the California Gold Rush. Many people moved to the West during those years to look for gold. By 1850, there were many new Gold Rush towns in California.

   Listing _____   Time order _____   Cause/effect _____   Comparison _____

8.   Cola and ginger ale are both kinds of soft drinks. Both these drinks have a lot of sugar in them, but cola has caffeine in it and ginger ale does not.

   Listing _____   Time order _____   Cause/effect _____   Comparison _____

Exercise 4

➤ *Read the following paragraphs quickly. Read only to find the pattern of organization. Put a checkmark beside the best answer. Try to finish the exercise in less than 60 seconds.*

1.　　Leif Ericson was probably the first European to see America. He visited some of the northern areas in about 1000. The next European visitor to America was Christopher Columbus in 1492.

　　Listing _____　　Time order _____　　Cause/effect _____　　Comparison _____

2.　　The Spanish kings and queens sent many people to find out about America. Christopher Columbus was one of these people. Ponce de Leon was another. Vasco da Gama was a third.

　　Listing _____　　Time order _____　　Cause/effect _____　　Comparison _____

3.　　Leif Ericson probably had a more difficult trip across the Atlantic Ocean than Christopher Columbus did. Ericson sailed across the cold northern part of the Atlantic, but Columbus sailed across the southern part, where it was warmer.

　　Listing _____　　Time order _____　　Cause/effect _____　　Comparison _____

4.　　Many American Indians died soon after the Europeans arrived. There was one important reason for this. The Europeans brought new kinds of diseases with them. These diseases caused thousands of deaths in a short time.

　　Listing _____　　Time order _____　　Cause/effect _____　　Comparison _____

5.　　Some of the early Americans did not want to come to this country. For example, many Africans had to come as slaves. Some Europeans had to come for religious freedom.

　　Listing _____　　Time order _____　　Cause/effect _____　　Comparison _____

6.　　When you study for an exam, you should follow three steps. First, you should make sure you have all the information you need. Next, you should put that information in order. Finally, you should make a list of the most important things.

　　Listing _____　　Time order _____　　Cause/effect _____　　Comparison _____

(continued on the next page)

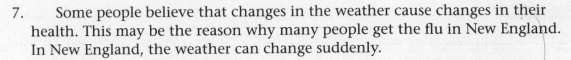

7. Some people believe that changes in the weather cause changes in their health. This may be the reason why many people get the flu in New England. In New England, the weather can change suddenly.

    Listing _____ *Time order* _____ *Cause/effect* _____ *Comparison* _____

8. Many American history books leave out some important information. For example, they often do not tell much about the American Indians. They also leave out some history about women.

    Listing _____ *Time order* _____ *Cause/effect* _____ *Comparison* _____

Skimming for ideas

You can also skim when you want to find out the general idea quickly. Speed is important for this kind of skimming, too. You should skim at least two times faster than you usually read.

You can do this only if you change the way you read. You cannot read every word or even every sentence. You have to leave out a lot. In fact, you should leave out everything except a few important words. These are the words that tell you the general idea.

Guidelines for Skimming for Ideas

1. Read the first few sentences at your usual speed. Ask yourself, "What is this about?"

2. As soon as you guess the general idea, go to the next paragraph. Remember, you do not need to know the details. You only want to learn something very general about the chapter or article.

3. Read only a few words in each paragraph after that. You should look for the words that tell you more about the general idea. Often they are at the beginning of the paragraph, but they may also be at the end.

4. Always work quickly. Remember that details are not important.

EXAMPLE

➤ *Skim the following newspaper article. Most of the words have been blacked out. You will find only a few sentences at the beginning and a few words in each paragraph. However, you should still be able to get the general sense of the article and to answer the questions.*

Big Macs in Russia

McDonald's hamburgers came to Russia not long ago. McDonald's is a world-famous company ▓▓▓▓▓▓▓▓▓▓▓. Started in California ▓▓▓▓▓▓▓ in Paris, Tokyo, and ▓▓▓▓▓▓▓ ▓▓▓▓▓▓▓ ▓▓▓▓▓▓▓ ▓▓▓▓▓▓ ,but not in Russia. Then the Russian government changed ▓▓ ▓▓▓▓▓▓▓

▓▓▓▓ open some McDonald's restaurants ▓▓▓ ▓▓▓▓▓▓▓ ▓▓▓ near Red Square ▓▓▓▓ "Big Mac," ▓▓ a popular sandwich ▓▓▓▓▓▓ ▓▓▓▓▓.

Some Russians are not happy ▓▓▓▓▓ ▓▓▓▓▓▓▓▓ eat only hamburgers and forget about Russian food.

➤ **Circle the letter of the best answer.**

1. McDonald's is a
   a. kind of Russian food.
   b. Russian company.
   c. restaurant company.
   d. kind of hamburger.

2. There were no McDonald's restaurants in Russia because
   a. Russians do not like hamburgers.
   b. Russians eat only Russian food.
   c. there were McDonald's restaurants in other countries.
   d. the Russian government did not want them.

3. The "Big Mac" is a
   a. restaurant.
   b. kind of hamburger.
   c. kind of Russian food.
   d. person who works for McDonald's.

Exercise 5

In this exercise you will skim a book review. A book review gives you some information about a book that helps you decide if you want to read it.

➤ *Skim as quickly as possible. Remember, you want to find out only the general ideas about the book. You should read only the underlined sentences. Then try to answer the questions below.*

Murder in the Language Lab

by M. L. Allen

This book is an unusual detective story. It begins with a crime, a murder. A scientist is killed in a laboratory. No one knows who killed the scientist. Inspector Barker is the detective. He must find the killer, but he needs help.

He gets help from Sally, a chimpanzee who lives in the laboratory. In this laboratory, scientists are studying language. They are interested in how animals like Sally can learn some language. Sally is one smart chimpanzee. She cannot talk, but she understands many words. She answers questions by using a computer. Sally saw the murder. She is afraid of Inspector Barker at first, but she wants to help. So she tells Inspector Barker who the murderer is.

If you like detective stories, you will enjoy this one. But you probably will not be able to guess who the murderer is!

➤ *Circle the letter of the best answer. You may check your answers by reading the rest of the review. The Answer Key is on page 286.*

1. This story is
   a. full of information.
   b. sad.
   c. fun to read.
   d. difficult to read.

2. Inspector Barker
   a. finds the murderer himself.
   b. never finds the murderer.
   c. is studying language.
   d. gets help from a chimpanzee.

3. Sally is
   a. a scientist.
   b. a smart animal.
   c. not a smart animal.
   d. a murderer.

Exercise 6

➤ *Skim the following review as quickly as possible for the general ideas about the book. Remember, you need to read only a few sentences and words. Then try to answer the questions below. You should finish in less than 60 seconds.*

The Hot Zone
A Terrifying True Story
by Richard Preston

In the 1980s and 1990s, people in many parts of the world began to catch strange and horrible illnesses. These new illnesses are caused by tiny viruses. The illnesses are a big problem, because no one knows how to cure them. Most people who catch these viruses die.

This book tells the story of how the killer viruses are moving around the world. Sometimes people carry them. Sometimes monkeys carry them. The stories in this book are true, but they are hard to believe because they are so terrible.

The author writes vivid descriptions of the illnesses. The reader can almost see the sick patients as they die horrible deaths, with blood coming out of their ears, nose, and mouth.

Near Washington, D.C., a special laboratory works on these dangerous viruses. In one of the best parts of this book, Preston tells how scientists at that lab work very carefully. They wear special clothes that make them look like astronauts. A tiny hole in their clothes could let a killer virus inside!

This book is perfect for people who like exciting stories and is not for people who are easily scared.

1. This book is
   a. not a true story.
   b. about killer viruses.
   c. for people who are scared to read.

2. Scientists work on the viruses
   a. until they die.
   b. in special laboratories.
   c. in exciting stories.

3. No one knows
   a. where the laboratories are.
   b. how the illnesses travel.
   c. how to cure the illnesses.

Exercise 7

➤ *Skim the following newspaper article. You should finish in about 60 seconds. Then answer the questions below.*

Teleshopping in Europe

by Victor Frank

For several years, Americans have enjoyed teleshopping—watching cable TV and ordering things by phone. Now teleshopping is starting in Europe. In a number of European countries, people can turn on their TVs to cable stations and shop for clothes, jewelry, wine, tools, toys, kitchen equipment, and many other things.

Teleshopping is becoming popular in Sweden, for example. The biggest Swedish company offers merchandise in 15 European countries, and in one year it had sales of $100 million. In France there are two teleshopping channels, and the French spend about $20 million a year to buy things through those channels.

In Germany, until recently teleshopping was only possible on one channel for 1 hour per day. Then the government decided to allow more teleshopping. Other channels can open for telebusiness, including the largest American teleshopping company and a 24-hour teleshopping company. German businesses are hoping these new teleshopping possibilities will help them increase their sales.

Some people like teleshopping because it allows them to do their shopping without leaving their homes. With all the problems of traffic in the cities, this is an important factor. However, other Europeans do not like this new way of shopping. A German journalist, for example, called teleshopping "junk on the air." In general, many Europeans are concerned about the quality of the things for sale on TV. Good quality is important to them, and they believe they cannot be sure about the quality of the things on TV.

This demand for high quality means that European teleshopping companies will have to be different from the American companies. They will have to be more careful about the quality of the things they sell. They will also have to work harder to sell things that the customers cannot touch or see in person.

1. Teleshopping is
   a. not popular in Europe.
   b. growing in Europe.
   c. not possible in Europe.
   d. cheap in Europe.

2. People like teleshopping because it is
   a. easier.
   b. cheaper.
   c. American.
   d. more popular.

3. Some Europeans don't like teleshopping because they
   a. don't like to buy things.
   b. want to shop at home.
   c. think the things sold on TV are poor quality.
   d. don't watch TV.

Exercise 8

➤ *Skim the following newspaper article. Try to finish in less than 60 seconds. Then answer the questions below.*

What Is Hurting the Environment?

by Faith Silver

Scientists are working hard to clean up our environment. Air pollution is one of the most serious problems they face. They know that a lot of the pollution is caused by people burning fuels such as gasoline, wood, and oil.

In many big cities now, the air is gray and dirty. This is caused mostly by the gasoline burned in car engines. For every gallon of gasoline that a car burns, a half pound of carbon monoxide goes into the air. This is what makes the air so gray. Scientists and car makers are making changes in car engines. New cars will not put so much carbon monoxide into the air. Then the air will be cleaner, and cities such as Los Angeles and Mexico City will have blue skies again.

But carbon monoxide pollution is only one form of air pollution. Another kind of air pollution that comes from gasoline and other fuels is carbon dioxide. For every gallon of gasoline a car burns, $5^1/2$ pounds of carbon dioxide go into the air. You cannot see carbon dioxide in the air, since it is a clear gas, and you cannot smell it. But the effects of carbon dioxide on the environment are very serious.

Carbon dioxide has made a clear cloud over the earth. This cloud is called the "greenhouse effect." Like a blanket, this clear cloud has made the earth warmer. As the earth becomes a lot warmer, many things may change. First of all, the weather may change. There may be more violent storms in many parts of the world. In many places the summers may become hotter and drier. In these places, it may be more difficult to grow food, and that means more people may die of hunger.

What can we do about carbon dioxide pollution? We need to burn fuels to keep warm in the winter, we need to cook, and we need to have transportation. In the past, we did all these things and there was no greenhouse effect. However, in the past there were far fewer people. Now, the number of people in the world is growing every year. So the amount of fuel we burn is growing, and the pollution problem is growing, too. Scientists say that the earth is in danger from the greenhouse effect. They also say the real problem is not carbon dioxide. The problem is too many people!

1. This article says that carbon monoxide pollution
   X a. comes from gasoline burned in cars.
   b. comes from the earth.
   c. is caused by scientists.

2. Carbon dioxide is a problem because it
   a. is a fossil fuel.
   X b. makes the earth warmer.
   c. is burned by cars.

3. Scientists say the real problem is
   a. carbon monoxide.
   b. the air in Los Angeles and Mexico City.
   c. too many people in the world.

Exercise 9

➤ *Skim the following magazine article. You should finish in about 60 seconds. Then answer the questions.*

Shannon Lucid, Space Pioneer

by Valentina Gold

On September 26, 1996, Shannon Lucid set a record for astronauts. She was the first woman in the world and the first American astronaut to live in a space station for 188 days. For all that time, she shared the Russian Mir Space Station with two Russian cosmonauts.

Shannon Lucid was born in 1943 in Shanghai, where her parents were working. Her family left China and moved to Oklahoma when she was a child, and from the time she was 13 years old, she knew she wanted to be a space pioneer. When she told this to her teacher, the teacher said, "That's impossible. You're a girl!"

Shannon never forgot her dream. When she was in high school, she learned to fly a plane, and soon after her graduation she earned a pilot's license. She went to study at the university, and she earned a doctoral degree in biochemistry. Then she joined the United States astronaut program.

Shannon was thrilled to be chosen for a long stay on the Russian Mir Space Station.

She wants to study how the human body reacts to long trips in space. She wants to help people prepare to fly to Mars someday. While Shannon was on the Mir Space Station, she and the Russians spent their time performing scientific experiments and exercising to stay in good physical condition. She also taught the Russian cosmonauts to enjoy her favorite American desserts. They especially enjoyed eating Jell-O, a cold, fruit-flavored jelly.

Astronaut Lucid and her husband, an oil company executive, have three children. Their family home is in Texas. While she was away, Shannon did not lose touch with her family: They sent each other e-mail messages every day.

1. Shannon Lucid was the first American to
   a. earn a pilot's license.
   b. study the human body.
   c. stay in space for 188 days.
   d. enjoy eating Jell-O.

2. Shannon and the Russians
   a. did not have anything to do.
   b. spent some time exercising.
   c. all came from Oklahoma.
   d. tried to fly to Mars.

3. Shannon showed her teacher that women can
   a. make good desserts.
   b. go to the university.
   c. become space pioneers.
   d. exercise to stay in good condition.

Exercise 10

➤ *Skim the following magazine article. You should finish in about 60 seconds. Then answer the questions.*

Burning Trees to Save a Forest

by Ken Gordon

Burning trees to save a forest! Strange as it sounds, that is the U.S. Forest Service's new idea for saving America's forests.

For more than a hundred years, Americans were taught that fires in a forest were always bad. When trees burned in the forest, it was a disaster which would ruin the forest. The Forest Service promoted this idea in many ways. They even invented a character named Smokey the Bear, who always said, "Remember, only you can prevent forest fires."

Whenever there was a fire in the forest, the rangers immediately put it out. No fires were allowed to burn, even in places where many of the trees were dead or diseased. This did not help the forests, however. In fact, with so many dead and diseased trees, the forest fires in the western United States have been far worse in recent years.

The new chief of the U.S. Forest Service recently explained that there is a new and better way to save our forests. He said, "Small, limited fires are part of nature. That is the way that old, dead and diseased trees are cleared away to make room for new trees."

Now the Forest Service has new plans. They will start small fires in forests, but they will control the fires. The fires will be started in parts of the forest which are old and full of diseased trees. The rangers plan to burn about 30,000 acres a year for the next 20 years.

As the chief said, "It took many years for the forests to become old and diseased, and so it will take more than 20 years to correct the problem by using controlled fires."

1. In the past, Americans thought
   a. forests were dead and diseased.
   b. there would be too many rangers.
   c. forest fires were bad.
   d. forest fires were good.

2. Forest fires help forests because they
   a. burn the dead and diseased trees.
   b. burn the new trees.
   c. are worse in the western United States.
   d. are a disaster.

3. Now the Forest Service plans to
   a. stop all fires immediately.
   b. find a new chief.
   c. make fires worse.
   d. start small, controlled fires.

Part Three

Thinking Skills

How to think in English

If you want to read English well, you must think in English. The Thinking Skills exercises in this part will help you learn to think in English.

EXAMPLE

➤ *This paragraph is incomplete: The ending is missing. Read the paragraph and the four possible endings. Decide which is the best ending and circle the letter.*

In the morning the language lab was full of people. Many students were waiting. Joe could not find a seat. He decided to come back later when the lab was

a. closed.   c. more crowded.
b. busy.   (d.) less crowded.

The right ending is d. Joe could not get a seat because the lab was full. He had to come back when it was not full. What is another word for "full"? "Crowded." What is another way to say "not full"? "Less crowded."

Ending a is not right. When the lab is closed, Joe cannot get in.

Ending b is not right. "Busy" is another way to say "crowded." Joe probably could not find a seat in a busy lab.

Ending c is not right. "More crowded" means "even more students than before, and fewer seats."

Guidelines for Thinking Skills Exercises

1. Do some Thinking Skills exercises every week.
2. Each time you work on an exercise, write the date in the margin at the side of the page.
3. Work quickly. Your first guess will often be the right one!
4. Do not use a dictionary. Try to guess the meaning of new words from the context.
5. You can follow the ideas better—and get the right answer—if you think in English!
6. When you finish an exercise, check your answers in the Answer Key on page 286.
7. Write the date and the number of questions you answered correctly in the Thinking Skills Progress Chart on page 271.

Exercise 1

➤ *Choose the best ending for each paragraph.*

1. It used to take months to cross the Atlantic Ocean in a ship. But now a plane can cross the Atlantic in

    a. a few months.   c. a few hours.
    b. a long time.   d. more time.

2. The easiest way to travel is to walk. You don't need anything special. All you need is

    a. two feet.   c. a car.
    b. to hurry   d. gasoline.

3. Cars are a problem in big cities. There are too many cars in the streets. Most city streets are noisy and

    a. safe.   c. parking.
    b. large.   d. crowded.

4. Alexander Graham Bell made the first telephone in 1876 in the United States. Now the telephone is international. You can use it to talk to someone anywhere

    a. in the city.   c. in history.
    b. in the world.   d. on time.

5. Henry went to the doctor because he could not see well. The doctor told him he should get a new pair of

    a. shoes.   c. gloves.
    b. pants.   d. glasses.

Exercise 2

➤ *Choose the best ending for each paragraph.*

1. New York is one of the biggest cities in the world. It has about 7 million people. But Tokyo is larger. It has more than

    a. a million people.   c. as many people.
    b. thousands of people.   d. 8 million people.

2. In cold climates, plants grow quickly in the spring and summer. This is partly because the weather is warmer. It is also because the days are longer and plants get more

    a. air.   c. water.
    b. sunlight.   d. leaves.

Thinking Skills

3.   Some plants grow in very dry places. These desert plants can live for a long time with no

      a. flowers.   c. food.
      b. sun.   d. water.

4.   People used to wake up when it was light. They went to bed when it was dark. The sun was their

      a. star.   c. clock.
      b. time.   d. bed.

5.   What is your favorite color? If it is red, you may be a lively kind of person. If you like blue, you may be a person who likes peace and quiet. Your favorite color tells something about

      a. colors.   c. you.
      b. life.   d. peace.

Exercise 3

➤ *Choose the best ending for each paragraph.*

1.   Sometimes children get sick because of problems at home. Then doctors like to meet with the children's

      a. friends.   c. teachers.
      b. parents.   d. patients.

2.   Dentists think that eating candy is bad for the teeth. If children eat candy, they will probably have tooth trouble

      a. before.   c. someday.
      b. in the past.   d. in the morning.

3.   Some birds fly many miles every year. In the fall they leave their homes in the north and fly south to warmer places. In the spring, they leave their winter homes and go back

      a. north.   c. around.
      b. south.   d. away.

4.   Many farmers in Florida grow oranges. They also grow lemons, limes, and grapefruit. Florida is famous for its

      a. apples.   c. weather.
      b. vegetables.   d. fruit.

5.   Some people prefer warm climates. They do not like cold weather or snow. They enjoy the heat and feel happy in the

      a. climate.   c. sun.
      b. snow.   d. night.

Exercise 4

➤ *Choose the best ending for each paragraph.*

1. Some people enjoy the winter. They like winter sports such as skiing and skating. They enjoy ice and

    a. weather.   c. sun.
    b. snow.   d. rain.

2. Jazz started in the United States around 1900. Now there are jazz musicians around the world. But the most famous jazz musicians are

    a. English.   c. European.
    b. dead.   d. American.

3. In very hot countries, the sun can hurt your eyes. It is a good idea to wear a hat when you are outside. You should also wear

    a. shoes.   c. a swimsuit.
    b. sunglasses.   d. gloves.

4. Last week Mr. Thomas rented a new apartment. He does not have a table, chairs, or any other furniture yet. The apartment looks

    a. comfortable.   c. empty.
    b. full.   d. crowded.

5. On special days, the whole family has dinner at our house. Everyone came last week for my father's

    a. parents.   c. house.
    b. family.   d. birthday.

Exercise 5

➤ *Choose the best ending for each paragraph.*

1. The police stopped a man. They said he took some money from a store. They found the money in his pocket. So they took him to

    a. the hospital.   c. the bank.
    b. the police station.   d. his home.

2. People used to learn the news from the newspaper. But today many people do not read the paper. They prefer to learn the news

    a. from a movie.   c. from books.
    b. from TV.   d. from friends.

3.   The whale swims like a fish and lives in the ocean, but it is not a fish. Fish stay under water all the time. Whales must have air. They can go down deep in the ocean for many minutes, but they always need to

    a. find a fish to eat.   c. act like a fish.

    b. swim a long way.   d. come up again for air.

4.   Whales are the largest animals in the ocean, but some whales eat only very tiny fish. That means they must

    a. eat larger fish.   c. drink a lot of water.

    b. eat a lot of fish.   d. travel far.

5.   Curtains on the windows can make a room cooler in the summer. They let air come into the room, but they

    a. stop the wind.   c. are dark.

    b. keep out the sun.   d. are light.

Exercise 6

➤ *Choose the best ending for each paragraph.*

1.   Coffee grows in places with warm climates. In some parts of the world, the land is good for growing coffee, but the winters are too

    a. cold.   c. short.

    b. dry.   d. cloudy.

2.   In Sweden, the summer days are long and the sun shines for many hours. But the winter is very dark. The days are short because the sun rises late and sets

    a. late.   c. at midnight.

    b. beautifully.   d. early.

3.   In Europe there are many small countries. Each country has its own kind of money. This sometimes is a problem for the traveler. It means you often have to change

    a. cash.   c. languages.

    b. money.   d. airplanes.

4.   In New England, the weather changes often. It may be sunny in the morning. Then it can be very cold and rainy in the afternoon. That is why a famous writer said, "If you don't like the weather in New England,

    a. go home."   c. bring an umbrella."

    b. wait a few hours."   d. listen to the radio."

5.   My favorite book is about the life of Charles Dickens. He was a famous English writer. It is an interesting story. The best part is about

    a. airplanes.   c. his childhood.

    b. the economy.   d. the mountains.

Exercise 7

> *Choose the best ending for each paragraph.*

1. Clocks were first made in Europe in about 1500. Before then, people looked at the sun

    a. to tell the time.   c. in the morning.
    b. to get places.   d. to read.

2. The piano is a popular instrument for children. It is easy to make a nice sound on the piano. The violin is less popular, because it is more

    a. fun.   c. boring.
    b. beautiful.   d. difficult.

3. In California, the time is three hours earlier than the time in New York. If it is 11 o'clock in New York, it must be

    a. 3 o'clock in California.   c. 11 o'clock in California.
    b. 8 o'clock in California.   d. later in California.

4. Glassmaking is an old art. The Romans and the Egyptians made glass many years ago. Now we can make many different kinds of glass in all colors, but the art is

    a. the same.   c. beautiful.
    b. very new.   d. not old.

5. Thousands of years ago, people loved gold. They wore gold rings, earrings, and bracelets. Today, people still like to wear jewelry made of

    a. rings.   c. bracelets.
    b. gold.   d. wood.

Exercise 8

> *Choose the best ending for each paragraph.*

1. Some people like history. They like to look at old buildings and old streets. They like to know that many others lived there before them. These people have a strong feeling for

    a. cities.   c. buildings.
    b. people.   d. the past.

2. Other people prefer new cities. They like to see modern buildings and clean streets. They feel that new things are exciting. These people don't think much about the past. They are interested in

    a. the present.   c. history.
    b. cities.   d. old times.

3.   The best way to learn about a new city is to walk around. You can watch people and listen to their conversations. You can look at things in the shop windows. This way you will get to know

     a. the price of food.   c. how the people live.
     b. the language.   d. the history of the city.

4.   Denver, Colorado, is next to the Rocky Mountains. In fact, the city is partly in the mountains. That is why it is called the

     a. "low city."   c. "flat city."
     b. "mile-high city."   d. "city of dreams."

5.   Every year more people move to cities. They think they will find better jobs in the city. They do not want to work on farms and live in small towns. So cities are growing larger all the time and

     a. more people are living on farms.   c. there are no jobs in small towns.
     b. people are more interesting.   d. fewer people are living on farms.

Exercise 9

➤ *Choose the best ending for each paragraph.*

1.   In every country people drink something different at mealtime. The French and the Italians like to drink wine with their dinner. The English and the Germans often drink beer. Many Americans drink coffee with their meal. And in Poland, people often have

     a. food.   c. glasses.
     b. tea.   d. dinner.

2.   You can tell a horse's age by looking at its teeth. You can learn about its health by looking at its eyes. So before you buy a horse, look carefully at its

     a. chest.   c. tail.
     b. feet.   d. head.

3.   Summer sports are popular even in northern countries with short summers. For example, in Sweden, sailing is an important national sport. So is

     a. tennis.   c. cooking.
     b. ice skating.   d. skiing.

4.   Reading is a good way to learn a new language. You can learn new vocabulary. You can also learn to think in that

     a. book.   c. comprehension.
     b. language.   d. word.

5.   "April showers bring May flowers." People say this in some places because April is the time for planting flowers. It is usually a

     a. rainy month.   c. long month.
     b. dry month.   d. hot month.

Exercise 10

> *Choose the best ending for each paragraph.*

1. When people get older, their eyes often get weak. They need to wear glasses to see things up close. They especially need glasses for

    a. driving a car.
    b. watching a movie.
    c. reading a book.
    d. looking out the window.

2. People used to think that the sun moved around the earth. They thought the earth stayed in one place and the sun

    a. never rose.
    b. moved across the sky.
    c. never moved.
    d. also stayed in one place.

3. One hundred years ago, there were no radios, CD players, or TVs. If people wanted to hear music, they had go to a concert, or they had to

    a. go to the city.
    b. play music themselves.
    c. change the station.
    d. stay home.

4. Franz Joseph Haydn wrote music in the 1700s. He lived to be 77 years old. Many younger musicians loved him, and they learned a lot from him. To them, Haydn was like

    a. a son.
    b. a father.
    c. other old men.
    d. a violinist.

5. Many great singers are Italian. In fact, singing is an important part of Italian culture. Some people say that even the Italian language sounds

    a. like English.
    b. like music.
    c. different.
    d. the same.

Exercise 11

> *Choose the best ending for each paragraph.*

1. Siberia is the coldest part of Russia. When people in Europe talk about a wind from Siberia, they mean

    a. a warm wind.
    b. a soft wind.
    c. a strong wind.
    d. a cold wind.

2. Some kinds of trees are always green. They do not lose their leaves in the winter, so they are called

    a. flowers.
    b. lifeless.
    c. evergreens.
    d. leafless.

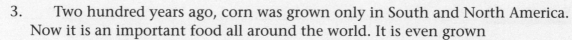

3.   Two hundred years ago, corn was grown only in South and North America. Now it is an important food all around the world. It is even grown

     a. in South America.   c. on farms.

     b. in China.   d. in the United States.

4.   Tomatoes are a new vegetable in Europe. They arrived from South America in the sixteenth century. At first people thought they were not good to eat. They believed that tomatoes made you

     a. live longer.   c. fatter.

     b. hungry.   d. sick.

5.   Every country has a national holiday. This holiday usually is an important date in the history of

     a. the United States.   c. the world.

     b. the summer.   d. that country.

Exercise 12

➤ *Choose the best ending for each paragraph.*

1.   In the United States, many children watch TV for hours every day. They never read books, except at school. It is not surprising that these children

     a. have no books.   c. can read well.

     b. go to school.   d. cannot read well.

2.   In cold weather, it is important to wear a hat. In fact, without a hat, you lose 60 percent of your body heat through your

     a. hands.   c. hat.

     b. body.   d. head.

3.   New Yorkers generally love city life. They like noisy places and bright lights. They often are not happy in the country. To them, the country seems too

     a. noisy.   c. bright.

     b. loud.   d. quiet.

4.   Cooking is different in the mountains. You have to cook things longer. For example, it usually takes about an hour to bake bread, but in the mountains, it may take

     a. an hour and a half.   c. less time.

     b. half an hour.   d. 45 minutes.

5.   In Tokyo, the subway station is like a small city. You can shop, eat, or get a haircut underground. You can spend a day in Tokyo and never see

     a. the subway.   c. the station.

     b. the sky.   d. the driver.

Exercise 13

➤ *Choose the best ending for each paragraph.*

1. Seagulls are birds that live near the ocean. But you can also find seagulls near garbage dumps. Their favorite food is fish, but they will eat

   a. at the beach.   c. near the ocean.
   b. only fish.   d. almost anything.

2. Penguins are unusual birds. They can swim very well. But they are heavy and have very small wings, so they cannot

   a. sing.   c. fish.
   b. talk.   d. fly.

3. Penguins are funny-looking birds. They look like little men with black suits and white shirts. They are friendly, and they are not afraid of people. In zoos, penguins

   a. hide from people.   c. sometimes wear clothes.
   b. are very popular.   d. never eat.

4. In a civil war, people in the same country fight each other. This can be the most terrible kind of war. Sometimes even people from the same family

   a. work together.   c. live near each other.
   b. fight each other.   d. move to another country.

5. New ideas travel from one country to another quickly now. Businesses try to sell new things in other countries. TV carries new ideas everywhere. The countries of the world are becoming more and

   a. crowded.   c. more alike.
   b. different.   d. empty.

Exercise 14

➤ *Choose the best ending for each paragraph.*

1. The idea of flying is old. Many years ago, people watched birds in the air. They studied the birds' wings, and they made wings with bird feathers. Then they

   a. flew.   c. will fly someday.
   b. tried to fly.   d. told stories.

2. The Wright brothers are famous in the history of flying. In 1903, they flew 120 feet in the world's first

   a. automobile.   c. airplane.
   b. machine.   d. wings.

3. Sputnik was the first spaceship. The Russians sent it up into space in 1957. Soon after that, the Americans sent up a spaceship, too. That was the beginning of the

    a. Scientific Age.   c. Nuclear Age.
    b. Space Age.   d. Industrial Age.

4. Jules Verne is called the "father of science fiction." He wrote novels in the 1800s. In his novels he described many things that really happened in the future. For example, he told about airplanes and submarine ships. He also told about a trip to

    a. the moon.   c. America.
    b. the seaside.   d. the sun.

5. In 1785, two men flew from England to France in a balloon. They began to have trouble with the balloon. It went lower and lower. They threw out everything they had. It went even lower. It almost touched the water. Finally, they took off their clothes and threw them out, too. When they arrived in France, they were safe, but

    a. wet.   c. unhappy.
    b. happy.   d. cold.

Exercise 15

➤ *Choose the best ending for each paragraph.*

1. Sometimes distant mountains look blue. When you look closer, you see that they are not blue. They just look blue when they are

    a. near the sky.   c. large.
    b. under the clouds.   d. far away.

2. On some days, the clouds are thin and high in the sky. These clouds may mean rain in the next few days. On other days, there are heavy, dark clouds. They often mean rain is coming soon. Clouds can tell you a lot about the

    a. sky.   c. weather.
    b. air.   d. temperature.

3. Many Americans drive their car to work every day. Around the cities, the highways are full of cars every morning and afternoon. Cars are an important cause of air pollution. This is one reason why many U.S. cities

    a. have such clean air.   c. have a problem with dirty air.
    b. are so large.   d. have little air pollution.

4.   If you work on a computer, you can work anywhere. In fact, many people now don't go to an office every day. They go to the office for meetings, but they do most of their work

      a. for the company.   c. in the office.

      b. at school.   d. at home.

5.   In the past, Italy was not really a country. It was many small countries with different governments. In 1870, all these small countries came together. Then

      a. modern Italy died.   c. the old Italy was born.

      b. modern Italy was born.   d. they started a war.

Exercise 16

➤ *Choose the best ending for each paragraph.*

1.   The Hebrides Islands are in the northwest of Scotland. The sea is beautiful there, but the water is cold, even in summer. It is not a good place to go

      a. fishing.   c. shopping.

      b. swimming.   d. walking.

2.   Tweed is a special kind of cloth. The Scottish island of Harris is famous for its tweed. All around the world, people pay a lot of money for

      a. Scottish bread.   c. the island of Harris.

      b. cloth.   d. Harris tweed.

3.   Fishermen today have large boats and special nets. They can catch thousands of fish in a short time. This may be a problem. Some scientists are afraid

      a. there will be too many fish soon.   c. the fish will swim away.

      b. the boats will not be large   d. there will soon be no more fish.
         enough.

4.   Violins are made from special kinds of wood. The wood is important to the sound of the violin. A violin made from the wrong wood will

      a. sound better.   c. not sound as nice.

      b. sound the same.   d. have no sound.

5.   Some birds travel long distances. They may fly thousands of miles to a winter home. Then they fly back to their old home in the spring. They always return to the same place. No one knows how they do it. Scientists think these birds have some kind of

      a. language in their heads.   c. special wings.

      b. map in their heads.   d. special food.

Exercise 17

➤ *Choose the best ending for each paragraph.*

1. In New England, the worst winter storms come from the northeast. If you are building a house, you should not put windows on that side. To stay warm, put your windows on

    a. the south side of the house.
    b. the northeast side of the house.
    c. all sides of the house.
    d. the second floor.

2. Some scientists used to have strange ideas about the size of a person's head. They thought that people with large heads were the smartest and that people with smaller heads were

    a. not as smart.
    b. also smart.
    c. the smartest.
    d. even smarter.

3. Strong muscles are less important than a strong heart. A healthy and strong heart is necessary for a long life. People with weak hearts usually

    a. live longer.
    b. die at a younger age.
    c. get better.
    d. do not die young.

4. Doctors often say that you should not smoke cigarettes, you should not be too heavy, and you should not work too hard. All these things can give you heart trouble. Some doctors get heart attacks. Maybe they don't

    a. smoke cigarettes.
    b. work too hard.
    c. do what they say.
    d. eat too much.

5. Are you going out? The weather report says rain is coming later tonight. Before you leave the house, please be sure to

    a. watch the news.
    b. close the windows.
    c. lock the door.
    d. read the newspaper.

Exercise 18

➤ *Choose the best ending for each paragraph.*

1. On weekends, people in Boston like to go away. They go to the country, to the mountains, or to the sea. Every Friday evening, the roads going out of Boston are

    a. empty.
    b. crowded.
    c. wet.
    d. wide.

2.   The American Civil War was a difficult time. The North was fighting the South. People who lived in the central states often did not agree about which side was right. Even members of the same family sometimes disagreed. Sometimes, one son was fighting for the North and another

  a. was fighting for the South. c. stayed home.
  b. moved to another state.   d. had more children.

3.   Brighton Beach is a neighborhood in New York City. There are many Russian people living there, and many of the shops and restaurants are Russian. In fact, the neighborhood is sometimes called

  a. "Little New York."   c. "Little Beach."
  b. "Little Odessa."   d. "Little Tokyo."

4.   Every year the Italian neighborhood in New York has a special day. There is Italian food. There are Italian songs and dances. There are games and exciting rides. The streets are full of people and noise.

  a. No one is happy.   c. Everyone has a good time.
  b. Few people enjoy themselves. d. Many people do not have fun.

5.   World War I ended in 1918. It was a terrible war that killed millions of people. Many Europeans believed there would be no more wars. They called World War I

  a. "the first of many."   c. "only the beginning."
  b. "the war to end all wars." d. "a war to be proud of."

Exercise 19

▶ *Choose the best ending for each paragraph.*

1.   Two thousand years ago, the Romans ruled much of the Western world. The city of Rome was in the center. Writers like to say that in those days

  a. "no roads led to Rome." c. "all roads led to the West."
  b. "all roads led to Rome." d. "all roads led to the East."

2.   A bicycle is useful in the city. It is faster than walking. It can go more places than a car. Also, with a bicycle, you don't have to look for a

  a. parking space.   c. wheel.
  b. road.   d. driver.

3.   The violin, viola, and cello all belong to the same family of musical instruments. The violin is the smallest, with the highest sound. The viola is larger, with a lower sound. The cello is largest, with the lowest sound. In this family,

      a. larger instruments have lower sounds.
      b. the size makes no difference to the sound.
      c. large instruments have higher sounds.
      d. the sizes are all the same.

4.   Some people say that photographs are not art. They say that a photograph is just a copy of the real world. A photograph does not tell you what the artist was thinking. These people believe that art

      a. is a true picture.
      b. must be the same as what we see.
      c. must show you what someone thinks.
      d. must not show you what someone thinks.

5.   Most European languages came from one language thousands of years ago, so in some ways they are alike. But Hungarian and Finnish are different from the other European languages. In fact, they

      a. came from Europe.
      b. are spoken only in Hungary and Finland.
      c. are also alike in some ways.
      d. came from a different language.

Exercise 20

➤ *Choose the best ending for each paragraph.*

1.   One hundred years ago, the British Empire was very strong. It sent ships and soldiers to North and South America, Africa, and Asia. There were British ships all around the world. The British were proud of this. They liked to say, "The sun never sets

      a. in England."   c. on the far side of the world."
      b. in our hearts."   d. on the British Empire."

2.   In some movies, there are only good cowboys and bad cowboys. The good cowboys are great men who help everyone. The bad cowboys are robbers and killers. But in real life, most cowboys were just like other men—not all good or bad. The idea of cowboys we get from movies is

      a. true.   c. good.
      b. not true.   d. helpful.

3.   Scientists say that Americans move often. The average American moves to a new home every seven years. But some Americans never move. They live all their lives in the same place. So there must be other Americans who

    a. move to new homes.
    b. move more than once in seven years.
    c. never move.
    d. move every seven years.

4.   It is harder to learn some things when you get older. Your brain does not work as quickly. That is why we sometimes say, "You can't teach

    a. a young dog anything."
    b. an old dog new tricks."
    c. a young dog new tricks."
    d. a dog when you are old."

5.   The Potato Famine happened in Ireland in the 1840s. The Irish people were poor. They couldn't buy meat or bread, because they were too expensive. They ate mostly potatoes. Then a disease killed many of the potato plants. With no potatoes to eat, the people

    a. were happier.
    b. ate meat instead.
    c. died of hunger.
    d. were ill.

Exercise 21

➤ *Choose the best ending for each paragraph.*

1.   A beaver is a small animal that lives in northern forests. It cuts down trees with its teeth, and it puts the trees and some dirt across a small river. This stops the river water and makes a lake. Then the beaver makes a home in the middle of the lake under the water. The beaver has to work long and hard to do all this. That's why we sometimes say that someone is as

    a. lazy as a beaver.
    b. wet as a beaver.
    c. small as a beaver.
    d. busy as a beaver.

2.   "An apple a day keeps the doctor away." That is what mothers used to say to their children. People believed that it was good to eat lots of apples, but they didn't know why. Now, scientists know that this is true and they know why. Apples really are

    a. good for your health.
    b. bad for your teeth.
    c. unhealthy.
    d. good for your doctor.

3.   Some people like to dream about things that are not possible. They plan wonderful vacations, but they have no money. They think of getting married to someone they do not even know. These people, we say, are

    a. building a solid future.
    b. making a new life for themselves.
    c. building castles in the air.
    d. telling tall tales.

4.   A few days ago, Sarah found a chair. It was lying on a pile of garbage outside her house. She did not understand why it was there. It was not broken or old. In fact, it was quite new. She needed a chair, so she

     a. left it there.   c. took it home.

     b. sat on it.   d. looked at it.

5.   Many Americans like to keep dogs as pets. Some dogs help with work on a farm. Others may help hunt wild animals. And many dogs are just nice to have in the house. Dogs are often called

     a. bad names.   c. farmers and hunters.

     b. man's worst enemy.   d. man's best friend.

Exercise 22

➤ *Choose the best ending for each paragraph.*

1.   In many countries, jogging is a popular sport. Some people jog to lose weight. Others jog because they like to feel strong. But the best reason for jogging is for your health. Doctors say it makes

     a. your heart stronger.   c. you go faster.

     b. your heart weaker.   d. you eat a lot.

2.   Many of the most famous marathon runners today are from Africa. Young African men and women work very hard at running. That is why they

     a. are not very good.   c. win so many races.

     b. are young.   d. travel a lot.

3.   Today, people run much faster than they did in the past. Before 1954, the record time for running a mile was over four minutes. That year, Bannister ran a mile in less than four minutes. After that, many other runners also

     a. ran very slowly   c. ran a mile in over four minutes.

     b. could run a mile.   d. ran a mile in less than four minutes.

4.   Many English words come from Greek words. For example, the Greek word for "star" is "aster." So the scientists who study the sky are called

     a. philosophers.   c. astronomers.

     b. sky-gazers.   d. archaeologists.

5.   In the last few years of his life, Beethoven could not hear. In his earlier life, he always tried out his music on the piano. Later, however, he could not do that. When he wrote his music, he had to

     a. listen to an orchestra.   c. sing it to someone.

     b. play the violin.   d. think it in his head.

Exercise 23

➤ *Choose the best ending for each paragraph.*

1.   Many New Yorkers live in tall apartment buildings. The nicest apartments with the best view are the ones at the top. These are called "penthouse apartments." Everyone wants these apartments, of course, but they are usually

       a. empty.   c. the last ones to be rented.
       b. the most expensive.   d. the least expensive.

2.   Some penthouse apartments are nice for another reason. You can open a door onto the roof of the building. It may even be possible to bring lots of dirt to the roof, put in some plants, and make a rooftop

       a. garden.   c. bathroom.
       b. restaurant.   d. apartment.

3.   One very large apartment building in New York is like a small city. In the building, you can shop for food, meet friends in a restaurant, go for a swim, or get a haircut. If you live there, you never need to go

       a. shopping.   c. home.
       b. outside.   d. to New York.

4.   Strange things happen when there is a full moon. More babies are born. Cats and other pets become restless. Some people cannot sleep. So it is not surprising that when the moon is full

       a. people sleep well.   c. the sky seems darker.
       b. there are more car accidents.   d. dogs are quiet.

5.   In the country, you can see many things in the night sky. If you know some astronomy, you can find stars, the Milky Way, and sometimes some planets. In the city, it is different. You cannot see many stars, because

       a. they are too far away.   c. there are no stars near cities.
       b. there is not enough time.   d. the city lights are too bright.

Exercise 24

➤ *Choose the best ending for each paragraph.*

1.   There are not enough apartments in New York City. More than 20,000 poor people have no place to live. The city government tries to help. It gives some poor people money to live in cheap hotels. The people can stay in the hotels

    a. because hotels are cheaper than apartments.
    b. with penthouse apartments.
    c. because they do not want apartments.
    d. until they find apartments.

2.   In England, "tea" does not mean just something to drink. Teatime is a special part of the day. With their cup of tea, English people like to have something to eat. They eat beautiful little sandwiches, sweet breads, and cake. When you have tea in England, be ready for

    a. a hot drink.   c. a quick sandwich.
    b. a nice meal.   d. breakfast.

3.   Tea is a popular drink in many countries. In Russia, the people use a special pot to make tea. It is called a "samovar." This pot is important to Russian families. Even a poor family usually

    a. has a samovar.   c. does not drink tea.
    b. drinks milk.   d. makes tea.

4.   People who live alone sometimes feel ill and unhappy. Their doctors may tell them to get a pet. Their "medicine" can be a dog, cat, bird, or goldfish. They are not sick. They just need

    a. some medicine.   c. something to love.
    b. a new doctor.   d. to find a new job.

5.   Elephants and whales are a lot alike. Elephants are the largest animals on land. Whales are the largest animals in the sea. People hunt and kill both whales and elephants, and now there are many fewer than in the past. Someday

    a. elephants will not be large anymore.
    b. there may be more whales and elephants.
    c. there may not be anymore whales or elephants.
    d. whales will move to different parts of the sea.

Exercise 25

➤ *Choose the best ending for each paragraph.*

1.　All living things change because of where they live. For example, there are fish in rivers deep underground. There is no light there, so these fish have no

　　a. food.　　　　　　　　c. eggs.
　　b. eyes.　　　　　　　　d. babies.

2.　On a map, Italy looks like an old-fashioned knee-high boot. The top of the boot is the border with France, Switzerland, and Austria. The bottom of the boot goes out into the Mediterranean Sea. It seems to have a

　　a. heel and a toe.　　　　c. shoe.
　　b. hand.　　　　　　　　d. mountain.

3.　In the past, people did not know much about faraway countries. News traveled slowly around the world. Nowadays, TV, telephones, faxes, and computers make countries seem close together. People know a lot about every part of the world. A famous writer says that the world is becoming

　　a. far apart.　　　　　　c. larger.
　　b. a big village.　　　　　d. a strange place.

4.　What happens in one place is important all over the world. If a factory makes the air dirty in one country, the air of the whole world is changed. We are all part of the same world. We all travel around the sun together. In fact, we can think of the world as

　　a. spaceship earth.　　　　c. many separate islands.
　　b. strangers in strange lands.　d. a big, round ball.

5.　In some countries, people are open to new foods. The English, for example, like to eat Indian and Chinese foods. In other countries, people prefer their own food. The Italians are a good example. Most of the restaurants in Italy serve Italian food, and when Italians go to other countries, they often

　　a. love the food.　　　　　c. eat Chinese food.
　　b. don't eat the food.　　　d. don't like the food.

Part Four

Reading Faster

Why read faster?

Reading faster helps you understand more. This may seem surprising to you, but, in fact, your brain works better when you read faster.

Try reading this:

Many	students	are	surprised	when	the
teacher	tells	them	to	read	faster.	But
they	soon	find	out	that	they
understand	more	that	way.		

If you read slowly, you read one word at a time, and you must remember many separate words. Soon you can get tired or bored.

Many students find that they read between 50 and 200 words per minute. If you read less than 200 words per minute, you are probably reading one word at a time. You may have trouble understanding the important ideas quickly.

If you read faster, you can read groups of words together. Then you can think about ideas and not just single words. That is why you will understand better and remember more.

How to read faster: three steps

1. Check your reading habits

Some bad habits can slow down your reading.

a. Do you try to pronounce each word as your read? Pronunciation is not necessary for comprehension. In fact, if you try to say the words, even silently, you will probably understand less.

b. Do you usually move your lips while you read silently? If you do, you will never be able to read faster than about 200 words per minute. That is the fastest speed you can speak in English.

c. Do you follow the words in the text with your finger or a pencil? This is another habit that can slow down your reading. It also limits the way you read. If you point at the words, your eyes will follow the lines of text. But good readers often skip parts, or they may look back at something again. *Your eyes should follow your thoughts, not your finger!*

d. Do you translate into your native language when you are reading in English? Do you often write the words in your language next to the English words? This slows your reading speed. It also means that you are thinking in your native language and not in English!

Reading Faster

2. Skip words

Good readers often skip many words. They skip over words they do not know. They also skip many other unimportant words. In fact, many words are not necessary for comprehension. You can get the general meaning without them.

➤ *Try reading the following passages. Many words are missing.* **Do not** *try to guess the missing words. Try to understand the general meaning of the passage. Then answer the questions below. The Answer Key is on page 286.*

EXAMPLE A

Mike loves to cook. He cooks all xxxxx *kinds* of food, but he likes best to xxxxx *cook* cakes. He says making cakes is very xxxxxxxx. When he is cooking, he does not xxxxx about work or bad things. He xxxxxx only about the cake. He can make very beautiful xxxxx with fruit or with xxxxxxxxx. On Saturdays, when Mike has xxxxxx of time, he makes a xxxxxxxxx good cake. After dinner, the xxxxxx family sits down xxxxxxxx to enjoy Mike's cake.

1. What does Mike like to do in his free time?

_____

2. Why does he like it?

_____

3. What does he do on Saturdays?

_____

EXAMPLE B

Do you have an e-mail (electronic mail) address? Xxxxxxxx of people have e-mail addresses xxxxxx the world. With e-mail you can xxxx with people from Montevideo to Kyoto. Many xxxxxx use it for fun. They talk with their xxxxxx or family through e-mail, or they xxx e-mail to "meet" with xxxxxx who have the same interests. E-mail is also very xxxxxx for people at work. Many offices and stores now xxxx e-mail addresses. They use e-mail for all kinds of xxxxxxxx. It is much faster than xxxxxxx mail. It can take xxxx time even than a phone call.

1. Where do people use e-mail?

_____

2. Why do people use e-mail for fun?

_____

3. Why do people use e-mail at work?

_____

3. Time yourself

In this part of *Reading Power,* there are 40 passages about an American family. In Examples C and D, time your reading of each passage and answer the comprehension questions.

➤ *Use Examples C and D to find out your reading rate.*

EXAMPLE C

Before you begin reading, write your starting time _____

Introduction to "An American Family"

Rosebud is a small town in New Jersey. It looks like many other towns in the United States. On Main Street there is a post office and a police station. The drugstore and the library are down the street. There is also a shopping center, with a supermarket and a department store.

In the middle of Rosebud, near the post office, is the office of Dr. Sam Diamond. Everybody in town knows Dr. Diamond. He's a good dentist. He's also a popular person. He likes to tell funny stories to his patients. They forget about their teeth when they listen to him.

Susan Conley is Sam Diamond's wife. She is a scientist with a Ph.D. in chemistry. She works in a laboratory in New York City. She and some other scientists are studying freshwater ponds. They test the water from these ponds for dangerous chemicals.

Every day, Susan takes the train to the city. Many other people take the train or drive to New York. Rosebud is a popular place to live because it is near the city. It is still a quiet town and a good town for families. But there are new houses every year, and it is growing fast.

Write the time you finished reading _____

Subtract your starting time – _____

Your reading time is _____

➤ *Answer the questions on the following page.*

➤ *Circle the best answer. Do not look back!*

1. This passage is about
   a. New Jersey.
   b. Main Street in Rosebud, New Jersey.
   ✓ c. two people who live in Rosebud, New Jersey.
   d. Susan Conley.

2. Rosebud is
   a. different from most towns in the United States.
   ✓ b. like many other towns in the United States.
   c. like no other towns in other countries.
   d. different from towns in other countries.

3. In Rosebud, there
   a. isn't a shopping center.
   b. are many shopping centers.
   c. is a laboratory.
   ✓ d. is a shopping center.

4. Dr. Diamond is popular because
   a. everyone in town knows him.
   b. he listens to his patients.
   ✓ c. his office is in the middle of Rosebud.
   ✓ d. he tells his patients funny stories.

5. Susan Conley is
   ✓ a. Sam Diamond's wife.
   b. Sam Diamond's patient.
   c. very popular.
   d. a good wife.

6. Susan is a
   a. dentist.
   b. housewife.
   ✓ c. chemist.
   d. student.

7. Many people in Rosebud
   a. work at home.
   ✓ b. take the train to New York.
   c. don't have work.
   d. like to take trains.

8. Rosebud is
   a. now a city.
   b. getting smaller.
   c. not changing.
   ✓ d. getting bigger.

➤ *Check your answers in the Answer Key on page 287. The number of correct answers is your comprehension score. Write your score in the space for Example C on the Faster Reading Progress Chart on page 273.*

➤ *Find your reading rate on the Reading Rate Tables on page 272. Write your rate in the space for Example C on the Faster Reading Progress Chart on page 273.*

EXAMPLE D

Susan and Sam

Susan Conley and Sam Diamond live in an old white house on Cleveland Road. They have two children, Ted and Jane. Ted and Jane are grown up now. They both live far away. Ted lives in Brazil with his wife, Maria, and Jane lives in Alaska. Ted and Jane's old rooms are always ready for them, and sometimes they come to visit.

Now Susan and Sam share their home with their pets: a cat, a dog, and a bird. In their free time, they like to work in the yard. In the front yard, Sam grows roses and other flowers. In the back, Susan has a large vegetable garden. Sam uses the fresh vegetables in his cooking. He likes to cook special dinners and invite their friends.

In their free time, Susan and Sam also help the town of Rosebud. Every Tuesday, Susan goes to the meetings of the town planning committee. This important committee decides about the future of the town. Every Saturday, Sam goes to help the Rosebud Food Bank. The Food Bank gets food from stores or people in town. It gives the food to people without homes and jobs.

Finishing time _____   *Reading time* _____

➤ **Answer the questions on the following page.**

➤ *Circle the best answer. Do not look back!*

1. This passage is about
   a. family life.
   b. Rosebud, New Jersey.
   ✓ c. Susan and Sam.
   d. Susan and Sam's children.

2. Susan and Sam's children
   ✓ a. are grown up.
   b. live on Cleveland Road.
   c. live in Brazil.
   ✓ d. are very young.

3. Jane and Ted
   ✓ a. sometimes go to Alaska.
   ✓ b. have two children.
   c. have a white house.
   d. sometimes visit.

4. Susan and Sam
   a. have some pets.
   b. do not like pets.
   c. have no pets.
   ✓ d. want more pets.

5. Susan and Sam both like to work
   a. in the house.
   b. in the garden.
   ✓ c. with animals.
   d. in a store.

6. When they invite their friends for dinner,
   ✓ a. Susan often cooks the meal.
   b. Sam cooks fish.
   c. Ted and Jane cook the meal.
   d. Sam cooks the meal.

7. Susan helps decide about the future of
   a. New York.
   b. the planning committee.
   ✓ c. Rosebud.
   d. her friends.

8. Sam helps poor people
   ✓ a. get enough food.
   b. in New York.
   c. plan their future.
   d. go to the bank.

➤ *Check your answers in the Answer Key on page 287. Write your comprehension score in the space for Example D on the Faster Reading Progress Chart on page 273.*

➤ *Now find your reading rate on page 272. Write your rate in the space for Example D on the chart on page 273.*

Guidelines for Faster Reading

1. Try to read each passage a little faster.

2. Do not look back at the passage when you are answering the questions.

3. Check your answers in the Answer Key on page 287. If you have some incorrect answers, look back at the passage. Think again about your answer.

4. Find your reading rate on the Reading Rate Tables on page 272.

5. For each passage, write your reading rate and comprehension score (number of correct answers) on the Faster Reading Progress Charts (pages 273–274).

6. After reading four or five passages, look at the chart and check your progress.
   • If your reading rate stayed the same, you must push yourself to read a little faster.
   • If you have more than two incorrect answers on any passage, you might be reading too quickly too soon. Slow down a little and read more carefully.

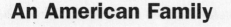

An American Family

1. Dreaming of Travel   *Starting Time* _____

Susan and Sam are different in many ways. Susan is tall and thin. Sam is short and heavy. Susan has blond hair and blue eyes. Sam has dark hair and brown eyes. Susan is a quiet kind of person. She can work for hours alone in her laboratory. Sam loves to talk and meet people. He can talk for hours with his patients.

But Susan and Sam think the same way about a lot of things. They both care a lot about their children and their home. They care about their town and their work. They both like to go to the seaside in the summer. At the seaside, Susan reads a lot and Sam goes fishing. The neighbors take care of their pets and their yard back in Rosebud.

Usually, they are happy to come home to Rosebud. But sometimes they think about other parts of the world. They want to visit new places and have new experiences. They went to Hawaii once, after they were married. But that was 30 years ago!

"We're not getting any younger!" Sam often says to Susan.

"You're right," says Susan. "Let's go somewhere next year. Not now. We're too busy."

Finishing time _____   *Reading time* _____

➤ *Answer the questions on the following page.*

➤ *Circle the best answer. Do not look back! Then, check your answers and record your reading rate.*

1. This passage is about
    a. how Susan and Sam are different.
    b. Susan and Sam's life and dreams.
    c. Susan and Sam's vacation.
    d. how Susan dreams of going to Hawaii.

2. Susan and Sam
    a. look the same.
    b. look different.
    c. are both tall and thin.
    d. both like to work alone.

3. Sam likes to
    a. work alone.
    b. work in a laboratory.
    c. listen to his patients.
    d. meet people and talk.

4. Susan and Sam both care about
    a. reading and fishing.
    b. different things.
    c. the same things.
    d. their pets.

5. In the summer, Susan and Sam
    a. go to the seaside.
    b. visit their children.
    c. travel to other parts of the world.
    d. take care of their house.

6. Susan and Sam are usually
    a. happy in other parts of the world.
    b. not happy in Rosebud.
    c. happy in Rosebud.
    d. not at home.

7. Some day they would like to
    a. go to the seaside.
    b. get married.
    c. go to Hawaii.
    d. visit new places.

8. They can't go away now because they are
    a. too busy.
    b. too young.
    c. happy at home.
    d. too old.

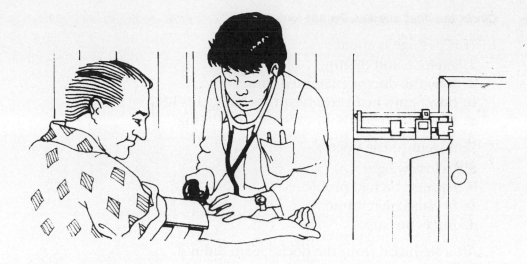

2. A Visit to the Doctor

Starting Time _____

One day in March, Sam Diamond went to the doctor for a checkup. He felt fine. He told the doctor he had no problems. The doctor examined him carefully and did some tests.

The next day, the doctor called Sam. He said, "I have some bad news for you. You'll have heart trouble soon if you don't change your way of life. You must lose weight. You must exercise more, and you must get more rest."

Sam was worried. He told Susan the bad news. "What should I do?" he said. "I know I eat too much, but I like good food! I don't have time to exercise!"

"Well, the doctor knows best," said Susan. She was worried, too. "We should do what he says."

"That's easy for you to say!" said Sam.

"I'll help you," said Susan. "I'll exercise with you and I'll help you cook healthy meals. Maybe we should think about some other changes, too. You're always talking about a vacation. Well, let's do it! Let's go some place where you can really rest."

"We can visit Ted in Brazil!" said Sam.

"Or Jane in Alaska!" said Susan.

Finishing time _____   *Reading time* _____

➤ **Answer the questions on the following page.**

> *Circle the best answer. Do not look back!*

1. This passage is about
   a. exercise and dieting.
   b. how the doctor examined Sam.
   c. how Sam's heart trouble may change his life.
   d. how Sam feels about exercise and dieting.

2. Sam went to the doctor
   a. to lose weight.
   b. because he had problems.
   c. because he felt fine.
   d. for a checkup.

3. After he heard from the doctor, Sam did not
   a. worry.
   b. go home.
   c. have any problems.
   d. feel happy.

4. The doctor told Sam he must
   a. change his life.
   b. work harder.
   c. feel sick.
   d. feel happy.

5. Sam worried because he
   a. wanted to exercise.
   b. was in danger of heart trouble.
   c. did not have heart trouble.
   d. did not want to eat good food.

6. When she heard the bad news, Susan was
   a. sad.
   b. happy.
   c. sick.
   d. worried.

7. Susan told Sam she
   a. did not want to exercise.
   b. did not want to go to Alaska.
   c. wanted to lose weight.
   d. wanted to help him get exercise.

8. Susan wanted to go to Alaska
   a. to visit her friends.
   b. because it is far away.
   c. to visit Jane.
   d. to get some exercise.

3. Changes for Susan and Sam

Starting Time _____

   The next day, Sam began to make changes in his life. He went on a diet. No more cookies at lunch, no more ice cream after dinner. It was hard. All day his stomach made funny noises. At night he dreamed about big pieces of chocolate.

   He also began to exercise with Susan. They jogged every morning before work. This was even harder than the diet.

   "We're crazy," Sam told his wife one morning. It was cold and raining. "My legs hurt and I'm freezing."

   "Think about our vacation," Susan said.

   Sam really just wanted a warm bath and breakfast. But he thought about hot, sunny beaches. He thought about tropical fruits and strong coffee.

   "Let's go to Brazil," he said to Susan. "Everyone says the food is great and the people are friendly."

   "Jane says you can see lots of animals in Alaska," said Susan. "And the mountains are beautiful."

   They decided to get more information from a travel agent. She gave them some articles from a travel magazine. She told them that Alaska and Brazil were very different, but they were both wonderful places. "You have to decide what you want for your trip," she explained. "They're both beautiful places."

Finishing time _____   *Reading time* _____

➤ **Answer the questions on the following page.**

➤ *Circle the best answer. Do not look back!*

1. This passage is about
   a. new problems and questions in their life.
   b. how crazy Susan and Sam are every morning.
   c. taking a vacation.
   d. what their children and friends tell them.

2. Sam had dreams about
   a. jogging.
   b. food.
   c. Brazil.
   d. a vacation.

3. Sam did not enjoy
   a. jogging.
   b. eating.
   c. traveling.
   d. dreaming.

4. Susan told Sam to think about a vacation
   a. because she was tired.
   b. to make him tired.
   c. because she was jogging.
   d. to help him.

5. Sam said the food in Brazil was
   a. terrible.
   b. Italian.
   c. very good.
   d. hot and strong.

6. Jane said Alaska has
   a. wonderful food and friendly people.
   b. strong American coffee.
   c. lots of animals and beautiful mountains.
   d. many dangerous animals in the mountains.

7. Susan and Sam went to a travel agent to
   a. find out more about Alaska and Brazil.
   b. buy plane tickets.
   c. spend less money.
   d. find out about other beautiful places.

8. The travel agent told them that
   a. Alaska is the best place for a vacation.
   b. Alaska and Brazil are both good places for a vacation.
   c. Alaska and Brazil are both very expensive places.
   d. Brazil was farther away.

4. **Travel Magazine** *Starting Time* _____

Alaska: Animals Everywhere

by Michael Wharton

Animals are everywhere in Alaska. If you go out to the wild areas, you can see a lot of wild animals. Some large animals, like the caribou, live in groups, and you can see hundreds of them. You can also see other large animals, such as moose and deer. There are also bears and wolves, of course. But these animals are not really dangerous. If you stay away from them, they will stay away from you. They usually are afraid of people.

Sometimes the wild animals come to areas with people. You may see deer or moose, for example, in someone's backyard. This makes the children and the tourists happy, but it's a problem for Alaskan gardeners! These animals like to eat the plants in gardens, and they walk all over the grass and flowers.

A lot of people in Alaska have animals at home, too. Dogs are the favorites, especially huskies. The Eskimos used these dogs to pull sleds in the winter. Many Alaskans now keep huskies and go dog-sledding as a sport. There are competitions for the most beautiful dogs and the strongest dogs. Of course, there are dog-sled races, too.

Finishing time _____ *Reading time* _____

 Answer the questions on the following page.

➤ *Circle the best answer. Do not look back!*

1. This article is about
   a. animals.
   b. Alaska.
   c. animals in Alaska.
   d. travel in Alaska.

2. In Alaska, you can see many
   a. people.
   b. mountains.
   c. wild animals.
   d. wolves.

3. Bears and wolves usually
   a. kill people.
   b. stay away from people.
   c. stay in the mountains.
   d. like people.

4. You can sometimes see wild animals in
   a. the city park.
   b. the zoo.
   c. backyards.
   d. people's houses.

5. Moose and deer sometimes eat
   a. garden plants.
   b. food in the kitchens.
   c. fruit in stores.
   d. tourists in cars.

6. Moose and deer
   a. are good for gardens.
   b. don't go in gardens.
   c. don't like gardens.
   d. are bad for gardens.

7. Many Alaskans
   a. have pets.
   b. don't like pets.
   c. have gardens.
   d. eat fruit.

8. Dogsledding
   a. is fun for children.
   b. stopped years ago.
   c. is not very popular.
   d. is a popular sport.

5. Travel Magazine   *Starting Time* _____

A Taste of Brazil

by Ella Bowen

Brazilian food is like Brazil itself. It's a rich mixture of many things from many places. Some dishes are like Portuguese dishes. That is because many Portuguese people went to live in Brazil. Other dishes are not like any European dishes. The flavors are special to Brazil.

Brazilian cooks are lucky. They can get excellent fish from the ocean. They can get good meat from the farms. And they can get all kinds of tropical fruits and vegetables. These fruits and vegetables give Brazilian dishes their special, delicious taste.

Brazil is a large country. Each area has its own history and traditions, and so each area also has its own way of cooking. If you are in Rio de Janeiro, for example, you should try the "feijoada." It is a very rich mixture of different meats with black beans. Brazilians usually eat it on the weekend. It's not a dish to eat in a hurry!

After your meal, you must try Brazilian coffee—"cafezinho." The Brazilians have a special little machine for making coffee, and their coffee is special, too. It's not like American coffee or Italian coffee. It's Brazilian, and it's very good.

Finishing time _____   *Reading time* _____

➤   **Answer the questions on the following page.**

Reading Faster

> *Circle the best answer. Do not look back!*

1. This article is about
   a. Brazilian cooks.
   b. traveling in Brazil.
   c. Brazil.
   d. Brazilian food.

2. Brazilian food is
   a. like Italian food.
   b. a mixture of different foods.
   c. is all the same.
   d. very different from Portuguese food.

3. Brazilian cooks
   a. can get lots of good things to cook with.
   b. can't get any good things to cook with.
   c. can get lots of Portuguese foods to cook with.
   d. can cook only Brazilian foods.

4. The special taste of Brazilian food comes from
   a. the ocean.
   b. tropical fruits and vegetables.
   c. Portugal.
   d. the farms.

5. The history and traditions are
   a. different in different parts of Brazil.
   b. similar all over Brazil.
   c. different from those in Argentina.
   d. very old.

6. "Feijoada" is a special dish from
   a. Brazil.
   b. Rio de Janeiro.
   c. many areas of Brazil.
   d. Europe.

7. Brazilians usually eat "feijoada"
   a. on the weekends.
   b. on holidays.
   c. at the seaside.
   d. during the week.

8. Brazilians make coffee in
   a. American coffee machines.
   b. a special kind of machine.
   c. Italian coffee machines.
   d. coffee shops.

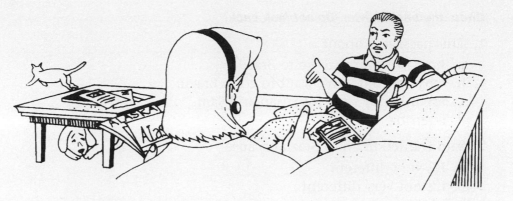

6. An Unhappy Time

Starting Time _____

    This was the beginning of an unhappy time for Susan and Sam. They could not agree on their travel plans. Susan preferred to go to Alaska, but Sam preferred to go to Brazil.

    "We want to change our lives, don't we?" he asked Susan. "Then we should go somewhere really different!"

    "Yes, but the plane tickets for Brazil are so expensive," Susan answered. "We're not millionaires!"

    "This will be our first trip in 30 years!" said Sam. "We may not take another one for a long time."

    "You just want to go to Brazil because of the food," said Susan.

    "That's not true!"

    "You'll eat too much of that rich food," said Susan. "I know you. You'll never be able to diet in Brazil."

    And so, they began to argue. They argued while they were jogging. They argued at breakfast. They argued at dinner. And all the time they were in a terrible mood. They didn't enjoy the things they used to enjoy. They stopped going to parties, and they didn't invite friends over for dinner. Sam didn't talk much to his patients. Susan didn't want to work in her vegetable garden. Even the pets were unhappy. The cat ran away, and the dog hid under the bed.

Finishing time _____   *Reading time* _____

➤ **Answer the questions on the following page.**

➤ *Circle the best answer. Do not look back!*

1. This passage is about
    a. how Sam wants to go to Brazil.
    b. why Susan doesn't want to go to Brazil.
    c. an unhappy time for Susan and Sam.
    d. a terrible mood.

2. Sam wanted to go to Brazil because
    a. it's very different.
    b. it's not very different.
    c. it's expensive.
    d. he's not a millionaire.

3. Susan thought Sam wanted to go to Brazil because of
    a. his heart.
    b. his diet.
    c. the Brazilian food.
    d. her diet.

4. Sam thought they might
    a. take another vacation soon.
    b. not like Brazilian food.
    c. not take another trip for a long time.
    d. have more fun in Alaska.

5. Susan and Sam were arguing about
    a. where to take their vacation.
    b. Sam's diet.
    c. their friends.
    d. their food.

6. They were in a terrible mood because they
    a. wanted to go eat rich food.
    b. stopped arguing.
    c. were always arguing.
    d. couldn't find the dog and cat.

7. They did not visit their friends because they were
    a. not getting any younger.
    b. not millionaires.
    c. not home.
    d. unhappy.

8. The dog hid under the bed because it
    a. liked arguing.
    b. was not getting any younger.
    c. didn't like Susan.
    d. didn't like Sam and Susan's arguing.

7. A Phone Call from Jane

Starting Time _____

One evening in the middle of an argument, the telephone rang. Susan answered it. Jane was calling from Alaska, and she was very excited.

"Guess what?" she said. "I have a new job! With American Airlines! I'll be living in New York, and I'll be flying all over, even to Europe!"

"That's wonderful!" said Susan. "When are you coming?"

"I start with American next month," said Jane. "So, I'll be coming at the end of this month."

"How did this happen?" Susan asked.

"I wanted to work for a bigger airline," said Jane. "I wanted to fly to new places and see more of the world. Alaska is a nice place to live, but I don't want to stay here all my life! So I applied for this job."

"Are there any other women pilots with American Airlines?" asked Susan.

"I don't know," said Jane. "I hope so. It's hard to be the only one. The men pilots say such stupid things to me sometimes."

"Here comes your Dad. He'll want to hear about this, too! He's picking up the other phone. Now tell us all about this new job!"

Finishing time _____ *Reading time* _____

➤ **Answer the questions on the following page.**

> *Circle the best answer. Do not look back!*

1. This passage is about
    a. a phone call from Susan.
    b. women pilots.
    c. living in Alaska.
    d. a phone call from Jane.

2. Jane was very
    a. angry.
    b. sad.
    c. excited.
    d. upset.

3. Jane is going to work for
    a. a new airline.
    b. a European airline company.
    c. a woman pilot.
    d. American Airlines.

4. Jane is a
    a. pilot.
    b. travel agent.
    c. flight attendant.
    d. secretary.

5. She said she is going to move to
    a. Europe.
    b. New York.
    c. Alaska.
    d. New Jersey.

6. She wanted a new job so she could
    a. go to new places.
    b. stay in Alaska.
    c. work at home.
    d. meet other pilots.

7. She liked Alaska,
    a. and she wanted to stay there.
    b. but she didn't want to stay there.
    c. but she preferred California.
    d. and she was looking for a job there.

8. Men pilots
    a. were always nice to Jane.
    b. sometimes were not nice to Jane.
    c. didn't talk to women pilots.
    d. didn't fly to Europe.

8. A Phone Call from Ted

Starting Time _____

"Well, isn't this exciting," said Sam after their phone conversation with Jane. The telephone rang again. This time it was Ted.

"Ted!" said Sam. "Jane just called, too."

"Yes, I know," said Ted. "She sent me an e-mail yesterday, and we decided to call you tonight. I've got some big news, too."

"Wait! Your mother wants to hear. She's running to the other phone. Susan? Are you there?"

"Hello! Ted!"

"Yes, it's me, Mom. Are you ready for this? You're going to be a grandmother!"

"Oh, how exciting!"

"When?"

"How's Maria?"

"A boy or a girl?"

Susan and Sam were both talking at once.

Ted laughed. "Slow down! One at a time!" He told them all about it. He said Maria was fine, just a little tired. She was still working on her painting, but she wasn't teaching classes anymore.

Ted also told them about another big change in their lives. He and Maria were moving back to New York from Brazil. He was going to work for the newspaper in New York. Maria was not from New York, but she went to art school there. She liked the city very much. It was a good place for an artist.

Finishing time _____   *Reading time* _____

➤ **Answer the questions on the following page.**

➤ *Circle the best answer. Do not look back!*

1. This passage is about
    a. a phone call from Ted.
    b. a phone call from Sam.
    c. Ted's wife, Maria.
    d. Ted's conversation with Jane.

2. Ted was calling from
    a. New York.
    b. Alaska.
    c. Brazil.
    d. his office.

3. Ted and Jane
    a. write lots of letters.
    b. talk every day on the phone.
    c. never talk.
    d. use e-mail to "talk."

4. Ted's wife, Maria, is going to
    a. send an e-mail message.
    b. have a baby.
    c. talk on the phone.
    d. stop painting.

5. When they heard the news, Susan and Sam
    a. were excited.
    b. didn't say anything.
    c. weren't interested.
    d. were upset.

6. Ted said that Maria was
    a. still teaching.
    b. not painting.
    c. still painting.
    d. not well.

7. Ted and Maria are going to
    a. work for a newspaper.
    b. move to another city.
    c. stay in Brazil.
    d. move to New York.

8. Maria likes New York because it is a
    a. good place for a baby.
    b. good place for an artist.
    c. big city.
    d. good place for teaching.

9. Jane Arrives

Starting Time _____

That night Susan and Sam could not sleep. They talked and talked about the news from their children.

The next day, Susan laughed and said, "I guess we won't be going to Alaska *or* Brazil."

"We'll go somewhere else, later on," said Sam. "We've got more important things to think about now."

Susan and Sam stopped arguing, and the time passed quickly. They cleaned out Ted and Jane's old bedrooms. They called many of their old friends and their aunts, uncles, and cousins. They wanted everyone to know all the good news.

Jane was the first to arrive. Susan and Sam went to the airport to meet her. They were surprised when they saw her. She had short hair before, but now it was very long.

"It's my new hairstyle, for my new lifestyle!" she said. She was full of ideas for her new life in New York. She wanted to find an apartment in the city. She wanted to go to concerts, the theater, and the movies. "I couldn't do those things in Alaska," she said, "and I missed them. I'll be away a lot. But when I'm home, I want to enjoy the city."

Finishing time _____   *Reading time* _____

➤ **Answer the questions on the following page.**

> *Circle the best answer. Do not look back!*

1. This passage is about
    a. a trip to the airport.
    b. Susan and Sam's children.
    c. news from the children.
    d. Jane's arrival in New York.

2. Susan and Sam decided
    a. to go on a vacation to Alaska and Brazil.
    b. to take a vacation later.
    c. not to take a vacation.
    d. to leave for their vacation that night.

3. Susan and Sam were busy
    a. working in the garden.
    b. arguing about their vacation.
    c. getting ready for their vacation.
    d. getting ready for Ted and Jane.

4. They wanted to tell everyone about
    a. Jane's long hair.
    b. the news from their children.
    c. their new jobs.
    d. their vacation plans.

5. They were surprised to see Jane's new
    a. hairstyle.
    b. clothes.
    c. apartment.
    d. bedroom.

6. Jane was excited about
    a. her job.
    b. her new life in New York.
    c. her friends and relatives.
    d. the airport.

7. She wants to live
    a. in Rosebud.
    b. near the airport.
    c. with her parents.
    d. in New York.

8. In Alaska, she couldn't
    a. go to concerts or the theater.
    b. have a new hairstyle.
    c. go away.
    d. talk to Susan and Sam.

10. An Airline Accident

Starting Time _____

One evening, Susan, Sam, and Jane were watching the news on TV. They heard about a terrible airline accident in Oklahoma. A DC9 jet was flying from Dallas to Kansas City. Suddenly, it began to burn and then it fell. All the people on it were dead. The pilot was a woman, Carmen Kreeger.

Susan turned off the television. "Did you know her?" she asked Jane.

"No," said Jane. They were all quiet for a while. Then Jane said, "But I know that airline company. It's like a lot of other small companies. They buy old airplanes and they don't take care of them. They just want to make a lot of money fast. And look what happens!"

Jane was very upset. "Now they'll say it was the woman pilot. They'll say she made a mistake or didn't have enough experience. But did you hear what they said? That plane was 27 years old! It was the company that made a mistake!"

"Was your company in Alaska like that company?" asked Susan.

"Yes, it was. I didn't tell you because I didn't want you to worry," said Jane. "But I'm glad to be with a better company now."

"I'm glad, too," said Susan.

Finishing time _____   *Reading time* _____

➤ **Answer the questions on the following page.**

➤ *Circle the best answer. Do not look back!*

1. This passage is about
   a. an airline company.
   b. a woman pilot.
   √ c. an airline accident.
   d. the news on TV.

2. An airplane
   ' a. burned and then fell.
   b. landed in Kansas City.
   c. burned in the airport.
   d. was on TV.

3. The pilot of the plane was
   a. Jane.
   b. Jane's friend.
   √ c. a woman.
   d. a man.

4. The airline company wanted to
   a. burn the airplane.
   √ b. make a lot of money fast.
   c. buy new planes.
   d. be on TV.

5. When she heard the news, Jane was
   a. excited.
   b. glad.
   c. happy.
   √ d. angry.

6. Jane thought the accident was caused by the
   √ a. airline company.
   b. pilot.
   c. TV.
   d. weather.

7. The airplane in the accident was
   a. new.
   √ b. 27 years old.
   c. 5 years old.
   d. very large.

8. The airline company in Alaska
   √ a. also used old planes.
   b. never used old planes.
   c. never had accidents.
   d. was a good, safe company.

11. Ted and Maria Arrive

Starting Time _13.30_

Before long, it was time for Susan and Sam to go to the airport again. Jane went, too. At the airport, they heard some bad news. The flight from Rio was two hours late.

"Oh, no!" said Susan. "Poor Maria."

The two hours passed slowly, but at last the flight arrived. Then they had to wait some more in the arrivals hall. There were a lot of people on the flight, and there were a lot of people waiting. Susan and Sam couldn't find Ted and Maria.

"Maybe they missed the flight," said Jane.

"Here we are!" said a voice from behind them. And there was Maria with Ted beside her. They all hugged and kissed and talked at once. Susan was even crying a little.

"You look wonderful," she said to Maria. She gave her another hug. "I'm sure you miss your mother."

Maria's parents both died a few years before. Now she had only her brother, Gilberto.

"Come on," said Sam. "Let's go home. I'll cook up a nice dinner for us all. It's time to celebrate! How about spaghetti with Bolognese sauce? I can forget about my diet for once, can't I?" he asked Susan.

Finishing time _____   *Reading time* ___60 sec.___

➤ **Answer the questions on the following page.**

209

➤ *Circle the best answer. Do not look back!*

1. This passage is about
   a. Ted and Maria's arrival in New York.
   b. Gilberto's arrival in New York.
   c. Susan and Sam's trip to Brazil.
   d. Ted and Maria.

2. Ted and Maria's flight
   a. was early.
   b. was canceled.
   c. was two hours late.
   d. never left.

3. Susan was worried about
   a. the airplane.
   b. Maria.
   c. Ted.
   d. the people on the plane.

4. When the flight arrived, Susan and Sam
   a. were at home.
   b. couldn't find Jane.
   c. didn't know where to go.
   d. couldn't find Ted and Maria.

5. The arrivals hall was
   a. crowded.
   b. empty.
   c. quiet.
   d. dark.

6. Susan was crying because she was
   a. upset.
   b. excited.
   c. happy.
   d. sad.

7. Maria has
   a. a large family.
   b. only a brother.
   c. no family.
   d. a mother and father.

8. Sam wanted to
   a. go to a restaurant.
   b. eat dinner at the airport.
   c. drink some champagne.
   d. cook a nice dinner.

12. Gilberto Comes to Rosebud

Starting Time _____

Maria talked with Susan and Sam about Maria's brother, Gilberto. Gilberto was 19. He wanted to be an engineer. He also wanted to go to college in the United States, but he didn't know enough English and he didn't have enough money.

"Why doesn't he come here?" said Sam. "He can take English courses at New Jersey Community College. I'm sure he can find a job here, too."

"He can stay here in the extra bedroom," said Susan. "Jane is moving to her new apartment next week. You'll probably find a home soon, too. It will be nice to have someone in the house."

So the next month, Gilberto came to Rosebud. He was soon busy. He took English classes in the morning. In the afternoon he worked at the supermarket. And in the evening he studied.

He was quiet at first. Susan was worried. "He doesn't seem happy," she said to Sam.

"Well, it's hard for him," said Sam.

"But he never says anything, except to Maria." said Susan. "It makes me uncomfortable."

"Think how he feels." said Sam. "I'm sure he'll be fine. Just give him some time."

Finishing time _____   *Reading time* __53 sec.____

➤ **Answer the questions on the following page.**

➤ *Circle the best answer. Do not look back!*

1. This passage is about
   a. how Gilberto came to Rosebud.
   b. Maria's family.
   c. how Gilberto studied English.
   d. Gilberto's plans.

2. Gilberto did not have enough money to
   a. go to college in Brazil.
   b. go to college in the United States.
   c. study English.
   d. be an engineer.

3. Susan and Sam wanted to
   a. send Gilberto some money.
   b. help Maria.
   c. take courses at New Jersey Community College.
   d. help Gilberto.

4. Susan said Gilberto can stay
   a. in a hotel.
   b. in their extra bedroom.
   c. in Jane's apartment.
   d. at New Jersey Community College.

5. In Rosebud, Gilberto was
   a. busy.
   b. not busy.
   c. happy.
   d. worried.

6. Susan thought Gilberto was
   a. uninterested.
   b. unhappy.
   c. busy.
   d. happy.

7. Gilberto
   a. didn't talk very much.
   b. talked a lot.
   c. worried a lot.
   d. wanted to have more time.

8. Sam thought Gilberto was
   a. not going to be fine.
   b. never uncomfortable.
   c. very sick.
   d. going to be fine.

13. A Day in New York

Starting Time _____

One Friday evening Jane called from New York.

"What are you and Dad doing tomorrow?" she asked. "Would you like to meet me in the city?"

"Why not?" said Susan. "We don't go into the city together very often."

Ted, Maria, and Gilberto decided to go, too. They met Jane at her apartment on the West Side. It was small but comfortable, and it had a nice view of Riverside Park. From there, they went to the Metropolitan Museum of Art. They looked at many pictures, and Maria told them all about the painters.

After they left the museum, they had lunch in a coffee shop. Then they went to Macy's department store. Susan, Jane, and Maria found some nice comfortable dresses for Maria. Ted helped Gilberto buy some new running shoes. Sam bought some, too.

Next, they went down to SoHo and walked around. Susan and Maria were interested in the new shops and galleries. Sam was more interested in the restaurants. On every street there were wonderful smells. Finally, he said, "How about dinner? I'm hungry!"

Everyone else was hungry, too. They stopped at a Thai restaurant and had a delicious meal.

Finishing time _____   *Reading time* _____

➤ **Answer the questions on the following page.**

➤ *Circle the best answer. Do not look back!*

1. This passage is about
   a. shopping in New York.
   b. New York.
   c. Jane's apartment in New York.
   d. the Diamonds in New York.

2. Susan and Sam
   a. never go to New York.
   b. don't go to New York together very often.
   c. don't ever go to New York.
   d. often go to New York.

3. They met Jane at
   a. the train station.
   b. her apartment.
   c. the Metropolitan Museum of Art.
   d. a park.

4. At the Metropolitan Museum of Art, Maria told them about the
   a. museum.
   b. city.
   c. views.
   d. painters.

5. They had lunch in
   a. the museum.
   b. a fancy restaurant.
   c. a coffee shop.
   d. Jane's apartment.

6. At Macy's, Maria bought some
   a. shoes.
   b. dresses.
   c. pictures.
   d. coffee.

7. In SoHo, they saw many
   a. new shops and galleries.
   b. coffee shops.
   c. museums.
   d. interesting people.

8. Sam often thinks about
   a. art.
   b. clothes.
   c. shoes.
   d. food.

14. Two Different Jobs

Starting Time _____

At the Thai restaurant, Jane and Maria talked about their jobs. They agreed that there are a few similarities. For both pilots and artists, there is a lot of competition and there are few famous women. In both jobs, you have to be very strong and sure of yourself.

Of course, there are also many differences between the two jobs. Pilots and artists have to be strong in different ways. Pilots have to stay awake for long hours, and sometimes they have to make important decisions quickly. Artists, however, have to be strong in their ideas about art and life.

People in the two jobs also work in different ways. Pilots usually work with other people, but artists usually work alone. Pilots must understand other people. Artists must understand themselves.

Finally, there is an important difference in lifestyle. Pilots travel for their job and are often away from home. Artists, however, work at home or in a studio near home. Also, unlike pilots, artists can start and stop working when they want.

"I could never be a pilot," Maria said to Jane. "I hate airplanes."

"And I could never be an artist," said Jane. "I hate working alone!"

Finishing time _____ *Reading time* _____

➤ **Answer the questions on the following page.**

➤ *Circle the best answer. Do not look back!*

1. This passage is about
   a. how pilots and artists are strong.
   b. working women.
   c. Jane's job and Maria's job.
   d. women pilots.

2. There are
   a. many famous women pilots and artists.
   b. few famous women pilots and artists.
   c. no famous women pilots and artists.
   d. no famous pilots and artists.

3. Women pilots and artists both have to be
   a. strong.
   b. young.
   c. famous.
   d. nice.

4. Pilots sometimes have to
   a. work alone.
   b. do two jobs.
   c. think about life.
   d. make quick decisions.

5. Artists have to
   a. sleep often.
   b. have strong ideas about art.
   c. think about people a lot.
   d. make quick decisions.

6. Pilots
   a. usually work with other people.
   b. often work alone.
   c. sometimes work with artists.
   d. never work with other people.

7. Artists
   a. don't have to travel for work.
   b. have to travel for work.
   c. don't like to travel.
   d. are often away from home.

8. Jane and Maria
   a. don't like their jobs.
   b. both like their jobs.
   c. wish they had other jobs.
   d. both hate working alone.

15. Save the Lake!

Starting Time _____

One Saturday morning Susan and Sam went jogging around Clear Lake, a small lake in Rosebud. There was a dirt road all the way around it without any houses. The woods were beautiful and filled with birds and small animals.

Susan and Sam stopped to look at some ducks on the lake. Then they saw two men with some equipment in the woods. "What are you doing?" Susan asked them.

"We're measuring the land for a shopping center," said one of the men.

"A shopping center! Oh no!" Susan said. She and Sam started to walk back home.

"That's terrible," said Sam. "A shopping center in a beautiful place like this. You're on the Planning Committee, Susan. Can't you stop it?"

"I'm going to try! But it may not be easy. Some people want another shopping center in Rosebud. They think it will bring more money to the town," Susan said.

"But this is a small town!" said Sam. "One shopping center is enough!"

"I know," said Susan. "Soon this town is going to be all buildings. It doesn't need a new shopping center. It needs a nice big park!"

Finishing time _____   *Reading time* _____

➤ **Answer the questions on the following page.**

Reading Faster

➤ *Circle the best answer. Do not look back!*

1. This passage is about
   a. some good news about Clear Lake.
   b. how Susan and Sam went jogging around Clear Lake.
   c. some bad news about Clear Lake.
   d. how Susan and Sam wanted a shopping center in Rosebud.

2. The woods around Clear Lake were
   a. dangerous.
   b. beautiful.
   c. full of flowers.
   d. dirty.

3. At the lake, there were lots of
   a. birds and small animals.
   b. people fishing.
   c. dogs and cats.
   d. large buildings.

4. The two men in the woods were
   a. jogging.
   b. shopping.
   c. measuring the land.
   d. cutting down trees.

5. Susan and Sam
   a. don't want a shopping center at the lake.
   b. want a shopping center at the lake.
   c. don't want any shopping centers in Rosebud.
   d. want to build a house at the lake.

6. The Planning Committee
   a. measures the land in Rosebud.
   b. builds shopping centers in Rosebud.
   c. is not interested in land in Rosebud.
   d. decides how land is used in Rosebud.

7. Rosebud
   a. already has one shopping center.
   b. already has two shopping centers.
   c. doesn't have any shopping centers.
   d. is building a new shopping center.

8. Susan said she would like
   a. another road at Clear Lake.
   b. a park at Clear Lake.
   c. more money for the town.
   d. lots of new buildings in town.

16. Gilberto Helps Out

Starting Time _____

That evening the whole family was talking about the new shopping center.

"Mom, you need some pictures of the lake and the woods," said Ted. "Then you can show them to the Planning Committee."

"That's a good idea," said Jane. "They must know that it's an important place for birds and animals. And also a nice place to go for a walk."

"Who's going to take the pictures?" asked Sam. "I'm a terrible photographer."

"So am I," said Jane. "What about you, Ted?"

"Well, I don't have much time this week," he said. "Maria and I are going to look at some houses tomorrow, and I'm very busy. I could do it next week."

"I think we need them sooner than that," said Susan. "I'd like them for the next meeting of the Planning Committee."

"I can do it," said Gilberto. "I like to take pictures."

"Oh, yes! Gilberto is a good photographer!" said Maria.

"Okay," said Susan. "The meeting is on Thursday."

On Wednesday evening, Gilberto showed everyone his pictures.

"This is Rosebud?" said Sam. "Look at the lake! Look at all the birds on the water!"

"Gilberto, they're beautiful," said Susan. "Thank you so much. These pictures may save the lake."

Finishing time _____   *Reading time* ___50___

➤ **Answer the questions on the following page.**

➤ *Circle the best answer. Do not look back!*

1. This passage is about
   a. beautiful pictures of the lake.
   b. a meeting of the Planning Committee.
   c. how Gilberto went to the meeting.
   d. how Gilberto helped Susan and Sam.

2. Ted said Susan should
   a. talk to the Planning Committee.
   b. get some pictures of the lake.
   c. go for a walk at the lake.
   d. talk about the shopping center.

3. The lake is an important place for
   a. the Planning Committee.
   b. photographers.
   c. animals and birds.
   d. Ted and Maria.

4. Sam and Jane both
   a. are terrible photographers.
   b. like looking at pictures.
   c. are interested in photography.
   d. like to take pictures.

5. Ted couldn't take the pictures because he
   a. had a new house.
   b. was very busy.
   c. was a terrible photographer.
   d. didn't have a camera.

6. Susan needed the pictures
   a. in just a few hours.
   b. in several weeks.
   c. later that year.
   d. for Thursday.

7. Gilberto's pictures of the lake were
   a. terrible.
   b. beautiful.
   c. interesting.
   d. unusual.

8. Susan said the pictures may save
   a. the shopping center.
   b. Rosebud.
   c. the Diamond family.
   d. the lake.

17. Time for a Vacation

A week later, Ted and Maria found a house in Hartwell. It was small, but it had a large yard and it was only 6 miles from Rosebud. They were very happy. Now they could make a home for their family.

"We're going to move there in a few weeks," Ted told Susan and Sam. "Maybe this is a good time for your vacation. Gilberto can stay in the house and take care of everything."

"What about Maria?" said Susan.

"There's lots of time, more than two months," said Ted. "You know what the doctor said. Dad needs some rest."

"But where should we go?" said Susan.

"How about England?" said Ted.

"That's a good idea," said Sam. "I hear they have great breakfasts."

"Well, language is not a problem in England," said Susan.

"And we can visit the famous English gardens," said Sam.

"True," said Susan. "There are Kew Gardens and Kensington Gardens and all those big houses."

"So it's England?" asked Sam.

"If you don't eat too many of those big breakfasts!" said Susan.

"I won't eat anything until teatime," said Sam.

"Okay, okay," said Susan, laughing. "England, here we come."

Finishing time _____   *Reading time* _____

➤ **Answer the questions on the following page.**

➤ *Circle the best answer. Do not look back!*

1. This passage is about
    a. how Susan and Sam go to England.
    ✓b. how Susan and Sam decide to go to England.
    c. how Sam eats large breakfasts.
    d. vacations in England.

2. Ted and Maria wanted to
    a. buy an apartment.
    b. find a home in Rosebud.
    c. have a large family.
    ✓d. find a home for their family.

3. Ted and Maria found a house
    a. in Rosebud.
    ✓b. 6 miles from Rosebud.
    c. next door to Susan and Sam's house.
    d. close to New York City.

4. When Susan and Sam are away,
    ✓a. Gilberto will stay in their house.
    b. Maria will stay in their house.
    c. Jane will stay in their house.
    d. no one will stay in their house.

5. Maria is going to have her baby
    (a.) in two months.
    b. next week.
    c. next year.
    ✓d. in two weeks.

6. According to Sam, England has good
    a. doctors.
    b. tea.
    c. houses.
    ✓d. breakfasts.

7. Susan and Sam want to
    a. visit English museums.
    ✓b. visit English gardens.
    c. drink English coffee.
    d. speak another language.

8. Susan is afraid
    ✓a. Sam will eat too much.
    b. she will eat too much.
    c. Sam won't like English breakfasts.
    d. she won't like English breakfasts.

18. At the Airport

Starting Time _____

Soon the big day came for Susan and Sam. They were ready to leave on their trip to England. Ted, Maria, and Jane went with them to the airport.

"I'm sure we forgot something," Susan said to Sam. "Do you have the plane tickets?"

"Oh yes. They're in my pocket."

"What about our passports?" Susan asked.

"They're in my pocket, too," Sam said, and he looked in his pocket to make sure. There were the tickets, but no passports! "I was sure I put them in this pocket," he said. "Maybe they're in my jacket pocket."

He looked in his jacket pocket, in his travel bag, and in his suitcase. "They must be on my desk at home!" he said.

"Oh no!" said Susan.

"But they were with the travel information. I thought you had all that."

"Wait a minute. Maybe I do," said Susan. She looked in her bag. There were the passports.

"Let's go drink a cup of coffee," said Ted. "You have lots of time, and I think you need to relax."

"No, coffee will just make us more nervous!" said Susan.

So they all said good-bye, and Susan and Sam went to the gate for their flight.

Finishing time _____   *Reading time* _____

➤ **Answer the questions on the following page.**

Reading Faster

➤ *Circle the best answer. Do not look back!*

1. This passage is about
   a. Susan and Sam's passports.
   b. traveling to the airport.
   c. how Susan and Sam forgot their tickets.
   d. how Susan and Sam left for their trip.

2. At first, Susan was worried about
   a. the plane tickets.
   b. forgetting something.
   c. leaving soon.
   d. going to the airport.

3. Sam thought the passports were
   a. on the plane.
   b. at the airport.
   c. in his pocket.
   d. in the car.

4. After Sam looked for the passports,
   a. he decided they were at home.
   b. he found them.
   c. he went back home.
   d. they all ran to the plane.

5. Susan and Sam's passports were
   a. in Sam's pocket.
   b. lost.
   c. on Sam's desk.
   d. in Susan's bag.

6. Susan and Sam were feeling
   a. nervous.
   b. happy.
   c. unhappy.
   d. relaxed.

7. Ted thought a cup of coffee might
   a. give them more time.
   b. make them late.
   c. make them more worried.
   d. help them relax.

8. Susan and Sam were worried about
   a. saying good-bye.
   b. the tickets.
   c. flying to England.
   d. missing their flight.

19. Sam Calls Ted

Starting Time _____

"Hello!"

"Hi, Dad! How was the trip?"

"Well, we had to wait for two hours on the runway!"

"Oh no! What for?"

"Technical problems with the plane. They didn't tell us exactly what kind of problems."

"How awful!"

"Yes, it was a long wait. But they gave us free champagne."

"After that, everything went okay?"

"Yes, the flight was fine."

"So how are you feeling today?"

"Pretty tired. We went out this morning and walked around a little. This neighborhood of London is nice, and so is the hotel. Your mom is sleeping now. I couldn't sleep, so I decided to call you. How is Maria? Is she there?"

"No, she's in New York at the gallery. She's a little nervous about her show. It's opening in a few days, you know. In Brazil, she was already well known, but here people are harder to please."

"I'm sure it will go well. But she must not do too much now. She must be careful, you know. Don't let her pick up those big paintings!"

"No, no. She'll be careful. Don't worry!"

"Well, maybe I'll try to sleep, too. We'll call again soon."

"Bye, Dad."

"Bye."

Finishing time _____   *Reading time* _____

➤ **Answer the questions on the following page.**

➤ *Circle the best answer. Do not look back!*

1. This passage is about
   a. Sam's phone call to Ted.
   b. Susan's phone call to Sam.
   c. a phone call.
   d. problems on the airplane.

2. Susan and Sam waited for two hours
   a. in the airport.
   b. in England.
   c. in the hotel.
   d. on the runway.

3. They got free champagne because
   a. the flight was two hours late.
   b. they had a good flight.
   c. their plane didn't leave.
   d. the pilot was late.

4. Sam was
   a. happy.
   b. excited.
   c. tired.
   d. nervous.

5. Their hotel was in a
   a. bad neighborhood.
   b. busy neighborhood.
   c. country town.
   d. nice neighborhood.

6. When Sam called Ted, Susan was
   a. sleeping.
   b. eating.
   c. walking around the neighborhood.
   d. reading.

7. Maria was nervous about
   a. walking around New York.
   b. having a baby.
   c. her show at the art gallery.
   d. picking up paintings.

8. Sam didn't want Maria to
   a. go to the art gallery.
   b. pick up heavy paintings.
   c. have a baby.
   d. have a show.

20. The New York Gazette

A New Artist in New York

by Sandra Woolf

A wonderful new show of paintings opened in New York last week. Maria Arroyo, the artist, is new to New York. She is not new to art, however. She grew up in Mexico. She studied with several famous artists in Mexico City and then in New York. Five years ago, she married Ted Diamond, a reporter for the *New York Times*. They moved to Brazil, where her work became quite popular. She won several important awards in Brazil and showed her work in Mexico and other countries.

Ms. Arroyo is a small, quiet person, but her paintings are very large. They are full of color and excitement. She explained that the colors she uses are Mexican colors. In Mexico, the sky and the sea are usually very bright blue. The houses are often bright colors, too.

In her paintings, the excitement comes partly from these colors. It also comes from her style. She likes to paint large shapes that seem to move. Ms. Arroyo's paintings do not show us the real world. Instead, they show us her feelings about the world.

We look forward to seeing more work from this very fine artist.

Finishing time _____   *Reading time* _____

➤ *Answer the questions on the following page.*

Reading Faster

➤ *Circle the best answer. Do not look back!*

1. This article is about
   a. painting in Brazil.
   b. the style of Maria's paintings.
   c. Maria and her paintings.
   d. Maria and Ted.

2. This passage was written by
   a. Ted.
   b. a newspaper reporter.
   c. Maria.
   d. the author of a book.

3. When she was living in Brazil, Maria
   a. won several awards.
   b. studied painting.
   c. began to paint.
   d. didn't show her paintings.

4. Maria's paintings are
   a. small and neat.
   b. popular in New York.
   c. quiet.
   d. large.

5. The colors in Maria's paintings come from
   a. her Brazilian past.
   b. her Mexican past.
   c. New York City.
   d. paintings in the past.

6. This reporter says Maria's style is
   a. realistic.
   b. quiet.
   c. exciting.
   d. European.

7. Maria's paintings show
   a. life in Mexico.
   b. the real world.
   c. the sea, sky, and houses.
   d. large, colorful shapes.

8. This reporter thinks Maria
   a. is a good artist.
   b. is not a good artist.
   c. works hard.
   d. should make smaller paintings.

21. Jane Has an Accident

Late one night, the telephone rang at Ted and Maria's house.

"Ted?"

"Jane!"

"Could you come get me, Ted? I'm at the hospital in Hartwell. I had an accident. I'm okay, but my car is a wreck."

"Hold on. I'll be right there."

Ted brought Jane home with him. She didn't want to go to her apartment alone. She was still upset. Maria made some special tea for her. Then Jane told them about the accident:

She had spent the evening at a friend's house near Hartwell. It was late when she started to drive back to New York. The road was narrow and dark. Suddenly, a truck came around a curve from the opposite direction. It was going too fast, and it went onto Jane's side of the road. Jane had to turn very quickly and drive off the road.

Her car hit a tree. Luckily, she was not going very fast, and she was wearing her seatbelt. So she was not hurt. When she got out of the car, the truck was gone. But another car stopped, and a young couple jumped out and ran to help Jane. They had the license plate number of the truck.

The young couple brought Jane to Hartwell hospital and called the police. The police came to the hospital. They asked Jane and the young couple a lot of questions. The couple were from Japan, and they did not speak much English. They were also a little afraid of the police. However, with some help from Jane, they told everything they knew. They also gave the police the license plate number of the truck.

At the end of Jane's story, Ted asked, "Did you get the names and address of that couple?"

"Oh yes," Jane answered. "They were so nice to me. They said they both work in a company near here. They have to drive a long way from their home. They said they can't find a cheap place to live near their jobs. Maybe we can find some place for them in Rosebud or Hartwell."

"What about Mrs. Pierce's apartment?" Ted said. "I think it's empty now. I'll call her tomorrow."

"How are you feeling now?" Maria asked Jane.

"That tea was wonderful," said Jane. "I feel better. What a night! Well, I guess I was lucky I didn't get hurt."

Finishing time _____   *Reading time* _____

➤ **Answer the questions on the following page.**

➤ *Circle the best answer. Do not look back!*

1. This passage is about
   a. a young Japanese couple.
   b. Jane's accident.
   c. how Jane goes to the hospital.
   d. car accidents.

2. Jane called Ted from
   a. her apartment.
   b. her friend's house.
   c. the Hartwell Hospital.
   d. the police station.

3. When the accident happened, Jane
   a. was driving slowly.
   b. was driving fast.
   c. wasn't in the car.
   d. wasn't wearing a seatbelt.

4. The truck driver
   a. stopped to help.
   b. waved to Jane.
   c. tried to stop.
   d. didn't stop.

5. Soon after the accident, Jane got help from
   a. the police.
   b. Ted and Maria.
   c. a young Japanese couple.
   d. a truck driver.

6. The Japanese couple
   a. gave the police some important information.
   b. couldn't tell the police anything.
   c. didn't see the truck.
   d. told the doctors about Jane.

7. Ted wanted to help the
   a. police.
   b. truck driver.
   c. hospital.
   d. Japanese couple.

8. The Japanese couple work in Hartwell but live
   a. in New York.
   b. far away.
   c. nearby.
   d. in Hartwell.

22. *Susan and Sam in London*

Susan and Sam were enjoying themselves very much in London. They were lucky with the weather. Sunny skies for a week! They couldn't believe it. England is famous for rainy weather. Londoners couldn't believe it, either. Everyone was smiling all the time. At lunchtime, the parks were full of people sitting in the sun.

With the good weather, Susan and Sam spent many hours outside. They walked all around London and visited many historical places. They went to Westminster Abbey, the most famous church in London. Many famous people are buried there. Susan and Sam saw the names of kings, queens, poets, and scientists. They went to Buckingham Palace. They didn't see the Queen, but they watched the changing of the Queen's Guards. They also went to the "City," where they saw lots of men wearing the same gray business suits. Many of them even wore old-style hats! Susan and Sam thought they looked very funny—and uncomfortable!

They visited some of London's famous museums. In the British Museum they found interesting, old art from Greece and Rome. They were surprised to see all these things in England. In the National Gallery, they saw fine examples of English art. Susan decided her favorite painter was J. M. W. Turner. She liked the soft colors of his pictures of the sea.

Sam's favorite museum was the Victoria and Albert Museum. He enjoyed looking at all the old things in this museum. He saw old clothing and jewelry, weapons, musical instruments, and old toys.

Susan and Sam also took two boat rides on the Thames River. They liked looking at London from the boat. One afternoon, they went down the river to Greenwich. There they visited the famous Royal Observatory. The old scientific instruments were very interesting. On another day, they took the boat up the river to Kew Gardens. They liked Kew Gardens very much, especially the roses.

For lunch, Susan and Sam often ate sandwiches in a park. There were so many parks in London, and they were all so beautiful. For dinner, they sometimes went to an Indian restaurant and sometimes to a pub. After that, they were usually very tired. One evening, they went to a concert, but they both fell asleep in the middle of it.

Finishing time _____   *Reading time* _____

➤ **Answer the questions on the following page.**

Reading Faster

➤ *Circle the best answer. Do not look back!*

1. This passage is about
   a. how Susan and Sam walk around the parks.
   b. sightseeing in London.
   c. London's museums.
   d. Susan and Sam's visit to London.

2. Londoners were smiling all the time because of the
   a. rain.
   b. good weather.
   c. tourists.
   d. the men in funny hats.

3. Susan and Sam enjoyed
   a. walking around new places.
   b. riding the trains to new places.
   c. taking taxis around new places.
   d. driving around new places.

4. In the "City," they saw
   a. many women in suits.
   b. many men in business suits.
   c. the changing of the Queen's Guards.
   d. lots of rain hats.

5. Susan liked J. M. W. Turner's paintings because
   a. they had soft colors.
   b. he was English.
   c. they were old.
   d. he painted London.

6. Sam liked best the
   a. old things at the British Museum.
   b. new things at the Victoria and Albert Museum.
   c. old things at the Victoria and Albert Museum.
   d. new things in Westminster Abbey.

7. Greenwich and Kew Gardens are
   a. far from London.
   b. always full of people.
   c. in the "City."
   d. on the Thames River.

8. At the end of every day, Susan and Sam
   a. went to a concert.
   b. were very tired.
   c. ate in a park.
   d. took a boat ride.

232

23. Susan Calls Home

"Hello, Maria?"

"No, this is Jane. Mom, is that you?"

"Jane, what are you doing there? Is everything okay? Maria? The baby? Don't tell me . . ."

"No, Mom. Maria's just fine. She's at the gallery now. No baby yet! Ted's at work. I'm staying here for the day because I had an accident last night."

"You had a what? I'm sorry, you'll have to speak louder. I can't hear you very well."

"I had an *accident* last night."

"Oh, Jane! Are you okay?"

"My car is a wreck, but I'm okay. My neck hurts a little. The doctor said I should rest for a few days."

"Test? What kind of test?"

"Not test—*rest*. I should *rest!*"

"Yes, that's a good idea. How did it happen?"

"A truck came around a corner too fast, so I had to go off the road. I hit a tree."

"How scary!"

"Then a very nice young couple stopped and took me to the hospital. But don't worry about me. I'll be okay. How are you and Dad? Are you calling from London?"

"No, we're in Salisbury now. We came down here by train for the day. This morning we took a bus out to Stonehenge. It's quite amazing. The stones are enormous, all in a circle. But there were too many people! Everyone was talking and taking pictures. This afternoon we looked at the church here. It's very old and beautiful, really special. Now we're waiting for the train back to London."

"How do you like London?"

"It's wonderful! We're having such a good time. But you know, it's a bit expensive here. Everything costs much more than at home. We're also getting tired of the city. I think we'll leave tomorrow."

"Are you going to rent a car?"

"Yes. That's the plan. We want to drive north to Scotland."

"Who's going to drive out of London, you or Dad?"

"I don't know. That's going to be hard! These English people are crazy! Why do they have to drive on the left!"

"You'll get used to it."

"What did you say? Oh dear, now there's noise again on the line. This is a bad connection! Listen, we'll call again in a few days. Thank goodness you didn't get hurt! Take care of yourself. Give my love to Ted and Maria and say hello to Gilberto for me."

"Okay, Mom. Bye."

"Bye."

Finishing time _____   *Reading time* _____

➤ **Answer the questions on the following page.**

➤ *Circle the best answer. Do not look back!*

1. This passage is about
   a. Susan's phone conversation with Jane.
   b. Sam's phone conversation with Susan.
   c. a car accident.
   d. Susan and Sam's visit to Salisbury.

2. At first, Susan thought that
   a. Jane was at work.
   b. Ted was in an accident.
   c. Maria had her baby.
   d. Jane had a baby.

3. Then Susan was afraid Jane
   a. couldn't speak loud.
   b. was hurt.
   c. was at the gallery.
   d. was driving too fast.

4. The doctor told Jane she should
   a. have some tests.
   b. get a new car.
   c. go back to work the next day.
   d. get some rest.

5. Susan was calling from
   a. Salisbury.
   b. London.
   c. Rosebud.
   d. Stonehenge.

6. At Stonehenge, there
   a. was a beautiful church.
   b. were no other people.
   c. were lots of people.
   d. was a train station.

7. Susan and Sam wanted to leave London because it's
   a. crowded and dirty.
   b. tiring and expensive.
   c. wonderful.
   d. too crowded.

8. They are worried about
   a. driving on the left side of the road.
   b. leaving London.
   c. renting a car.
   d. the noise on the telephone line.

24. Gilberto's New Friend

Starting Time _____

Back in Rosebud, Gilberto was learning English quickly. He was earning some money at the supermarket. He was taking good care of Susan and Sam's house. Ted and Maria were worried about him. He didn't have any friends, and he spent all his free time alone. He often took the train and went in to New York.

"What do you do in New York?" Ted asked him.

"I like to walk around the city," said Gilberto. "I like to visit the different neighborhoods and take pictures."

"Will you show us some of your pictures?" asked Ted.

"Yes, but not yet. I'm not ready yet."

"Well, on Saturday we're having a barbecue in our new yard. Why don't you come and bring someone with you?" said Ted.

But Gilberto arrived at the barbecue alone. He helped Ted cook the chicken on the barbecue, and he helped Maria serve the food. He didn't talk much, and he didn't smile. Then a car drove up to the house, and a young woman stepped out. Gilberto walked quickly toward her.

"Hello, I'm sorry I'm late," she said. Everyone turned to look at her. She was very pretty. "I had to wait for my sister. She works late on Saturdays," she told Gilberto.

Now Gilberto was smiling. He introduced his friend to Ted and Maria. Her name was Milena. She was from Sarajevo, in Bosnia.

Gilberto and Milena sat down together and talked all evening. Milena was 18. She was living with her sister and her sister's little boy, Niko. Niko's father died in the war a few years earlier. Niko, now 4, had problems with his eyes. That's why he and his mother were in the United States. A doctor in New York was trying to save his eyes.

Milena was there because of her parents. They didn't want her to stay in Sarajevo. But she was not happy now. In Sarajevo, she studied music and played the violin in an orchestra. In Rosebud, she could not study music, and she didn't have time for her violin. She had to work part of the day at a restaurant, she had to study English, and she often had to stay with Niko.

Gilberto invited Milena to go to New York with him on Sunday. She didn't know the city. She only knew how to get to the hospital. "Maybe we can go to a concert in the park," said Gilberto. At last, Milena was smiling, too.

Finishing time _____   *Reading time* _____

➤ **Answer the questions on the following page.**

➤ *Circle the best answer. Do not look back!*

1. This passage is about
   a. Gilberto and his friend, Milena.
   b. how Milena came to Rosebud.
   c. how Gilberto met Milena.
   d. Ted's barbecue.

2. Gilberto liked to
   a. go to the theater in New York.
   b. go to barbecues in New York.
   c. meet people in New York.
   d. take pictures in New York.

3. Ted invited Gilberto to
   a. help serve the food.
   b. a barbecue.
   c. dinner.
   d. take pictures.

4. Gilberto came to the barbecue
   a. with Milena.
   b. alone.
   c. with Maria.
   d. with Susan and Sam.

5. Milena was living with
   a. a friend and her husband.
   b. her sister and her sister's husband.
   c. her sister and her sister's son.
   d. her sister and her father.

6. Niko
   a. had heart trouble.
   b. was very sick.
   c. was healthy.
   d. had trouble with his eyes.

7. Milena was unhappy in Rosebud because
   a. she couldn't study English.
   b. she couldn't study music.
   c. she didn't like the town.
   d. her father was dead.

8. Milena smiled when
   a. Gilberto asked her to go to New York.
   b. Ted invited her to eat some chicken.
   c. Gilberto asked her to go to the hospital.
   d. she talked about Niko.

Starting Time _____

Neighborhoods in New York

by Sarah Cather

Most tourists think that New York is one big city, but in fact, it is made of many different neighborhoods. There are rich neighborhoods and poor neighborhoods, of course. And there are neighborhoods full of people from the same country. These neighborhoods sometimes don't even look like they are part of the same city. The people are different, and so are the buildings.

For example, in the southern part of the city is New York's Chinatown. This neighborhood has many Chinese stores and restaurants. It also has some Vietnamese and Thai shops and restaurants. New Yorkers from all parts of the city like to go Chinatown, but most of the people who live there are Asian. The shop signs are all written in Asian languages. Everyone in the shops speaks Chinese, Vietnamese, or Thai. This is one of the most crowded and colorful neighborhoods in the city. It is also one of the fastest growing neighborhoods. New families move in every day.

Not far from Chinatown is Little Italy. Many Italians moved there from Italy in the early 1900s. Some of them stayed in the neighborhood. There are still good Italian shops, restaurants, and cafés in Little Italy. You can hear Italian spoken on the streets. Every year there is a big Italian festival.

Greenwich Village is another kind of neighborhood. There the buildings are small, old, and comfortable. In the 1950s and 1960s, the rent for apartments in Greenwich Village was cheap. Young people with little money lived there. For many years writers, artists, and students also lived there. Famous books were written in the neighborhood. Famous artists painted their first pictures there.

Greenwich Village became more expensive in the 1960s. So some artists and writers moved down the street to SoHo. There were many old factories in this area. Artists made their studios in these buildings, but then this neighborhood also became too expensive. The artists moved to Brooklyn, and SoHo filled up with fashionable restaurants and shops.

The most beautiful and expensive neighborhood in New York is the Upper East Side. That is where many of the city's richest people live. The apartment buildings are large and fancy. The streets are always clean. The shops sell all kinds of special foods and clothing. People from all over the world come to the Upper East Side to shop or just to look in the store windows and dream.

Finishing time _____   *Reading time* _____

➤ **Answer the questions on the following page.**

➤ *Circle the best answer. Do not look back!*

1. This article is about
   a. Greenwich Village.
   b. people who live in New York.
   c. New York.
   d. the neighborhoods of New York.

2. Chinatown is one of New York's
   a. slowest growing neighborhoods.
   b. fastest growing neighborhoods.
   c. quietest neighborhoods.
   d. largest neighborhoods.

3. Little Italy is
   a. near Chinatown.
   b. far away from Chinatown.
   c. growing faster than Chinatown.
   d. farther south than Chinatown.

4. Greenwich Village used to be popular with
   a. Italians.
   b. New Yorkers.
   c. students and artists.
   d. rich people.

5. Apartments in Greenwich Village were usually
   a. expensive.
   b. large.
   c. lively.
   d. inexpensive.

6. Now SoHo has many
   a. factories.
   b. restaurants and shops.
   c. offices.
   d. expensive apartment buildings.

7. In general, the neighborhoods of New York
   a. often change.
   b. always stay the same.
   c. aren't as nice as they used to be.
   d. are all the same.

8. The Upper East Side is for people
   a. with only a little money.
   b. in fancy clothing.
   c. with a lot of money.
   d. from around the world.

The Man with the Gloves

by Eliza Alcott

Michael Greenberg is a popular New Yorker. He is not in the government, and he is not famous in sports or the arts, but people in the streets know about him, especially poor people.

For these poor people, he is not Michael or even Mr. Greenberg. For them, his name is "Gloves" Greenberg. "Here comes Gloves," they say when they see him walking down the street. How did he get that name? He looks like any other businessman. He wears a suit and carries a briefcase. He is different, however. His briefcase does not just have papers and books. It also has several pairs of gloves.

On cold winter days, Mr. Greenberg does not act like other New Yorkers. He does not look at the sidewalk and hurry down the street. He looks around at people. He is looking for poor people with cold hands. That is why he carries gloves in his briefcase. He stops when he sees someone with no gloves. If the person looks poor, he gives him or her a pair of gloves. "Merry Christmas!" he says. He shakes the person's hand. Then he moves on, looking for more people with cold hands.

Every day during the winter, Mr. Greenberg gives away gloves. During the rest of the year, he buys gloves. People who know about him send him gloves. He has a mountain of gloves in his apartment. There are gloves of all colors and sizes: children's gloves, work gloves, and evening gloves for ladies.

Mr. Greenberg began giving away gloves 21 years ago.

Now, many of the poor people in New York know him. They know why he gives away gloves. Some people, however, are surprised by him. They think he wants money for the gloves. They don't understand that he just wants to help them be a little warmer and happier.

The Greenberg family was poor, but Michael's father always gave things away. He believed it made everyone happier. Michael Greenberg feels the same way. He wants to do something for the poor people in New York. He feels that winter is a hard time for them. Many of these poor people have no warm place to go and no warm clothing. A pair of gloves may be a small thing, but he feels it can make a big difference in the winter. No wonder he is popular among the street people of New York.

Finishing time _____   *Reading time* _____

 Answer the questions on the following page.

➤ *Circle the best answer. Do not look back!*

1. This article is about
   a. gloves.
   b. winter in New York.
   c. Michael Greenberg.
   d. poor people in New York.

2. The people who like Michael Greenberg most are
   a. famous.
   b. poor.
   c. businessmen.
   d. rich.

3. Mr. Greenberg is called "Gloves" because he
   a. looks like any other businessman.
   b. always wears gloves.
   c. makes gloves.
   d. gives away gloves.

4. In the winter, Mr. Greenberg looks for
   a. his briefcase.
   b. clothing.
   c. friends.
   d. people with cold hands.

5. Mr. Greenberg gives the gloves to
   a. his family.
   b. poor people in New York.
   c. businessmen.
   d. New Yorkers.

6. In his apartment, Mr. Greenberg has
   a. many gloves.
   b. only gloves for children.
   c. a few pairs of gloves.
   d. lots of briefcases.

7. People are sometimes surprised because
   a. Mr. Greenberg wants money.
   b. they want money.
   c. gloves usually aren't free.
   d. they have gloves already.

8. Greenberg wants to
   a. be famous.
   b. keep warm.
   c. make people happier.
   d. make a lot of money.

27. Churches, Cows, and Pubs

When Susan and Sam drove out of London, on their way to Scotland, they were nervous. Sam drove, and Susan looked at the map. It was strange driving on the left side of the road! Once they were out of London, they relaxed a little.

They went first to Ely, a town north of London. There they visited a beautiful, old church. Beside the church there was an old school for boys and fields with cows. They went on to Lincoln to visit another beautiful, old church. This church was on the top of a hill, with old streets and shops all around it.

Late in the afternoon Susan and Sam arrived at a village north of Lincoln. In front of a house, there was a sign that said "Bed and Breakfast." It was a large house with a beautiful flower garden on one side and a vegetable garden on the other. Cows and sheep were in the nearby fields.

"This looks perfect," said Susan. "Let's stop." So they did. A smiling woman showed them to their room. It was once her daughter's room, but now the daughter lived in London, so she rented it to guests for the night. The room was large and pretty, with a nice view of fields and hills.

For dinner that evening they went to the village pub. It was called the Golden Horse, and a sign said it was built in 1705. Outside the pub was a garden with tables and a small playground. Some children were playing while their parents talked and had dinner.

Inside, the pub had beautiful dark wood all around. Susan and Sam ordered some beer. It was dark and strong and excellent. For dinner, Sam had steak and kidney pie, a traditional English dish. Susan had chicken curry, a spicy Indian dish. Their food was excellent, too.

"People told me that English food was terrible," said Susan. "But it's not true at all. We eat very well every day." She looked at Sam and said, "Too well, I'm afraid. We're not jogging anymore. And now, I think you're gaining weight."

"I'll eat less breakfast in the morning," said Sam.

But the next morning for breakfast, there were fresh-baked scones with butter. And there was fresh milk and sausages from the farm next door. It was impossible to eat only a little!

Finishing time _____   *Reading time* _____

➤ **Answer the questions on the following page.**

➤ *Circle the best answer. Do not look back!*

1. This passage is about
   a. eating dinner at the Golden Horse.
   b. how English food is terrible.
   c. churches in English towns.
   d. traveling around England.

2. Both Ely and Lincoln
   a. are in London.
   b. are north of London.
   c. are big cities.
   d. serve big breakfasts.

3. Susan and Sam liked
   a. visiting old churches.
   b. walking up hills.
   c. driving on the left side of the road.
   d. visiting schools.

4. A bed and breakfast is
   a. a school for boys.
   b. a restaurant.
   c. in a church.
   d. in someone's house.

5. At the pub, there were some
   a. people from India.
   b. very old people.
   c. families with children.
   d. people from London.

6. Susan and Sam thought the food was
   a. terrible.
   b. excellent.
   c. too spicy.
   d. too strong.

7. Susan was worried about
   a. the old buildings.
   b. English food.
   c. her weight.
   d. Sam's weight.

8. In the morning, Sam ate
   a. only a little.
   b. a lot.
   c. nothing.
   d. less.

Starting Time _____

Do You Speak British or American?

by John Eliot

American and British people both speak English, of course, but sometimes it does not seem like the same language. In fact, there are some important differences between British and American English.

First of all, they sound very different. Often, Americans don't say all the letters in each word, especially consonants like "t" and "d." For example, Americans may say "I dunno" instead of "I don't know," or they may say "Whaddya say?" instead of "What do you say?" However, the British usually pronounce their consonants more carefully.

Also, some letters have different sounds. For example, Americans say the "a" in "half" like the "a" in "cat," but the British say the "a" in "half" like the "o" in "soft." The "r" is sometimes said differently, too. When an American says "farmer," you can usually hear the "r." But you can't hear the "r" in British English. The British say "fahmah."

Sound is not the only difference between British English and American English. The two languages have different words for some things. For example, the words for clothing are different. Americans use the word "sweater," but the British say "jumper." Americans wear "vests" over their shirts, but in England they wear "vests" under their shirts. An American man wears a "tuxedo" to a very fancy party, but an Englishman wears a "dinner-jacket." Americans talk about "pants" or "slacks," but the British talk about "trousers."

Many expressions are also different in the two countries. In England, if you are going to telephone friends, you "ring them up." In America, you "give them a call." The British use the word "lovely" to describe something they like. Americans use the word "nice" or "great."

There are also some differences in grammar. For example, Americans almost always use the helping verb "do" with the verb "have." They might say, "Do you have an extra pen?" The British often ask the question a different way. They might say, "Have you got an extra pen?"

These differences can be confusing if you are learning English. But there is a reason for the differences. Languages change over time. When the same language is used in different places, it changes differently in each place. This is what happened to English. It also happened to other languages, such as French. Many people in Canada speak French, but their French is different from the French spoken in France.

Finishing time _____   *Reading time* _____

 Answer the questions on the following page.

➤ *Circle the best answer. Do not look back!*

1. This article is about
    a. English vocabulary.
    b. the way the British say words.
    c. how American sounds are different from British sounds.
    d. how American English is different from British English.

2. Compared to the British, Americans are usually
    a. more careful about saying consonants.
    b. less careful about saying consonants.
    c. easier to understand.
    d. slower speakers.

3. Some letters in English
    a. always sound the same.
    b. have different sounds in the United States and England.
    c. don't change.
    d. have an unusual sound.

4. The words for clothing are
    a. an example of British English.
    b. different in the United States and England.
    c. an example of modern technology.
    d. the same in the United States and England.

5. People in the United States and in England
    a. always use the same expressions.
    b. often say good-bye.
    c. don't use expressions often.
    d. sometimes use different expressions.

6. When Americans ask questions, they almost always
    a. use the helping verb "do."
    b. don't use the helping verb.
    c. don't use any grammar.
    d. cause confusion.

7. Learners of English can get confused
    a. because it never changes.
    b. because it is different in different places.
    c. when you ask questions.
    d. because British English is the only kind of English.

8. Languages
    a. change over time.
    b. are difficult to say.
    c. don't change much.
    d. are the same in all places.

29. Travel Magazine

An Unusual Place

by Walter Wharton

If you like unusual places, you should go sometime to the Hebrides Islands. Not many people live on these islands in the northwest of Scotland. The land is not good for farming. It's good only for keeping sheep. The winters are long, cold, and wet. It is hard to make a living in the Hebrides, but for a visitor, these islands can be very special.

They're not for everyone, however. Even summer days are cool and often windy. The water is too cold for swimming. There are no forests, and there are only a few trees and green fields. Instead of fields, there are just rocks and bushes. The hills, too, are just piles of rocks. Sometimes the scenery looks like pictures of the moon.

But there is beauty in this wild place. It's in the wide, wonderful views. From the beach you can often see all the way to the rocky hills. From the hills you can see far out to other islands and the open ocean. The colors, too, are special. Blue is everywhere. It's in the sky and in the ocean. It is in the tiny flowers that grow on the hills. In the spring there is also green in the hills. In the summer and fall the hills are more purple. Often the air is soft and gray with clouds and rain.

In these islands you can forget about the rest of the world. You can forget about city problems of noise, dirt, and crime. The evenings are quiet. The restaurants close early, and there isn't any nightlife. There aren't even many hotels. Most visitors stay at a guest house or a bed and breakfast. This is the best way to learn about life on the islands. The islanders are often friendly, and they like to talk.

If you want to meet islanders, you can also try the pubs or even the shops. People are in no hurry here. At the baker's or the grocer's they like to chat about the weather or the fishing. There are also some tourist shops, but not many. They sell the usual tourist things. They also sell some beautiful clothes made of wool from the islands. The wool cloth called "Harris tweed" is famous around the world.

Do not come to the Hebrides to go shopping. Come to walk in the clean, cool air. Come for the quiet beauty and for the views.

➤ *Answer the questions on the following page.*

➤ *Circle the best answer. Do not look back!*

1. This article is about
   a. islands.
   b. Scotland.
   c. the Hebrides Islands.
   d. vacations.

2. Not many people live in the Hebrides because
   a. the water is too cold.
   b. it is hard to make a living there.
   c. it is in the northwest of Scotland.
   d. the summers can be cool.

3. The weather in the Hebrides is
   a. usually warm and sunny.
   b. never warm and sunny.
   c. often cold and wet.
   d. nice in the summer.

4. Some of the scenery looks like the moon because
   a. it is green.
   b. it is rocky.
   c. the colors are beautiful.
   d. there is no sun.

5. The colors on the islands
   a. are unforgettable.
   b. are always the same.
   c. are like the colors everywhere else.
   d. make it look like the moon.

6. In the Hebrides you can forget about
   a. yourself.
   b. your vacation.
   c. noise, dirt, and crime.
   d. life.

7. Visitors usually
   a. stay in hotels.
   b. stay out late at night.
   c. stay at a bed and breakfast.
   d. buy a lot of gifts.

8. People usually come to the Hebrides to
   a. shop.
   b. go sightseeing.
   c. paint pictures.
   d. look at the views.

30. *Travel Magazine*   *Starting Time* _____

Health Tips for Travelers

by Sam Morrison

Travel is fun and exciting, but not if you get sick. You may think, "Not me. I won't get sick on my vacation!" However, for many people, that is what happens. You do not want to spend your vacation sick in bed, of course. If you have heart trouble, you do not want to make it worse. What can you do to stay in good health? These are the three things to remember when you travel: relax, sleep, and eat well.

A vacation is supposed to be a time for relaxing, but tourists often forget that. There are so many places to visit: museums, churches, parks, and shops. You want to see as much as possible, of course, and so you spend most of your days on your feet. This is tiring. Your feet may start to hurt. You may get a headache or a backache. If this is the way you feel, you should take a rest. Do not ask your body to do too much. A tired body means a weak body, and a weak body gets sick easily. So sit down for a few hours in a nice spot. In good weather, look for a quiet park bench or an outdoor café. You can learn a lot by watching people while you rest.

Sleep is also important. If you want to stay healthy, you need to get enough sleep. That is not always easy when you are traveling. You may have a noisy hotel room or an uncomfortable bed. If you do, don't be afraid to change rooms or even hotels. If you are young, you may have other reasons for not sleeping. In many cities the nightlife is exciting. You may want to stay out late at night. Then you should plan to sleep during the day. That extra rest can make a big difference.

Finally, whatever age you are, you must eat well. That means eating the right kinds of foods. Your body needs fresh fruits and vegetables and some meat, milk, or fish. You also need to be careful about eating new foods. Try small amounts first to make sure they are okay for you. And of course, stay away from foods that are very rich.

Remember this: If you want to enjoy your vacation, take care of yourself. Give your body some rest. Get enough sleep and eat good, healthy food.

Finishing time _____   *Reading time* _____

 Answer the questions on the following page.

247

➤ *Circle the best answer. Do not look back!*

1. This article is about
    a. what to eat when you travel.
    b. how exciting travel is.
    c. relaxing when you travel.
    d. how to stay healthy when you travel.

2. A vacation is not fun if
    a. you don't want to go.
    b. you go sightseeing.
    c. you get sick.
    d. you are in a new place.

3. Sightseeing is
    a. the best way to relax.
    b. tiring.
    c. never any fun.
    d. unhealthy.

4. It's a good idea to
    a. spend every day in bed.
    b. take short vacations.
    c. get some rest every day.
    d. take lots of medicines.

5. You can get sick more easily if you are
    a. tired.
    b. sleepy.
    c. in a hotel.
    d. strong and healthy.

6. Your body needs sleep to
    a. enjoy the nightlife.
    b. change hotels.
    c. stay strong and healthy.
    d. learn a lot about a new place.

7. When you travel, your body needs
    a. new foods.
    b. fresh fruits and vegetables.
    c. lots of rich foods.
    d. more food.

8. For good health, you need
    a. to travel.
    b. to get enough sleep and good food.
    c. to enjoy the nightlife.
    d. to eat new foods.

31. Trouble in Edinburgh

One Friday afternoon, Susan and Sam arrived in Edinburgh. It was their last stop in Scotland. They were going to leave the car there and take the train back to London and the plane back to New York. They were both tired. It had been a long drive from Ullapool, near the Hebrides Islands, and it was a cool, rainy day. They found a bed and breakfast on a quiet street. Edinburgh seemed large and noisy after the Hebrides. They had dinner in a pub, and it was crowded and noisy, too. There was also a lot of cigarette smoke. They finished their dinner quickly and started to walk home.

Suddenly, Sam stopped. He said he didn't feel well. He sat down on a doorstep.

"What is it?" asked Susan.

"I can't breathe," said Sam.

"Wait, stay there. I'll get—" But Sam tried to get up, and he fell over into the street.

Susan shouted for help, and several people came running. They called an ambulance and brought Sam to the hospital. Susan went, too. It was a terrible moment.

But very soon, Sam was awake and speaking again. At the hospital, the doctors did some tests on him. It was a heart attack, but only a small one. The doctors said he was out of danger. The important thing now was rest for Sam, but they also wanted to do some more tests and watch him carefully. He had to stay in the hospital for at least 10 days.

The next day, Susan called Jane and Ted. She told them all about Sam's heart attack. She told them how helpful everyone was at the bed and breakfast and in the hospital. And she told them about Dr. Campbell, the nice young doctor who was taking care of Sam. Dr. Campbell said that Sam was going to be fine.

"Don't even think of coming here," Susan said to Ted. "Jane said she'll be here tomorrow, and you can't leave Maria now! How's she doing?"

"She's a little tired after her show, but she's fine. She's getting very large. Only one more month!"

In fact, Ted did not want to leave Maria at that moment. He was a little worried about her. She was not very well. The doctor told her she must stay in bed, but Ted did not tell this to his mother. She had enough to worry about.

Finishing time _____   *Reading time* _____

➤ **Answer the questions on the next page.**

Reading Faster

➤ *Circle the best answer. Do not look back!*

1. This passage is about
   a. Sam's heart attack.
   b. Edinburgh.
   c. Dr. Campbell.
   d. how Susan calls Ted.

2. Susan and Sam
   a. still had many weeks of vacation left.
   b. had finished their vacation.
   c. had almost finished their vacation.
   d. were starting their vacation.

3. For dinner, Susan and Sam went to
   a. a smoke-free restaurant.
   b. Ullapool.
   c. a crowded, noisy, and smoky pub.
   d. a large, quiet pub.

4. On the way home, Sam
   a. said he was tired.
   b. suddenly fell down.
   c. talked with Susan.
   d. smoked a cigarette.

5. The doctor told Sam he
   a. was in serious danger.
   b. might die.
   c. did not have heart trouble.
   d. was not in danger.

6. Susan told Ted that
   a. no one was helpful.
   b. many people were helpful.
   c. only a few people were helpful.
   d. people didn't have time to help her.

7. Susan said that
   a. Ted must come to Edinburgh.
   b. Maria should come to Edinburgh.
   c. she wasn't feeling well.
   d. Jane was coming to Edinburgh.

8. Ted was worried about Maria,
   a. but he didn't tell his mother.
   b. so he told his mother.
   c. and also about his mother.
   d. but not about his father.

32. A Granddaughter for Susan and Sam!   *Starting Time* _____

"Mom?"

"Ted! Hello! What's up?"

"Guess what! You're a grandmother now!"

"Oh!!! So early! Is the baby okay? And Maria?"

"Everything is fine. Well, no, there were some problems. But now the baby and Maria are both okay. It's a girl. Her name is Elena. She's small—only five and a half pounds—but she's healthy."

"Tell me everything. How did it happen?"

"We went to the doctor for a checkup, and Maria started to feel something. The doctor sent us to the hospital. She went in at two o'clock in the afternoon on Monday. The baby was born at eight o'clock Tuesday night. That's 30 hours! Poor Maria. She had a difficult time. And then after the baby was born, she had some serious problems. She lost a lot of blood, and the doctors had to operate. Now she can't have anymore children. We were sad when the doctor told us. We always wanted to have two children."

"That is sad news. I'm really sorry. How is Maria now?"

"She's weak, of course. But Elena stays with her most of the day. She's such a pretty little baby. Not all babies are pretty, you know. Some of the other babies at the hospital are a little ugly, but Elena has beautiful big brown eyes, like Maria's. All the nurses love her, too. She doesn't cry very often. She's really a very happy baby."

"Oh, I wish I could see her! This is terrible. Now I can't help Maria when she comes home. Your father won't be able to travel for a few weeks."

"That's okay. My boss said I could work part-time now. I can do most of the work at home on my computer, too. That way, I can really help Maria. And I can spend a lot of time with Elena. I don't know much about babies, but I guess I'll learn! I can change her diapers already!"

"That's something your father never did. Men didn't do those things when you were a baby."

"How is Dad now?"

"Much better, much stronger. He can walk around the room and he wants to leave the hospital, but Dr. Campbell says he must stay another week. Dr. Campbell is such a nice person. He took Jane out to a concert last night."

"Oh, a Scottish romance, maybe?"

"Well, it's too early to tell, but it's possible!"

Finishing time _____   *Reading time* _____

➤ **Answer the questions on the following page.**

➤ *Circle the best answer. Do not look back!*

1. This passage is about
   a. how Maria had a little girl.
   b. how Maria had a little boy.
   c. how Ted changed Elena's diapers.
   d. what the doctor said about Maria.

2. The baby was
   a. small and unwell.
   b. large and healthy.
   c. small but healthy.
   d. large but unhealthy.

3. Maria
   a. had an easy time in the hospital.
   b. stayed a short time in the hospital.
   c. didn't want to go to the hospital.
   d. had a difficult time in the hospital.

4. Ted and Maria
   a. couldn't have anymore children.
   b. didn't want anymore children.
   c. didn't have any children.
   d. couldn't keep their baby.

5. Ted thought that
   a. Elena was an ugly baby.
   b. some babies were ugly.
   c. all the babies were beautiful.
   d. Elena was not a beautiful baby.

6. Susan was upset because
   a. Maria couldn't come to Edinburgh.
   b. she couldn't help Maria.
   c. Ted couldn't come to Edinburgh.
   d. Ted was working part-time.

7. Ted wants to
   a. travel soon.
   b. go back to full-time work soon.
   c. work a lot on the computer.
   d. stay home and help Maria.

8. According to Dr. Campbell, Sam
   a. can leave the hospital soon.
   b. must stay in the hospital another week.
   c. should travel around Scotland more.
   d. must have more tests.

Reading Faster

33. *The New York Gazette*   *Starting Time* _____

Family Life in the United States

by Jacob Sand

Family life in the United States is changing. Thirty or forty years ago, the wife was called a "housewife." She cleaned, cooked, and cared for the children. The husband earned the money for the family. He was usually out working all day. He came home tired in the evening, so he did not do much housework. And he did not see the children very much, except on weekends.

These days, however, more and more women work outside the home. They cannot stay with the children all day. They, too, come home tired in the evening. They do not want to spend the evening cooking dinner and cleaning up. They do not have time to clean the house and do the laundry. So who is going to do the housework now? Who is going to take care of the children?

Many families solve the problem of housework by sharing it. In these families, the husband and wife agree to do different jobs around the house, or they take turns doing each job. For example, the husband always cooks dinner and the wife always does the laundry. Or the wife cooks dinner on some nights and the husband cooks dinner on other nights.

Then there is the question of the children. In the past, many families got help with child care from grandparents. Now, families usually do not live near their relatives. The grandparents often are too far away to help in a regular way.

More often, parents have to pay for child-care help. The help may be a babysitter or a day-care center. The problem with this kind of help is the high cost. It is possible only for couples with jobs that pay well.

Parents may get another kind of help from the companies they work for. Many companies now let people with children work part-time. That way, parents can spend more time with their children. Some husbands may even stop working for a while to stay with the children. For these men there is a new word: They are called "househusbands." In the United States, more and more men are becoming househusbands every year.

These changes in the home mean changes in the family. Fathers can learn to understand their children better, and the children can get to know their fathers better. Husbands and wives may also find changes in their marriage. They, too, may have a better understanding of each other.

Finishing time _____   *Reading time* _____

➤ **Answer the questions on the following page.**

253

➤ *Circle the best answer. Do not look back!*

1. This article is about
   a. housewives.
   b. American men.
   c. how more American women are working.
   d. how family life in America is changing.

2. Forty years ago, most women
   a. had no children.
   b. worked.
   c. were not housewives.
   d. were housewives.

3. In those days, men
   a. did not see their children very much.
   b. spent a lot of time with their children.
   c. worked with the children all day.
   d. never saw the children.

4. Today there are
   a. more housewives.
   b. more women working outside the home.
   c. not as many women working.
   d. no jobs for women.

5. Day-care centers help
   a. working parents with their children.
   b. housewives.
   c. with cooking and cleaning.
   d. men become househusbands.

6. Some parents work part-time
   a. so they can be with their children.
   b. so they can earn more money.
   c. because they have no time.
   d. because they do not like their work.

7. Househusbands
   a. earn a lot of money.
   b. do not do any housework.
   c. do the housework and take care of the children.
   d. marry housewives.

8. These changes in the American home may
   a. not change the children at all.
   b. cause problems for a marriage.
   c. not happen.
   d. help families.

Starting Time _____

Househusbands

Dear Editor:

I read with interest the article on American families. In general I agree with it, but there are some important things it left out. It didn't tell the reader much about the life of a househusband. It's not an easy life. I know, because I'm now a househusband myself. A househusband has to change many of his ideas and his ways.

First of all, he has to change the way he thinks about time. Before I was a househusband, I worked full-time for the *New York Times*. I was a reporter, and time was always important. We had to finish our articles quickly and give them to the editor. Everyone was always in a hurry. This is the way many other men work, too. Businessmen, lawyers, bankers, and doctors all have to work quickly.

At home it's different. The househusband cannot be in a hurry all the time. If you rush around, you will make everyone unhappy! The children will be unhappy because they don't understand. For them, time is not important. Your wife will be unhappy because the children are unhappy. You will be unhappy, too, because they are all unhappy. So you have to learn to slow down. That is the first and most important rule for a househusband.

There is something else the househusband must learn. You must learn to show how you feel about things. At work, men usually do not talk about feelings. If they do, people think they are strange. So, many men are not used to telling anyone about their feelings. They do not know how to talk about their anger, worries, or love. But children need to know how you feel. They need to know how much you love them. If you are angry, they need to know why. Your wife also needs to know about your feelings. If you do not say anything, your family may get the wrong idea. Then there may be serious problems.

People talk a lot about househusbands these days. Usually they talk about men doing the housework, the cooking, cleaning, and shopping. But in my opinion, these are the easiest things to learn. It was much harder for me to change the way I think and the way I act with my family. I think other men will also find this harder, but, like me, will find it necessary if they want to have a happy family!

Ted Diamond
Hartwell, New Jersey

Finishing time _____   *Reading time* _____

 Answer the questions on the following page.

➤ *Circle the best answer. Do not look back!*

1. This article is about
   a. fathers and children.
   b. life as a househusband.
   c. ideas about time.
   d. American families.

2. This letter was written by
   a. Jacob Sand to Ted.
   b. a newspaper publisher to Ted.
   c. Ted Diamond to the editor.
   d. Maria Diamond for the newspaper.

3. At work, most people
   a. have to hurry.
   b. take their time.
   c. have lots of time.
   d. have to slow down.

4. The househusband has to learn
   a. to do things more slowly.
   b. to do things more quickly.
   c. the importance of time.
   d. how to understand his work.

5. Children
   a. are usually unhappy.
   b. are always in a hurry.
   c. usually don't think time is important.
   d. don't know how to show their feelings.

6. Many men
   a. like to talk about their worries.
   b. don't have any worries.
   c. don't often talk about their worries.
   d. have terrible problems.

7. Family problems can happen if
   a. men don't talk enough with their families.
   b. men talk too much with their families.
   c. men get wrong ideas.
   d. people talk about househusbands.

8. Ted thinks
   a. learning about housework is easy.
   b. learning about housework is a problem.
   c. cooking is the easiest thing to learn.
   d. being a househusband is easy.

35. News about Gilberto and Milena

Back in Rosebud, Gilberto was taking good care of everything. The garden looked beautiful, the house was clean, and the animals were healthy. Gilberto was very busy now. He still went to the English course. He still worked in the supermarket. And every free moment, he went to New York to take pictures. He was beginning to think he did not want to be an engineer. He wanted to go to art school and study photography. He felt happy when he was taking pictures. In fact, Gilberto was like a different person now. He was much more friendly, and he laughed a lot, especially when he was with Milena.

Milena was much happier, too. She sometimes went to New York with Gilberto. Her parents came to live in Rosebud, so she did not have to help take care of Niko. Now she had time to practice her violin. She wanted to go to a famous music school in New York, but she was afraid they might not take her. They took only the best students. She also worried about money. The school was expensive. And she could not continue to study without a good violin. But good violins were expensive, too. And her family didn't have much money.

Then one day two friends came to visit Ted and Maria and Elena. They both were musicians and teachers at the Julliard School of Music. Maria told them about Milena. They invited Milena to come to the school and play for them.

A few weeks later, Milena played the violin for the teachers at the school. They were all amazed. She played beautifully. They told her she could study at the school. They also told her not to worry about the money. She would almost certainly get a scholarship, and, furthermore, she could borrow a good violin from the school.

When Milena heard all this, she almost fell on the floor with happiness. Luckily, Gilberto was with her and held her up. Then he took her out to a Brazilian restaurant to celebrate.

The next week they went out to a Greek restaurant. This time they were celebrating for Gilberto. The New York Times was going to publish some of his pictures! It was Ted's idea. He really liked Gilberto's pictures of New York neighborhoods. Why not write an article and use those pictures? The editor thought this was a good idea, too. Now Gilberto was sure that he wanted to be a photographer, not an engineer.

Finishing time _____   *Reading time* _____

➤ **Answer the questions on the following page.**

➤ *Circle the best answer. Do not look back!*

1. This passage is about
   a. how Milena starts music school.
   b. how Gilberto decides to be a photographer.
   c. Gilberto and Milena.
   d. changes in the lives of Gilberto and Milena.

2. Gilberto had new ideas about
   a. his English course.
   b. his career.
   c. Susan and Sam's house.
   d. his job at the supermarket.

3. Milena now had more time because she didn't have to
   a. study English.
   b. go to New York.
   c. practice her violin.
   d. take care of Niko.

4. Milena was afraid she
   a. couldn't go to the Julliard School.
   b. didn't speak English well.
   c. was too young.
   d. didn't want to go to the Julliard School.

5. The teachers at the school were surprised because Milena
   a. didn't have a violin.
   b. didn't play very well.
   c. played beautifully.
   d. Gilberto was there, too.

6. They told Milena she
   a. couldn't go to the school.
   b. could go to the school.
   c. needed a lot of money.
   d. had a very good violin.

7. When she heard the news, Milena
   a. laughed.
   b. was happy.
   c. was unhappy.
   d. cried.

8. The *New York Times* was going to publish
   a. some of Gilberto's pictures.
   b. an article by Ted.
   c. news about Maria.
   d. an article by Gilberto.

The Secret of a Good Violin

by Susan Austen

Most musicians agree that the world's best violins were made in Cremona, Italy, about 300 years ago. These violins sound better than any others. They even sound better than violins made today. Violin makers and scientists now try to make instruments like the Italian violins, but they are not the same. Musicians still prefer the old ones. Why are these old Italian violins so special? No one really knows, but many people think they have an answer.

Some people think it is the age of the violins. They say that today's violins will also sound wonderful someday. The problem with this answer is that not all old violins sound wonderful. Only some old violins have a special sound. So age cannot be the reason. Other people think the secret to those violins is the wood. The wood of the violin is important. It must be from certain kinds of trees. It must not be too young or too old. Perhaps the violin makers of Cremona knew something special about wood for violins.

Other people say that the kind of wood is not so important and that it is more important to cut the wood a special way. The wood for a violin must be cut very carefully. It has to be the right size and shape. The smallest difference will change the sound of the violin. Some musicians think that the violin makers from Cremona knew a secret about cutting wood.

However, size and shape may not be the answer, either. Scientists measured the old violins from Cremona very carefully. They can make new ones that are exactly the same size and shape. The new violins still do not sound as good as the old ones. Other scientists think the secret may be the varnish. Varnish is what covers the wood of the violin. It makes the wood look shiny. It also helps the sound of the instrument. No one knows what the Italian violin makers used in their varnish. So no one can make the same varnish today.

There may never be other violins like the violins of Cremona. Their secret may be lost forever. Young musicians today hope this is not true. They need fine violins, and there are not very many of the old violins left. Also, the old violins are very expensive. Recently, a famous old Italian violin was sold for almost a million dollars!

Finishing time _____   *Reading time* _____

➤ **Answer the questions on the following page.**

Reading Faster

➤ *Circle the best answer. Do not look back!*

1. This article is about
   a. playing violins.
   b. musical instruments.
   c. scientific ideas.
   d. the old Italian violins.

2. The best violins
   a. are modern.
   b. were lost many years ago.
   c. were made in Italy 300 years ago.
   d. were made by scientists in Italy.

3. Some people think that modern violins
   a. will sound better in the future.
   b. will sound worse in the future.
   c. sound wonderful.
   d. are too old.

4. Other people think the Italian violin makers
   a. did not know much about violins.
   b. were lucky.
   c. used many kinds of wood.
   d. knew something special.

5. The size and shape of the violin
   a. do not matter.
   b. are a secret.
   c. can make a difference.
   d. are different today.

6. Violins made today
   a. have the same size and shape as the old ones.
   b. sound the same as the old ones.
   c. are better than the old ones.
   d. have the same varnish as the old ones.

7. Some scientists believe the secret to the sound of the old violins is
   a. their price.
   b. their color.
   c. their varnish.
   d. the music.

8. The old violins are
   a. lost forever.
   b. inexpensive.
   c. expensive.
   d. easy to get.

37. Looking into the Future

Sam was still in the hospital, but every day he was a little stronger. He was comfortable at the hospital. He could walk around, and he liked the doctors and nurses. However, he wanted to go home soon to see his new granddaughter.

One day, Dr. Campbell took Susan and Jane to a Scottish festival. In the afternoon, there were sheepdog trials outside. These dogs are used on the sheep farms in Scotland. They are very smart, and they can make the sheep go wherever the farmer tells them. In the evening, there was Scottish music and dancing. It was colorful and fun to watch. The men in the dance wore kilts, the traditional Scottish national costume. Susan and Jane tried dancing, too. It was fun but not easy!

On Jane's last evening in Edinburgh, she went out alone with Dr. Campbell. By now, she called him by his first name, Andrew. He told her he wanted to go to New York and work at a hospital there. She told him all about her life as a pilot. He said he hoped he could see her again. Jane was going to fly to London the next month, so they decided to meet in London.

Ted called one day with good news for Susan. The Planning Committee in Rosebud had decided not to allow a supermarket to be built near the lake. Instead they were talking about making a park. There was going to be another meeting next month to decide. Susan was very happy about that. She called Gilberto and thanked him again for his wonderful pictures.

That same day, Susan also got a call from the laboratory where she worked. They, too, had good news for her. The government was going to give a lot of money to the laboratory. They wanted Susan and the other scientists to do a big new study about lakes. That meant lots of work for Susan in the future. Susan was happy and excited. She loved her work, and she thought it was important.

She and Sam talked about their life in Rosebud. The doctors said that he must work less and rest more. Sam decided that he was going to work fewer hours. He had always been very busy when Jane and Ted were children. Now he wanted to be a good grandfather. He wanted to spend time with little Elena.

Finishing time _____   *Reading time* _____

➤ **Answer the questions on the following page.**

➤ *Circle the best answer. Do not look back!*

1. This passage is about
    a. Jane and Andrew Campbell.
    b. Sam in the hospital.
    c. Susan, Sam, and Jane in Edinburgh.
    d. life in Edinburgh.

2. Sam wanted to go home and
    a. return to work.
    b. see Elena.
    c. talk to his friends.
    d. see Jane.

3. Dr. Campbell took Susan and Jane to
    a. a sheepdog trial.
    b. the museum.
    c. London.
    d. a hospital.

4. At the Scottish festival, Jane and Susan
    a. tried working with sheepdogs.
    b. ate lots of food.
    c. tried Scottish dancing.
    d. listened to Scottish stories.

5. Jane and Andrew Campbell are planning to
    a. fly to New York.
    b. go to a Scottish dance.
    c. meet in London.
    d. travel together.

6. The Rosebud Planning Committee decided
    a. not to allow a supermarket to be built near the lake.
    b. to allow a supermarket to be built near the lake.
    c. to allow a supermarket to be built near Jane's house.
    d. not to make a park near the lake.

7. Susan's laboratory will
    a. study parks.
    b. make a lot of money.
    c. ask for money from the goverment.
    d. study lakes.

8. In the future, Sam is going to
    a. work the same hours.
    b. work fewer hours.
    c. spend more time with Susan.
    d. earn more money.

Men in Skirts

by Samuel Jewett

In Europe men do not usually wear skirts, but the Scottish national costume for men is a kind of skirt. It is called a "kilt." The Scottish like to be different. They are also proud of their country and its history, and they feel that the kilt is part of that history. That is why the men still wear kilts at traditional dances and on national holidays. They believe they are wearing the same clothes that Scottish men always used to wear.

That is what they believe. However, kilts are not really so old. In the early days, Scottish men wore a kind of long shirt that went below their knees. They wore long socks and a big wool blanket around their shoulders. These clothes were warm and comfortable for working outside on a farm, but they were not so good when men started to work in factories in modern times. So in 1730 a factory owner changed the blanket into a skirt: the kilt. That's how the first kilt was made, according to one historian.

In the late 1700s, Scottish soldiers in the British Army began to wear kilts. One reason for this was national feeling: The Scottish soldiers wanted to look different from the English soldiers. The British Army probably had a different reason: A Scottish soldier in a kilt was always easy to find! The Scottish soldiers fought hard and became famous. The kilt was part of that fame, and in the early 1800s men all around Scotland began to wear kilts.

These kilts had colorful stripes going up and down and across. In Scotland, this pattern is called a "tartan." Tartan cloth was used many centuries ago. In fact, Scottish literature talks about tartans in the 1200s.

At first, the tartans showed where people came from. Then they became important to Scottish families. We do not know when this happened. Some people say that the colors of the family tartans are many centuries old. Others say that they became important only in the nineteenth century.

In any case, by the early 1800s, most Scottish families had special colors for their tartans. The men always wore these colors on their kilts. For example, the Campbell family tartan was dark blue, with yellow and green stripes.

The exact history of the tartan kilt is not so important. To the Scottish people today, it is part of their tradition, and that is what matters.

Finishing time _____   *Reading time* _____

 Answer the questions on the following page.

Reading Faster

➤ *Circle the best answer. Do not look back!*

1. This article is about
    a. Scottish men.
    b. the history of Scotland.
    c. the history of kilts.
    d. Scottish families.

2. A kilt is
    a. a kind of shirt.
    b. a kind of blanket.
    c. a national holiday.
    d. a kind of skirt.

3. The first kilt was made
    a. in Paris.
    b. in the British Army.
    c. by a Scottish factory owner.
    d. by a Scottish family.

4. Scottish soldiers wore kilts partly because of
    a. the colors.
    b. the weather.
    c. national feeling.
    d. the style.

5. Kilts are made of
    a. old cloth.
    b. tartan cloth.
    c. old shirts.
    d. Army cloth.

6. The colors of the tartans
    a. may be many centuries old.
    b. are unimportant to Scottish people.
    c. are not Scottish.
    d. are for the Campbell family only.

7. By about the early 1800s, most Scottish families
    a. wore the same color kilts.
    b. had special colors for their kilts.
    c. wore blankets.
    d. wore green, yellow, and blue kilts.

8. Scottish people
    a. always wear tartans.
    b. are proud of their traditions.
    c. never wear kilts for dancing.
    d. wear kilts only in factories.

264

Starting Time _____

What Is Happening to Our Lake?

by Susan Conley

Thirty years ago, Lake Ponkapog in Hartwell, New Jersey, was full of life. Many birds and animals lived beside the water, which was full of fish. Now there are few birds, animals, and fish. The lake water is polluted. It is a dirty brown color, and it is filled with strange plants.

How did this happen? First, we must think about how water gets into Lake Ponkapog. When it rains, water comes into the lake from all around. In the past, there were woods all around Lake Ponkapog, so the rainwater was clean.

Now there are many homes on the lake shore. People often use chemicals in their gardens. They use other chemicals inside their houses for cleaning or killing insects. There are also many businesses. Businesses use chemicals in their machines or stores. Other chemicals fall onto the ground from cars or trucks. When it rains, the rainwater flows by these homes and businesses. It picks up all the chemicals and then pours them into the lake. They pollute the water and kill the animal life.

Boats on the lake are also a problem. Lake Ponkapog is a popular place for motorboats and jet-skis. But oil and gas from boats and jet-skis often get into the lake. They add more bad chemicals to the water.

There is still another problem at the lake: exotic plants. These plants come from other countries. They have no natural enemies here, and they grow very quickly. In a short time, they can fill up a lake. Then there is no room for other plants. The plants that normally grow there die. These plants gave many animals and fish their food or their homes. So now those animals and fish die, too.

People in Hartwell are worried. They love their lake and want to save it. Will it be possible? A clean lake must have clean rainwater going into it. Clean rainwater is possible only if people are more careful about chemicals at home and at work. They must also be more careful about gas and oil and other chemicals on the ground. And they must stop using motorboats and jet-skis on the lake.

All this may cause a lot of changes in people's lives. And then, scientists need to find a way to stop the exotic plants. Only then can Lake Ponkapog be a beautiful, clean lake again.

Finishing time _____   *Reading time* _____

 Answer the questions on the following page.

Reading Faster

➤ *Circle the best answer. Do not look back!*

1. This article is about
    a. boats on Lake Ponkapog.
    b. why the water is dirty in Lake Ponkapog.
    c. the exotic plants in Lake Ponkapog.
    d. dirty lakes.

2. Lake Ponkapog was
    a. always very polluted.
    b. much larger in the past.
    c. very dirty in the past.
    d. not always polluted.

3. The water in Lake Ponkapog comes
    a. from the land all around it.
    b. from a river.
    c. up from underground.
    d. from the sea.

4. Chemicals from homes and businesses
    a. are always cleaned up.
    b. can help the animals.
    c. are good for the lake.
    d. get into the rainwater.

5. Exotic plants grow quickly because they
    a. have a lot of water.
    b. have no natural enemies.
    c. are large.
    d. pollute the water.

6. Other plants and animals die when
    a. exotic plants die.
    b. people grow exotic plants.
    c. exotic plants fill the lake.
    d. motorboats pollute the lake.

7. Cleaner rainwater will mean
    a. a cleaner lake.
    b. more pollution in the lake.
    c. more boats on the lake.
    d. a dirtier lake.

8. To save Lake Ponkapog, people need to
    a. be more careful about chemicals.
    b. use less water.
    c. stop working in their gardens.
    d. stop fishing.

266

40. The Rosebud Record

Starting Time _____

Diamonds Return from Great Britain

by Alex Green

Yesterday afternoon Susan Conley and Sam Diamond returned to Rosebud after almost two months in England and Scotland. While they were in Scotland, Sam Diamond had a heart attack. Luckily, it was not a serious one. Dr. Diamond's patients and friends will be glad to know that he is now in good health. His dental office will be open next week in the mornings.

Susan Conley is returning to her work at the National Science Laboratory in New York. She tells us they are starting work on a new study for the government. They will study the water in lakes. Many of our lakes are very polluted. Dr. Conley and her laboratory will look for the harmful chemicals that pollute the water and try to find ways to stop these chemicals from going into the water. We all hope our lakes can be clean again someday. We are lucky to have people like Dr. Conley working on the problem.

Dr. Conley and Dr. Diamond were met at the airport yesterday by their son, Ted. He and his wife, Maria Arroyo, returned from Brazil this spring. Last month they had their first child, a girl named Elena. Ted is a reporter for the *New York Times*. Recently he wrote some articles about New York City neighborhoods. Some of our readers may remember the excellent photographs with those articles. They were taken by Maria Arroyo's brother. Gilberto Arroyo is only 20 years old, but his pictures are full of life. He shows us the people of New York in a new way.

Maria Arroyo, an artist, is well known in Brazil. She recently had a show in an important gallery in New York. A writer for the *New York Gazette* reported on a recent showing of Maria's paintings and spoke of her as a "very fine artist."

We also have news of the youngest member of the Diamond family. Many of us remember Jane Diamond as a person who liked excitement and change. In high school, she was always busy with sports, music, and other activities. As you may know, she became an airplane pilot and lived and worked in Alaska for several years. In March of this year, she moved back to our area. Now she is living in New York City and working as a pilot for American Airlines. She was not at the airport yesterday— she was in Paris!

Welcome home to the Diamonds, and good luck to all the family!

Finishing time _____   *Reading time* _____

 Answer the questions on the following page.

Reading Faster

➤ *Circle the best answer. Do not look back!*

1. This article is about
    a. the Diamond family.
    b. Susan and Sam.
    c. a new study of lake water.
    d. Rosebud.

2. The person who wrote this article
    a. probably lives in New York.
    b. probably lives in Rosebud.
    c. is a member of the Diamond family.
    d. does not know the Diamonds very well.

3. Susan and Sam Diamond
    a. are still in Scotland.
    b. are coming back soon.
    c. came back yesterday.
    d. are not coming back from Scotland.

4. This writer probably
    a. saw the Diamonds and talked to them.
    b. did not talk with the Diamonds.
    c. will talk with the Diamonds tomorrow.
    d. does not want to talk to the Diamonds.

5. People in Rosebud want to have
    a. a cleaner town.
    b. cleaner lakes.
    c. more water.
    d. better scientists.

6. This writer thinks Susan is
    a. a good mother.
    b. a good scientist.
    c. not a good scientist.
    d. not a scientist.

7. Susan and Sam were met at the airport by
    a. Sam's patients and friends.
    b. Jane.
    c. Ted.
    d. Dr. Andrew Campbell.

8. This writer thinks Jane always liked
    a. excitement and activities.
    b. a quiet life.
    c. children.
    d. painting.

Book Title _____

Author _____

RATE (words per minute)																									
480																									
460																									
440																									
420																									
400																									
380																									
360																									
340																									
320																									
300																									
280																									
260																									
240																									
220																									
200																									
180																									
160																									
140																									
120																									
100																									
80																									
60																									
40																									
20																									

Date

Reading for Pleasure Progress Chart 2

Book Title _____

Author _____

RATE (words per minute)																							
480																							
460																							
440																							
420																							
400																							
380																							
360																							
340																							
320																							
300																							
280																							
260																							
240																							
220																							
200																							
180																							
160																							
140																							
120																							
100																							
80																							
60																							
40																							
20																							

Date

Thinking Skills Progress Chart

Exercise	1	2	3	4	5	6	7	8	9	10	11	12	13	14	15	16	17	18	19	20	21	22	23	24	25
Number Correct																									
5																									
4																									
3																									
2																									
1																									

Date

Examples C and D

Passages 1–20 (200-word passages)

Reading Time (minutes)	Reading Rate (words per minute)
:30	400
:45	266
1:00	200
1:15	160
1:30	133
1:45	114
2:00	100
2:15	89
2:30	80
2:45	73
3:00	67
3:15	62
3:30	57
3:45	53
4:00	50
4:15	47
4:30	44
4:45	42
5:00	40

Passages 21–40 (400-word passages)

Reading Time (minutes)	Reading Rate (words per minute)
:30	800
:45	533
1:00	400
1:15	320
1:30	267
1:45	229
2:00	200
2:15	178
2:30	160
2:45	145
3:00	133
3:15	123
3:30	114
3:45	107
4:00	100
4:15	94
4:30	89
4:45	84
5:00	80
5:15	76
5:30	73
5:45	70
6:00	67
6:15	64
6:30	62
6:45	59
7:00	57

Faster Reading Progress Chart

Examples C and D

Passages 1–20

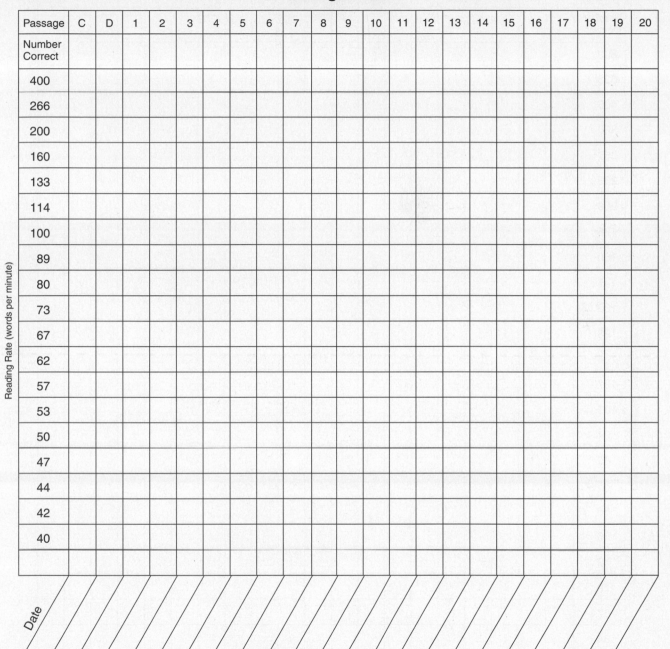

Passage	C	D	1	2	3	4	5	6	7	8	9	10	11	12	13	14	15	16	17	18	19	20
Number Correct																						
400																						
266																						
200																						
160																						
133																						
114																						
100																						
89																						
80																						
73																						
67																						
62																						
57																						
53																						
50																						
47																						
44																						
42																						
40																						

Reading Rate (words per minute)

Date

273

Faster Reading Progress Chart

Passages 21–40

Passage	21	22	23	24	25	26	27	28	29	30	31	32	33	34	35	36	37	38	39	40
Number Correct																				
800																				
533																				
400																				
320																				
267																				
229																				
200																				
178																				
160																				
145																				
133																				
123																				
114																				
107																				
100																				
94																				
89																				
84																				
80																				
76																				
73																				
70																				
67																				
64																				
62																				
59																				
57																				

Reading Rate (words per minute)

Date

Answer Key

Part Two

Unit 1: Scanning

Exercise 1 (p. 22)

1. 6
2. The Trouble with Jet Skis
3. 2
4. 6
5. Yes. 17
6. 23
7. Yes. John H. Mitchell
8. 14
9. Watcher at the Pond
10. 6

Exercise 2 (p. 24)

1. 132
2. 53
3. v, 12, 28 (and many more)
4. 63
5. 75, 76, 131 (and many more)
6. 9, 14, 53
7. 118
8. 127, 128, 132
9. 159
10. 66

Exercise 3 (p. 26)

1. 7:00 A.M. and 11:00 A.M.
2. 2:00 P.M. and 4:20 P.M.
3. No
4. June, July, August, September
5. February, March, April, October
6. $39
7. $93
8. 4:20 P.M.
9. 5 hours and 20 minutes
10. No

Exercise 4 (p. 28)

1. 2
2. $610
3. Susan or Mrs. Young
4. extra large studio
5. Yes
6. 954-4121
7. Brighton, Brookline, Concord
8. 598-8440
9. Concord
10. Lynn
11. $550, $525, $590
12. $565

Exercise 5 (p. 30)

1. 14
2. shoe store
3. 4:40 P.M.
4. Westchester County

Exercise 6 (p. 31)

1. 515
2. Monday
3. 445,000
4. Panay Island
5. Agnes
6. more than 400

Exercise 7 (p. 32)

1. 108
2. November 22
3. on a bridge
4. Washington, D.C.
5. 2
6. Frank Lautenberg
7. between New York and Newark
8. There may have been a gap in the track on the bridge.

Exercise 8 (p. 34)

1. Paqcomp
2. $3395
3. Data Systems International
4. 40
5. Paqcomp
6. $2595

Unit 2: Previewing and Predicting

Exercise 1 (p. 37)

Many different predictions are possible. Here are a few examples: go to the beach, go dancing, eat seafood, wear shorts or a bathing suit, buy hats, feel relaxed and happy when you come home.

Exercise 2 (p. 38)

Many different predictions are possible. Here are a few examples: go to museums during the day, go to a concert in the evening, wear comfortable shoes, eat good meals in fine restaurants, buy souvenirs and maybe postcards, feel refreshed but tired when she comes home.

Exercise 3 (p. 39)

1. d   2. e   3. a   4. b   5. c

Exercise 4 (p. 40)

1. yes	3. no	5. no	7. no	9. yes
2. yes	4. yes	6. yes	8. no	10. no

Exercise 5 (p. 40)

1. no	3. no	5. yes	7. no	9. no
2. yes	4. no	6. yes	8. yes	10. no

Exercise 6 (p. 41)

1. c	3. c	5. a
2. b	4. b	6. b

Exercise 7 (p. 42)

1. b	3. c	5. c	7. b
2. a	4. a	6. c	8. c

Exercises 8, 9, and 10

You may check your predictions by rereading the passages.

Unit 3: Building a Powerful Vocabulary

Exercise 1 (p. 48)

1. books	3. was	5. had
2. traveled	4. not	6. person

Exercise 2 (p. 49)

1. was	9. years	17. ran
2. when	10. They	18. to
3. became	11. But	19. teacher
4. that	12. not	20. find
5. parents	13. something	21. wrote
6. take	14. eat	22. a
7. not	15. noises	23. is
8. her	16. her	

Exercise 3 (p. 50)

1. wanted	8. that	15. not
2. she	9. not	16. take
3. be	10. It	17. teach
4. what	11. thought	18. of
5. to	12. could	19. Helen's
6. home	13. know	20. Annie
7. mother	14. to	

Exercise 4 (p. 51)

1. they	8. hand	15. Helen
2. very	9. Annie	16. learned
3. in	10. on	17. with
4. cup	11. water	18. words
5. was	12. was	19. ready
6. Then	13. name	20. in
7. finger	14. to	21. and

Exercise 5 (p. 52)

1. It	8. her	15. help
2. to	9. also	16. stop
3. college	10. her	17. thought
4. good	11. and	18. of
5. went	12. countries	19. she
6. graduated	13. world	20. That
7. together	14. blind	21. Annie

Exercise 6 (p. 54)

1. a pot for heating water
2. to make clothes
3. without clothes on
4. someone who says something that is not true
5. let your body rest against something
6. a horse with a bad leg

Exercise 7 (p. 55)

1. someone who has to leave his or her home because of war or other trouble
2. to look for, find and keep a lot of something you like
3. someone who is careful and does every part of his or her job
4. bread that is old and dry
5. an unwanted mark that ruins something
6. to stop going to work, usually because of old age

Exercise 8 (p. 56)

1. to tell others how good you are at something
2. an insect
3. a terrible taste
4. a boat that carries people and cars and trucks
5. to die
6. to like someone or something very much

Exercise 9 (p. 57)

1. the part of your leg that bends in the middle
2. someone who forgets things all the time
3. a place on the shore that is safe for boats
4. in general
5. a way of holding onto something tightly
6. reddish-brown stains on old or wet metal

Exercise 10 (p. 59)

A.			
1. c	4. h	7. l	10. e
2. k	5. i	8. b	11. g
3. d	6. f	9. a	12. j

B.				
1. c	2. d	3. b	4. b	5. d

Exercise 11 (p. 61)

A. 1. f 4. h 7. c 10. d
    2. a 5. j 8. k 11. e
    3. i 6. b 9. g

B. 1. c 2. b 3. c 4. b 5. c

Exercise 12 (p. 63)

1. Running
2. Runners
3. people give water to the runners
4. running
5. Africans
6. winners get large amounts of money

Exercise 13 (p. 64)

They	thousands of people
This	Boston Marathon
It	Boston Marathon
They	runners
them	runners
it	Marathon
It	the Boston race
them	runners
they	runners
them	runners
them	runners

Exercise 14 (p. 65)

it	jogging
it	the weather
This	Central Park
them	New Yorkers
They	dogs
them	joggers
them	dogs
They	dog owners
They	park police

Exercise 15 (p. 66)

They	Mary and Jim
It	large white dog
them	Mary and Jim
their	Mary and Jim
They	Mary and Jim
it	big stick
She	Mary
it	dog
her	Mary
It	large rock
she	dog's owner
It	dog
It	dog
she	dog's owner
He	park police officer
them	Mary, Jim, and dog's owner
This	fighting
he	park police officer

Exercise 16 (p. 67)

1.	They	two Frenchmen
	This	hot air
2.	He or she	pilot of the balloon
	That	raising and lowering the balloon
3.	they	early photographers
	this	carrying heavy equipment everywhere
4.	She	Helen Keller
	she	Helen Keller
	that	not speaking until age seven
	She	Helen Keller
5.	It	tornado
	it	tornado
	this	turning over cars, destroying houses, and killing people
6.	They	tornadoes
	this	cone shape in the sky
	they	people
7.	they	tornadoes
	they	tornadoes
8.	them	families
	this	lose their homes
9.	those	Kansas, Arkansas, Nebraska, Iowa, and Missouri
	they	people in those states
	It	cone-shaped cloud in the sky
	them	people in those states
10.	it	the wind of a tornado
	it	the wind

Exercise 17 (p. 68)

1. Music, rock music, twentieth-century music (2 1 3)
2. Japanese mountain, Mount Fuji, mountain (2 1 3)
3. problems, water pollution problems, pollution problems (3 1 2)
4. pine tree, evergreen tree, tree (1 2 3)
5. musicians, Sting, popular musicians (3 1 2)
6. Nicaragua, country, Central American country (1 3 2)

277

7. man, Dr. Diamond, dentist
   (3, 1, 2)
8. place, Boston, city
   (3, 1, 2)
9. The *New York Times*, newspaper,
   (1, 2)
   reading material
   (3)
10. group, Diamond family, people
    (2, 1, 3)
11. storm, tornado, windstorm
    (3, 1, 2)
12. president, person, political leader
    (1, 3, 2)
13. shirt, white shirt, clothing
    (2, 1, 3)
14. flute, musical instrument, wind instrument
    (1, 3, 2)
15. jet plane, Boeing 737, air transportation
    (2, 1, 3)

Exercise 18 (p. 69)

1. Scotland, home-land
2. stringed instru-ment
3. president
4. storm, winds
5. lemons, limes, and oranges; source of vitamin C
6. food in the morning, meal
7. fuel
8. lion with three little cubs, animals
9. season, time of year
10. illness, problem

Unit Four: Learning to Look for the Topic

Examples: *A. sports, color; B. Europe, head*

Exercise 1. (p. 71)

1. family
2. number
3. animal
4. house
5. kitchen
6. City
7. food
8. party
9. furniture
10. clothes

Exercise 2 (p. 73)

1. drink
2. money
3. travel
4. car
5. water
6. classroom
7. hospital
8. feeling
9. computer
10. gas

Exercise 3 (p. 74)

Many answers are possible.

Exercise 4 (p. 75)

1. countries
2. buildings (or institutions)
3. book
4. languages
5. sciences
6. dairy foods (foods made from milk)
7. times of the day and night
8. sports

Exercise 5 (p. 77)

1. rivers
2. workers in a hospital
3. money from differ-ent countries
4. where cars and trucks can go
5. states in the United States
6. feelings
7. former U.S. presidents
8. world problems

Exercise 6 (p. 78)

1. U.S. cities (not Paris)
2. what's in school (not ice cream)
3. clothes for cold weather (not bathing suit)
4. names of months (not Tuesday)
5. desserts or sweets (not carrots)
6. job titles (not husband)
7. what you can put things into (not table)
8. parts of a building (not tree)

Exercise 7 (p. 80)

1. African countries: Zimbabwe, Nigeria, Kenya, Ethiopia, Zambia
   World's religions: Catholic, Buddhist, Muslim, Christian, Jew
2. animals used by people: dog, horse, cow, camel, elephant, cat
   bodies of water: stream, ocean, canal, lake, sea, river
3. Western U.S. states: California, Washing-ton, Arizona, Nevada, Oregon
   English-speaking countries: Ireland, Scotland, Australia, England, Canada
4. ways to measure time: hour, year, minute, month, day, century
   sounds: tick, roar, bang, boom, thud, screech
5. winter weather: cold, windy, ice, sleet, snow
   geography: mountain, river, lake, hill, valley

Exercise 8 (p. 83)

1. furniture: chair, desk, table, bed, bookcase
   things to read: magazine, newspaper, letter, book, map

2. weather: rain, snow, hail, thunder, clouds, what you see in the sky: planet, sun, moon, stars, comet
3. medicines: aspirin, tetracycline, quinine, penicillin, antihistamine
   parts of the body: chest, arm, hip, leg, neck
4. cloth: cotton, linen, nylon, wool
   atom: proton, nucleus, neutron, electron
5. kinds of music: jazz, folk, rock, classical, blues
   musical instruments: trumpet, drum, clarinet, piano, accordion

Unit Five: Understanding Paragraphs

Exercise 1 (p. 85)
1. No   2. Yes   3. Yes   4. No

Exercise 2 (p. 87)
1. a. too specific
   b. too general
   c. topic
2. a. topic
   b. too specific
   c. too general
3. a. too general
   b. topic
   c. too specific

Exercise 3 (p. 88)
1. a. too general
   b. too specific
   c. topic
2. a. too specific
   b. topic
   c. too general
3. a. topic
   b. too specific
   c. too general

Exercise 4 (p. 89)
1. a. too general
   b. topic
   c. too specific
2. a. too general
   b. too specific
   c. topic
3. a. topic
   b. too specific
   c. too general

Exercise 5 (p. 90)
1. ideas about lightning
2. 3 kinds of clouds

Exercise 6 (p. 91)
1. where people in the United States get their drinking water
2. American problems with safe drinking water
3. ways to save water

Exercise 7 (p. 92)
1. how Galileo became a modern scientist
2. Galileo's experiments about how things fall
3. how Galileo's ideas caused problems for him

Exercise 8 (p. 93)
2. *Topic:* how coffee became popular around the world
   Cross out "They also liked other foods from the Middle East."
3. *Topic:* Florida orange juice in the United States
   Cross out "Another good snack is apple juice."

Exercise 9 (p. 95)
1. b. Clothes   2. b. Clothes   3. c. Clothes

Exercise 10 (p. 96)
1. c. Alchemists   3. a. Lavoisier
2. c. Boyle

Exercise 11 (p. 97)
1. c   2. b   3. c

Exercise 12 (p. 98)
1. c   2. b   3. c

Exercise 13 (p. 99)
You can write the main idea in many ways. Just be sure that the main idea is a sentence and that it tells the topic and the author's idea about the topic.

1. Some newspaper ads are about people and what they need.
2. "Personal" ads can tell us a lot about the people in a town or country.
3. Some "Personal" ads are not written for good reasons.

Exercise 14 (p. 100)
1. "Black Thursday" was a terrible day for many Americans.
2. The Great Depression was very serious and surprised many people.
3. The Great Depression ended because of Roosevelt's new laws and because of World War II.

Unit Six: Finding the Pattern of Organization

Exercise 1 (p. 104)
1. *Topic:* computers
   Main idea: Computers are helpful in many ways.

First	are fast
Second	work with lots of information
Third	do not forget information
Also	are almost always correct

2. *Topic:* ways to learn about computers
   Main idea: There are a number of ways to learn about computers.

Some	companies have computer classes
Also	universities offer courses
Another way	learn from a book
Or	learn from a friend

Exercise 2 (p. 105)
1. *Topic:* the many programs for computers
   Main idea: Today, computer companies sell many different programs for computers.

First	math problems
Second	scientific studies
Third	word processors
Other	CD-ROM
Finally	fun

2. *Topic:* computer language
   Main idea: Computer language can be funny at times.

For example	memory
Also	menus
Another	mouse

Exercise 3 (p. 106)
1. *Topic:* the many different sizes of computers
   Main idea: Computers come in all shapes and sizes.

For example	large, for companies and hospitals
other	for factories
also	small computers to use at home
and some	tiny, in phones and cars

2. *Topic:* problems of computers
   Main idea: Computers can cause several problems.

One kind	they sometimes lose information
Another	machinery can break down
another	they may be bad for your health

Exercise 4 (p. 107)
1. *Topic:* computers in many professions
   Main idea: Today, many people use computers in their work.

For example	scientists
And	business people
also	Doctors
too	writers
even	students
Finally	people at home

2. *Topic:* ways that computers talk to each other
   Main idea: There are many new programs that let computers work together.

For example	people's computers work together on a job
also	cash registers in supermarkets report to the company
finally	computers connect to the Internet

The Time Order Pattern Examples (p. 109)
Example A
Topic: Albert Einstein
Events: Einstein was born.
He graduated from the University of Zurich.
He did some of his most famous work in physics.
He won the Nobel Prize.
He lived in Germany and traveled a lot.
He left Germany.
He lived in Princeton, New Jersey.
He died.

Example B
The answers are the same as in Example A.

Exercise 5 (p. 111)
1. *Topic:* the first part of the Vietnam War

1946	The war began.
1953	The French Army was in trouble.
1954	The French Army left Vietnam.

2. *Topic:* the second part of the Vietnam War

| 1954 | the beginning of the second part of the war |

1954–60	North Vietnam and South Vietnam were fighting all the time.
1965	The North Vietnamese were winning the war.
March 1965	The United States began to help the South.
July 1965	There were about 75,000 American soldiers in Vietnam.

Exercise 6 (p. 112)

1. *Topic:* how the Vietnam War became an American war

1965	The Vietnam war became an American war.
That year	The United States bombed North Vietnam.
each year	The United States used more bombs and sent more soldiers.
the end of 1967	There were almost 510,000 American soldiers in Vietnam.

2. *Topic:* how the Americans stopped fighting in Vietnam

the early 1960s	A few Americans did not want the war.
the late 1960s	Many people did not want the war.
May 1968	The United States and North Vietnam began to talk about stopping the war.
For the next few months	There were fewer bombs.
By the end of the year	The U.S. bombing had stopped.
1970	American soldiers started to go home.
three years later	The last Americans left.

Exercise 7 (p. 113)

1. *Topic:* Anh Nguyen's early life

1960	Anh was born.
When she was four years old	Her family moved to Saigon.
1972	She finished grammar school.
In the fall	She won a prize.
That winter	She decided she wanted to study in France.
in the spring	She did well on her French exams.

2. *Topic:* how Anh's life changed because of the war

1973	Life in Saigon was changing.
1974	The North Vietnamese Army moved into Saigon.
that year	Troubles began for the people.

Exercise 8 (p. 114)

Topic: how Anh decided to leave Vietnam

The next few years	Anh had an unhappy and difficult time.
After a while	She stopped going to school and started working.
At last	She decided to leave Vietnam.
The day came	Anh said good-bye.
at night	The boat left Vietnam.
For several days	They sailed with no trouble.
then	boat stopped
Finally	A large Japanese ship picked them up.
right away	Anh wrote to her cousin in Boston.
Finally, almost one year later	She got her American visa.

Exercise 9 (p. 115)

Topic: what happened when Anh arrived in the United States

December 1979	Anh arrived in Boston.
That evening	She talked with Pho and To-van.
That night	She made a decision.
The first winter	Boston seemed very cold.
In January	She started studying at the high school.
By summer	The worst times were over.
For the next two years	She studied hard.
at the end of her last year	She won a college scholarship.
Finally	Anh had a plan.

Exercise 10 (p. 116)

Topic: Changes in Anh's life and in governments

during her college years	Anh was busy.
After studying for one semester	Anh began to feel lonely.
in the 1980s	The U.S. government was still unfriendly to Vietnam.
In 1988	Anh graduated from college.
In 1990	Anh became a U.S. citizen and she began to study for an MBA.
in 1992	The U.S. government began to do business with Vietnam. Young Vietnamese thought about going home.
in June 1994	Anh went to see Vietnam and look for her mother.

Exercise 11 (p. 118)

2. *Cause:* ice and snow on the road
   Effect: car accidents
   Signal words: because of

3. *Cause:* bad food and not enough sleep
   Effect: bad health
   Signal words: reasons for

4. *Cause:* smoking cigarettes
   Effect: cancer
   Signal words: leads to

5. *Cause:* drinking coffee
   Effect: some people become nervous
   Signal words: because of

6. *Cause:* careless smokers
   Effect: fires in homes
   Signal words: due to

7. *Cause:* eating too much
   Effect: heart disease
   Signal words: the result of

8. *Cause:* bright sunlight
   Effect: your eyes hurt
   Signal words: can cause

9. *Cause:* car accidents
   Effect: high insurance costs
   Signal words: result of

10. *Cause:* serious family problems
    Effect: illness
    Signal words: can cause

Exercise 12 (p. 119)

1. *Cause:* he had the highest score
   Effect: Sam won a prize
   Signal words: because

2. *Cause:* play football
   Effect: some students go to college
   Signal words: in order to

3. *Cause:* reading for pleasure
   Effect: a larger vocabulary
   Signal words: can result in

4. *Cause:* English skills
   Effect: Helen found a job quickly
   Signal words: because of

5. *Cause:* your phone call
   Effect: I could not go back to sleep
   Signal words: as a result of

6. *Cause:* students made too much noise
   Effect: he called the police
   Signal words: so

7. *Cause:* her computer program
   Effect: she received an award
   Signal words: because of

8. *Cause:* eating too much chocolate
   Effect: weight gain
   Signal words: can result in

9. *Cause:* regular exercise
   Effect: good health
   Signal words: comes from

10. *Cause:* they lost all their games
    Effect: the team needs a new coach
    Signal words: because

Exercise 13 (p. 121)

1. *Main idea:* Coffee is a drug, and it has many effects on your body.
   Signal words: effects, can help, makes, keep, can cause

Causes	*Effects*
Coffee	can help you stay awake
Coffee	can keep you awake at night
Coffee	makes some people feel alive and work better
Coffee	other people feel too nervous
Coffee	can help your stomach after a large meal
Coffee	too much can cause a stomachache

2. *Main idea:* Aspirin is a simple drug with many useful effects.
Signal words: effects, can stop, helps, can make, can result

Causes	Effects
Aspirin	can stop a headache or earache
Aspirin	helps take away pain in fingers or knees
Aspirin	can stop a fever
Aspirin	can make you feel better
Aspirin	can result in a healthy heart

Exercise 14 (p. 122)

1. *Main idea:* Americans are too fat for several reasons.
Signal words: One cause, another cause, third cause

Causes	Effects
food Americans eat	fat Americans
the way Americans eat	fat Americans
too little exercise	fat Americans

2. *Main idea:* Doctors say that if you are too fat you may soon have problems with your health.
Signal words: effects, effect, may lead, can also change, can cause, result, may make

Causes	Effects
being too fat	heart has to work harder
being too fat	can change the amount of sugar in your blood
being too fat	High blood pressure is another possible result
being too fat	Cancer can sometimes be a result

Exercise 15 (p. 123)

1. *Main idea:* The shorter days of winter can be a problem for some people.
Signal words: cause, are the result of, had to

Causes	Effects
winter	health problems
short and cloudy days	illness
short and cloudy days	unhappiness and illness

2. *Main idea:* Poor city children in the United States have some health problems.
Signal words: because, caused by, because of

Causes	Effects
children are ill	poor diet
children are ill	bad housing
children are ill	do not receive enough medical care

Exercise 16 (p. 126)

1. Different ideas about what to cook
Main idea: Peter cooks simple food, but Joe cooks special dishes.
Signal words: both, but

Differences	Likenesses
Peter cooks simple food.	Both like to cook good meals.
Joe cooks special dishes.	

2. The little food market of the past and today's supermarkets
Main idea: Shopping for food in the United States is different from the way it used to be.
Signal words: not the same, in the past, now, however

Differences	Likenesses
Old markets were small and friendly.	Both are for buying food.
People stopped there to hear news or to talk.	
Supermarkets usually are large and not very friendly.	
Supermarkets are not good places for meeting friends.	
Many people seem to be tired and in a hurry and are not polite.	

Exercise 17 (p. 127)

1. The food in India and China
Main idea: Food in India and China is similar in many ways.
Signal words: similar, both, Both, And, also

Likenesses
Rice is important.
Food is often spicy.
Many vegetables are used.

Meat is not important.
The food is different in each part of the country.

2. How people ate in Europe 1,000 years ago and how they eat now
Main idea: A thousand years ago, Europeans' ways of eating were very different from ways of eating today.
Signal words: Now, But, Today, In those days, Instead

Differences
now—Forks, knives, and spoons are used.
before—No forks were used.
now—People do not use their fingers.
before—People picked up food with their fingers.
now—People drink from glasses.
before—People drank from bowls or wooden cups.

Exercise 18 (p. 128)
1. How doctors work in England and Germany
Main idea: Doctors in England and Germany do their jobs differently in many ways.
Signal words: differences, but, on the other hand, but, six times as many, however

Differences
English doctors give strong antibiotics for colds; German doctors do not.
German doctors give medicine for low blood pressure; English doctors do not.
German doctors give six times as many heart drugs as English doctors do.
English patients do not question their doctors; German patients do.

2. Ideas about medicine in France and England
Main idea: French ideas about medicine are different from English ideas about medicine.
Signal words: different, However, but, however

Differences
French doctors give medicine to move blood to the brain; English doctors do not.
French doctors worry about the liver; English doctors do not.
French doctors take stomach illnesses seriously; English doctors do not.
French doctors try out new treatments; English doctors do not.

Exercise 19 (p. 129)
1. Poland and Italy
Signal words: but, both
Main idea: Poland and Italy are different in some ways and similar in others.

Differences
Poland is in northern Europe; Italy is in southern Europe.
Poland has cold winters; Italy has warmer winters.

Likenesses
Importance of Catholicism
Importance of history
Friendliness and good spirit

2. Medical care in the United States and Canada
Signal words: different, on the other hand, But, unlike
Main idea: Canada has nationalized health care, but the United States has private health care.

Differences
In Canada, everyone has health care.
In the U.S., many poor people do not have health care.
In Canada, everyone pays a tax to the government.
In the U. S., some people pay insurance companies.

Exercise 20 (p. 130)
2. TO, b   3. C, a   4. CE, e

Exercise 21 (p. 131)
1. TO, a   2. C, c   3. CE, d   4. L, b

Exercise 22 (p. 132)
1. C, c   2. L, a   3. TO, d

Unit 7: Making Inferences
For all the inference exercises, many answers may be correct. You should be able to explain your inference and show the words or phrases that led to your inference.

Exercise 1 (p. 134)
1. A newborn baby girl
2. In a neighborhood
3. she's, eight pounds, home from the hospital, congratulations

Exercise 2 (p. 134)
1. A car
2. At a car dealer's lot
   Keywords: miles, didn't use it much, engine

Exercise 3 (p. 135)
1. Mom and Dad arriving on a plane
2. At the airport
   Keywords: Swiss Air, no message on the announcement board, airline counter, flight

Exercise 4 (p. 135)
1. Someone hurt a leg
2. In a doctor's office

Exercise 5 (p. 136)
1. Someone is buying clothes
2. In a shop

Exercise 6 (p. 136)
1. Their language class
2. At school

Exercise 7 (p. 137)
1. Getting to the airport on time
2. In a taxi

Exercise 8 (p. 137)
1. Someone is leaving a job
2. At work

Exercise 9 (p. 138)
1. Being stuck in traffic
2. In a car

Exercise 10 (p. 138)
1. The bus schedule
2. Near the bus stop

Exercise 11 (p. 139)
1. An adventure or mystery story
2. In the present
3. In Julia's apartment
4. Julia almost fell into an elevator shaft.
5. Edward may help Julia.

Exercise 12 (p. 140)
1. An adventure story
2. In the present
3. In a jungle
4. Her plane crashed.
5. She will find her way out of the jungle.

Exercise 13 (p. 141)
1. A story about a family
2. In the present
3. A father and two children
4. Far from the city
5. The children's mother died.
6. Papa will have a new wife soon.

Exercise 14 (p. 142)
1. An adventure story
2. During World War II
3. Two children, a German Commandant, and a German lieutenant
4. Outside, near a cliff, in Norway
5. Making snowmen to hide bricks of gold
6. Peter is afraid of the Commandant.
7. Because the children will not speak to him
8. They are afraid they might give away their secret.
9. The Germans will go away.

Unit 8: Skimming

Skimming for point of view

Example B (p. 145)
For (*Keywords:* nicer, cooler in the summer, happy)

Exercise 1 (p. 145)
1. Against
2. Against
3. For
4. Against
5. Against
6. For
7. Against
8. For

Exercise 2 (p. 146)
1. Against
2. Against
3. Against
4. For
5. Against
6. For
7. Against
8. For

Skimming for pattern of organization

Example B (p. 147)
Listing

Exercise 3 (p. 148)
1. Comparison
2. Listing
3. Time order
4. Cause/effect
5. Listing
6. Comparison
7. Time order
8. Comparison

Exercise 4 (p. 149)
1. Time order
2. Listing
3. Comparison
4. Cause/effect
5. Listing
6. Time order
7. Cause/effect
8. Listing

Skimming for ideas

Example (p. 151)
2. d   3. b

Exercise 5 (p. 152)
1. c   2. d   3. b

Exercise 6 (p. 153)
1. b   2. b   3. c

Exercise 7 (p. 154)
1. b   2. a   3. c

Exercise 8 (p. 155)
1. a   2. b   3. c

Exercise 9 (p. 156)
1. c   2. b   3. c

Exercise 10 (p. 157)
1. c   2. a   3. d

Part Three: Thinking Skills

Exercises	Questions				
	1	2	3	4	5
1	c	a	d	b	d
2	d	b	d	c	c
3	b	c	a	d	c
4	b	d	b	c	d
5	b	b	d	b	b
6	a	d	b	b	c
7	a	d	b	a	b
8	d	a	c	b	d
9	b	d	a	b	a
10	c	b	b	b	b
11	d	c	b	d	d
12	d	d	d	a	b
13	d	d	b	b	c
14	b	c	b	a	d
15	d	c	c	d	b
16	b	d	d	c	b
17	a	a	b	c	b
18	b	a	b	c	b
19	b	a	a	c	d
20	d	b	b	b	c
21	d	a	c	c	d
22	a	c	d	c	d
23	b	a	b	b	d
24	d	b	a	c	c
25	b	a	b	a	d

Part Four: Reading Faster

Example A (p. 184)
1. He likes to cook.
2. He likes to cook because then he doesn't think about problems at work.
3. He makes a good cake.

Example B (p. 184)
1. They use it all around the world.
2. They use it so they can talk with their friends or family or to "meet" new people.
3. They use it at work because it is fast.

Passages	Questions							
	1	2	3	4	5	6	7	8
C	c	b	d	d	a	c	b	d
D	c	a	d	a	b	d	c	a
1	a	b	d	c	a	c	d	a
2	c	d	d	a	b	d	d	c
3	a	b	a	d	c	c	a	b
4	c	c	b	c	a	d	a	d
5	d	b	a	b	a	b	a	b
6	c	a	c	c	a	c	d	d
7	d	c	d	a	b	a	b	b
8	a	c	d	b	a	c	d	b
9	d	b	d	b	a	b	d	a
10	c	a	c	b	d	a	b	a
11	a	c	b	d	a	c	b	d
12	a	b	d	b	a	b	a	d
13	d	b	b	d	c	b	a	d
14	c	b	a	d	b	a	a	b
15	c	b	a	c	a	d	a	b
16	d	b	c	a	b	d	b	d
17	b	d	b	a	a	d	b	a
18	d	b	c	a	d	a	d	d
19	a	d	a	c	d	a	c	b
20	c	b	a	d	b	c	d	a
21	b	c	a	d	c	a	d	b
22	d	b	a	b	a	c	d	b
23	a	c	b	d	a	c	b	a
24	a	d	b	b	c	d	b	a
25	d	b	a	c	d	b	a	c
26	c	b	d	d	b	a	c	c
27	d	b	a	d	c	b	d	b
28	d	b	b	b	d	a	b	a
29	c	b	c	b	a	c	c	d
30	d	c	b	c	a	c	b	b
31	a	c	c	b	d	b	d	a
32	a	c	d	a	b	b	d	b
33	d	d	a	b	a	a	c	d
34	b	c	a	a	c	c	a	a
35	d	b	d	a	c	b	b	a
36	d	c	a	d	c	a	c	c
37	c	b	a	c	c	a	d	b
38	c	d	c	c	b	a	b	b
39	b	d	a	d	b	c	a	a
40	a	b	c	a	b	b	c	a

Reading Power is intended for students who need to develop their reading skills in English:

- ESL/EFL students who have studied English for about 100 hours and have acquired a vocabulary of about 600 words,
- students in developmental English classes,
- native speakers of English in adult literacy programs.

In appearance and approach, this book is different from other reading skills books. First, the focus is different. This book directs students' attention to their own reading processes, whereas most other books call attention to the content of the material.

In addition, *Reading Power* is organized in a different way from most textbooks. It contains four sections that correspond to four important aspects of the development of proficient reading, and whereas most books are meant to be used in a linear fashion from beginning to end, the four parts of this book are designed to be used concurrently. This means that each reading class should include several different kinds of activities and exercises from the different parts of the book. Using all the parts together in this way is a crucial aspect of a successful reading program.

Introduction

In this *Teacher's Guide,* you will find general guidelines and specific suggestions for making the most effective use of *Reading Power.* For a more complete explanation of the theory and methodology used in this book, see *A Short Course in Teaching Reading Skills,* by Beatrice S. Mikulecky (Addison Wesley Longman, 1990).

The purpose of *Reading Power* is to develop students' awareness of the reading process, so that they will be able to learn to read in ways that are expected in school, college, or business. In order to allow students to focus on the process of reading, the lexical and syntactical contents of the materials have been kept to a minimum (at the high-beginning level). No more than about 600 different vocabulary items have been used, and most sentences do not exceed 12 words in length. Verb forms used include present simple and continuous, past simple and continuous, future, and infinitives.

Many students have a conceptualization of reading that interferes with their reading in English. This book aims to help students acquire an accurate understanding of what it means to read in English. To accomplish this, the book addresses the reading process in a direct manner, and the various reading skills are presented as part of that process.

Student awareness of reading and thinking processes is further encouraged in many parts of the book by exercises that require them to work in pairs or small groups. In discussions with others, students have to formulate and articulate their ideas more precisely and acquire new ways of talking and thinking about text. Students are also asked to read each other's work, so they can experience the connections between reading and writing.

Using Reading Power in Your Class

Your role in the reading class

The teacher is the most important element in a successful reading class. A good teacher provides:

1. An anxiety-free environment in which students feel comfortable taking risks and trying new ways of reading,

2. Enough practice that students can master new strategies,

3. Friendly pressure in the form of persuasion and timing,

4. Positive examples of how to approach a text,

5. A model for the kind of thinking that good reading requires,

6. An inspiring example of an enthusiastic reader.

Planning your reading classes

The materials in this book were designed to take approximately 35 hours of class time. This will vary according to the language ability level of the students in your class and the amount of homework you assign. Classes and individual students also vary in the amount of time they need to complete different kinds of exercises in the book. Students should work at their own pace as often as possible.

Reading Power may be used in several different types of classes.

1. In an integrated skills class that meets for two to three hours per day, five days a week, for one semester, use *Reading Power* for a total of 30 to 40 minutes three times a week. A sample schedule is

    Monday—15 minutes of Reading Faster exercises, 20 minutes of Reading Comprehension Skills exercises;

    Wednesday—15 minutes of Thinking Skills exercises, 20 minutes of Reading for Pleasure exercises and book conferences;

    Friday—15 minutes of Reading Faster exercises, 20 minutes of Reading Comprehension Skills exercises.

    Homework assignments can include
    Reading for Pleasure exercises,
    Thinking in English exercises,

Selected Reading Comprehension Skills exercises* (further practice on skills introduced in class).

2. In an integrated skills class that meets for three hours per week for one semester, use *Reading Power* for about one-third of the class time, for a total of about one hour per week, divided approximately as follows:
    20 minutes of Reading Faster exercises,
    15 minutes of Thinking Skills exercises,
    20 minutes of Reading Comprehension Skills exercises.

    Homework assignments would be the same as above.

3. In a reading class that meets two hours per week for one semester, use the four parts of *Reading Power,* as well as the students' pleasure reading books, in every class. Work for about 20 to 30 minutes on each part of the book. Homework assignments can focus on reading for pleasure.

4. In a reading lab, as in the classroom, students should work regularly on all four parts of the book, dividing their time about equally among the four parts. It is essential that students be instructed on how to use each part of *Reading Power* before they begin to work on their own.

Making the reading class exciting and effective

The following are some general principles for using *Reading Power*:

1. Always involve students fully. Never allow class work to turn into busywork.

2. Explain to students the purpose of their work. Knowing why they are doing an exercise increases their sense of involvement and allows them to become more active learners (increasing their metacognitive awareness).

3. Always focus on the thinking process and not on the right answers. The answer itself

---

* Keep in mind that the Reading Comprehension Skills exercises in Part Two should be introduced in class and practiced before any of the exercises are assigned for homework.

matters far less than how the student arrives at it. Encourage students to take this same approach by frequently asking "Why?" or "How can you tell?" or "How do you know?" When students are required repeatedly to articulate answers to these questions, they become more conscious of their own thinking processes.

4. Ask students to work in pairs whenever possible, especially on the Reading Comprehension Skills exercises in Part Two. Having to talk about the exercises and explain the reasoning behind their answers reinforces students' awareness of process and purpose. It also facilitates language acquisition (when the conversation is in English).

5. Emphasize the importance of trying to guess the meaning of words from the context. Students should be discouraged from using dictionaries during the reading class or while doing their reading homework.

6. The Answer Key is intended to serve as more than just the repository of the right answers. Students should check their own answers so they can work independently when appropriate. When their answers differ from the Answer Key, they should try to figure out how and why they may have made a mistake. However, they should also be encouraged to question the Answer Key and to defend their answers and their reasoning. Some of the exercises, in fact, have alternative answers.

7. When students work individually (especially in Parts Three and Four), allow them to work at their own pace. In these exercises, speed should be encouraged, but each student must determine what "fast" is for him or her. Faster students should not have to wait for slower classmates, and slower readers should not be pressed too hard, or they may become anxious and incapable of comprehending.

Specific Suggestions for Using Reading Power

Introducing the book to the student

To encourage students to begin thinking about reading, you might start the first reading class with a questionnaire like this one:

Reading Questionnaire	Yes	No
1. It is important to read every word if you want to understand.	☐	☐
2. You will learn more if you look up every new word in the dictionary.	☐	☐
3. Reading stories and novels is not important.	☐	☐
4. If you read fast, you will not understand.	☐	☐
5. You should be able to say every word you read.	☐	☐
6. Reading class is the same as vocabulary class.	☐	☐
7. Books for ESL students must be simple. ESL students cannot read books for English speakers.	☐	☐
8. You should write the words in your own language above the English words in a book.	☐	☐

A good reader would answer "no" to all these statements. Students may answer "yes" to some questions, and it may be difficult to convince them otherwise. Do not press the point too much at this time, since students will come to understand the reasons as they use the book. However, discussion of these questions and students' answers will help raise students' awareness of the reading process in English and the differences between the reading process in English and the reading processes in other languages, as well as the different values cultures place on reading. This questionnaire will also help clarify for students their objectives in the reading class.

Later in the course, refer back to these questions and students' answers as a way for students to note changes in their thinking about reading.

Part One—Reading for Pleasure

Many students have never learned to enjoy reading for pleasure (reading extensively) in English, yet we know that to be a good reader, it is necessary to read a lot. However, to get students reading extensively, it is not enough to say, "Read a book." Students must first come to understand the importance of reading extensively, and then they must be encouraged to develop the habit of reading regularly for pleasure. *Reading Power* provides several motivating features: a rationale for pleasure reading, guidelines for success, goal setting, recordkeeping, a list of carefully selected books, and suggestions for how teachers can evaluate the students' reading.

Extensive versus intensive reading

Ongoing immersion in extensive reading is essential for practicing and applying reading skills and for developing all areas of language skill. Research shows that vocabulary acquisition and writing ability, for example, are directly related to the quantity of reading students engage in.

There is a great difference between extensive and intensive reading. Intensive reading is an activity in which students (usually in a class group, led by the teacher) carefully read and examine an essay, short story, or other reading material assigned by the teacher. Many traditional reading classes use this approach almost exclusively. Although intensive reading can play an important role in developing an appreciation of English language and literature, it is no substitute for extensive reading. Improvement in general reading and language ability comes with reading a lot.

Having students select books for extensive reading

Extensive reading is included in Part One: Reading for Pleasure. Students are instructed to select books to read for pleasure on an individual basis. These books should be neither too easy nor too difficult.

1. At this level, many students will be able to enjoy books written for native speakers of English, especially books in the Young Adult category. Others who are lacking confidence in their reading ability can select titles (at about level two) from the various series of graded readers written in simplified English for ESL/EFL learners. Publishing companies that publish graded readers include Addison Wesley Longman, Penguin,

Oxford University Press, Harcourt Brace, and Heinemann.

2. Students should not choose books that are required reading in other courses or books they have already read in translation. Most important, students should be encouraged to choose any book they want—fiction or nonfiction, literature or popular culture. What matters most is that the book is of interest to the student and that he or she actually wants to read it.

3. For pleasure reading, complete books are recommended. Newspapers, magazines, "readers" (collections of short passages), books made up of extracts of other books (such as *Reader's Digest* selections), and collections of short stories by many different authors are not recommended. There are several reasons for this. First, many students may have never before read a book in English that they chose for themselves. Thus the selection process will be a new experience for them, one that will help them form a new, literate identity. Second, although magazines, newspapers, and book selections provide reading practice, the goal of pleasure reading is for students to develop the habit of sustained silent reading, which is possible only with whole books. Reading a whole book by a single author also allows students to become comfortable with a writer's style and lexicon. This sense of ease is experienced as success and actually allows students to read faster as they proceed through their books.

4. One way to help your students select their books is to bring some of your favorite books to the reading class and talk about them. These "book talks" serve two purposes. First, students find out about books they might like to read. Second, you provide students with a model for how to talk about books, so that they will be able to talk about their own books and discuss them with others. Discussion about books can be an effective motivating tool.

5. Students can also find books by participating in a class trip to a bookstore or library, where they are allowed to browse and ask questions about books. If the classroom includes a library of suitable books, students can be guided to ones they might enjoy.

They also can be encouraged to exchange books with classmates or other students. Since students do not need to and, in fact, should not write notes or vocabulary in their pleasure reading books, there is no reason for them to buy the books (unless they want to be able to keep them afterward).

Motivating students to read for pleasure

Students tend to regard reading for pleasure as a less important element of the reading class. Since it is, in fact, a key to successful reading development, be sure to encourage your students to take it seriously.

1. Require your students to bring their pleasure reading books to class and regularly devote some class time to pleasure reading.

2. Assign reading for pleasure as homework and require your students to keep a record of how many pages they have read.

3. Establish a requirement for the number of pages to be read per week or semester.

4. Ask students to fill out a pleasure reading report (see the example in Part One, page 14). Full book reports are less useful, since the writing task tends to diminish the student's enjoyment of the book. Pleasure reading reports can be kept on file in the classroom for other students to consult when they want suggestions for a book to choose.

5. Ask students to write a letter to a friend about a pleasure reading book (see Part One, page 13). These letters can be exchanged in the classroom and discussed.

6. Ask students to respond orally to their book, giving their classmates a brief description of the book and their opinion of it.

7. Hold individual book conferences with the students. This is the surest way to evaluate a student's progress and promote pleasure reading. Conferences can be the key to a successful extensive reading program. Not only do they provide you with feedback on students' reading, but they also serve several other important purposes.

Your questions about the book often represent a true knowledge gap between you and the student: The student knows more about the book than you do, and your questions are authentic, not "school questions." Your questions model the kinds of questions a literate reader habitually asks while reading. The discussion may also help the student acquire fluency in evaluative and elaborative language, which will become the basis for good writing.

The scheduling of book conferences varies. Some teachers hold conferences during office hours or just before or after class. Others find that they can hold book conferences with one student while the rest of the class is engaged in another activity.

Having students practice improving their reading rate on their self-selected books

Included in Part One are instructions for how students can find their reading rate in their self-selected pleasure reading books. This use of the students' books adds to their motivation for improving their reading rate. The Progress Charts (pages 269–270) are intended as an additional incentive to work on reading faster.

You can also help students break slow reading habits by having them do reading sprints in their books. The following are some guidelines for using reading sprints in the classroom.

1. Be sure to study the procedure for reading sprints before using them with your students. Explain the procedure thoroughly to avoid confusion in the middle of the exercises. Students should use their pleasure reading books for the sprints.

2. After the first session of sprints, students should repeat the sprints at regular intervals in class (once a week, once a month, etc., according to the frequency of class meetings) and at home.

3. Given the concentration required for doing sprints, you should follow them with some relatively relaxing activity.

4. As they do the sprints at ever faster speeds, students may object that they can't understand what they're reading. Reassure them that this is not important for the purpose of this exercise. The sprints are intended to show students what it feels like to move their eyes quickly across the page and to demonstrate that they can, in fact, do so.

Also, though students may say they don't understand what they're reading, often, if they are questioned, they realize that they have in fact been able to follow the basic story line. In this way, sprints help students become aware of how much text they can skip when they read for the story or general ideas.

5. Note that in following the directions for calculating their reading rate and for reading sprints, students are also getting meaningful practice in the important skill of following directions.

Part Two—Reading Comprehension Skills

Reading comprehension means getting the writer's intended meaning. Many students for whom reading comprehension is a problem attribute their difficulties in comprehension to the English language, since they can read in their own language. Others feel that they are just not able to understand. In fact, the problem usually lies in their approach to a text. When students have a better understanding of how information is presented in English texts and a greater awareness of the cognitive processes involved in reading, comprehension will almost certainly improve.

In Part Two of *Reading Power,* eight essential comprehension skills are introduced, each with a rationale, and practiced in a series of exercises sequenced from simple to more difficult in order to build up the students' mastery of the skill. The skills covered include both top-down (concept-driven) and bottom-up (text-driven) modes of reasoning and comprehending.

Learning to read well can be compared, in some respects, to learning to play tennis well. The tennis player must learn how and when to use different shots or different strategies. He or she must work on various separate aspects of her game, practicing backhands, serves, volleys, etc. Then he or she can try to put it all together and win a match. This is the same process that students should follow in working on reading comprehension skills. As the "coach," you ensure that the students understand how and why to do the exercises and then stand by to provide advice, support, and increasing challenges.

How to use the Reading Comprehension Skills units in the classroom

1. Focus on one reading/thinking skill at a time.

2. Explain the purpose for doing the exercises and how this particular skill is important for effective reading.

3. Do an example or a sample exercise with the whole class. Model your thinking aloud as you do the exercise.

4. Put the students into pairs whenever possible and appropriate, and assign one exercise for practice.

5. When the pairs have completed the exercise, discuss it with the whole class. Ask students how they arrived at their answers. Encourage friendly disagreement among pairs and in the class as a whole. Ask, "What was your thinking as you decided on that answer?" Students are not necessarily wrong if they come up with an answer that is different from the Answer Key, as long as they can give a rationale for their choice.

6. In this and the next few classes, assign additional exercises that focus on the same skill, increasing the complexity of the tasks. Make sure the students work together whenever it is feasible.

7. Assign an exercise to be done by individual students, either in class or as homework, which they will use to check their own ability and confidence in using the skill.

8. Assign further exercises as needed, based on your sense of the students' mastery of the skill.

When working on comprehension exercises, keep these two principles in mind:

• Do not simply pronounce answers right or wrong. Instead, always respond to students' answers with questions such as "Why?" or "How can you tell?" to encourage them to examine their reasoning processes.

• Have students work in pairs or small groups whenever possible, since talking about the exercises helps develop awareness of thinking processes and also promotes general language improvement.

Unit 1: Scanning

1. Speed is essential in these exercises. To encourage speed, time students' reading, or have them do the exercises (in pairs) as a kind of race to see who can find all the answers first.

2. Do not spend time correcting or having students correct their answers, which are of little importance to the exercise. On the other hand, you may want to spend a few minutes discussing the cultural content of some of the scanning material, with which some students may be unfamiliar.

3. All of these exercises give students an opportunity to practice asking and writing questions. Formulating questions to ask another student helps students learn to ask themselves questions as they read.

4. In order to retain the skill, students should continue to practice scanning. You can devise scanning exercises similar to the ones in this book on all kinds of reading materials.

5. Notice that though scanning and skimming are often taught as the same thing, they are really two different skills. Scanning is a fairly simple skill that involves only a visual search for information on a page. Skimming, on the other hand, involves processing text for ideas, which requires more complex thinking skills. (Skimming is introduced in Unit 8.)

Unit 2: Previewing and Predicting

1. Students should be encouraged to preview everything they read for the following reasons:
   - It allows them to place the text in context or within a mental framework.
   - It helps them judge the level of difficulty of a text and the extent of their background knowledge of the subject.
   - It demonstrates to ESL/EFL students in particular that they can extract information from a text without reading every word.
   - It is the groundwork for improvement in reading rate and eventually for learning how to skim.

2. Encourage your students to discuss their answers to these exercises. Additional predictions often come up in the course of discussions. Point this out to your students when it happens, so they will be aware of the benefits of talking about their work.

Unit 3: Building a Powerful Vocabulary

1. The importance of trying to guess word meaning cannot be stressed too much. Students are often bound to their dictionaries. They need to learn that English discourse gives multiple clues to meaning. They also need to realize that there are many advantages to guessing meaning, as pointed out in the introduction to this section (page 47).

2. The first vocabulary exercises are designed to help students understand what context is and how it influences the choice of a word. Students should always read the entire passage first and then go back and try to write in the missing word.

3. Notice that the directions for the first exercises in this unit all require the students to work in pairs. This is important, because working with another student makes the exercises less intimidating and increases their value as language acquisition activities. In the later exercises (Exercises 6 to 11), however, students should work on their own to develop their individual ability and confidence in guessing word meaning.

4. The exercises in the section on using reference words are intended to help students become more aware of the way writers commonly use these words in English and how important they are for understanding a text. In fact, ESL/EFL students often run into comprehension problems because they cannot identify the referent for a pronoun or fail to notice the way hyponyms can connect ideas.

   Pronouns: The whole class should work together on the examples on page 62. Exercises 12 to 16 give students practice in identifying simpler pronouns. The next exercises include some pronouns that summarize earlier facts or ideas.

   Synonyms—general and specific: The whole class should work together on the examples on page 68. The exercises on synonyms are designed to alert students to their function in connecting ideas and to the way the related words usually are used progressively: A specific noun is used first, then a less specific one, and then a more general term.

Unit 4: Learning to Look for the Topic

1. Since discourse in English is usually topic-centered, finding the topic is key to understanding a text. Thus, work on finding main ideas must begin with teaching students to think in terms of topics.

2. Encourage your students to work quickly in order to develop efficiency.

3. Working in pairs on these exercises, students will begin to internalize the key questions: "What is this about? How do I know that?"

4. Writing practice: Being able to work with topics is a fundamental skill in writing as well as in reading. Exercises 4 through 6 require students to write out the details for given topics, the first step toward writing coherent paragraphs.

Unit 5: Understanding Paragraphs

1. In the first set of exercises, students are given three possible topics and asked to select the one that fits the paragraph best and is neither too specific nor too general. A visual representation may help clarify for the students the meaning of "specific" and "general," terms they will need to understand. You can draw this diagram on the board:

2. Alert students to the fact that the topic sentence of a paragraph is often the first sentence. In both oral and written English, people expect to find out right away what something is about. With English-language texts, readers expect to find the topic at the beginning, so they can orient their thinking. Thus, writers almost always provide the topic early on.

3. Point out to your students that the topic of a paragraph is usually mentioned more than once in the paragraph. This is the writer's way of ensuring that the reader understands.

4. In a class that combines work on reading and writing, the introductory section of Unit 5 can also be used to discuss the concept of unity, or the idea that a paragraph has a single topic and all the sentences in the paragraph relate to it.

5. In Exercises 9 through 14, students learn how to go beyond the topic to find the main idea of a passage by asking, "What is the author saying about that topic?" Go through the examples on page 94 with the whole class. Note that the main idea of any passage should be stated in a complete sentence to ensure that it is really an idea and not just a topic. All the exercises in this unit require students to form main idea sentences. In Exercises 9 and 10, students simply complete the best main-idea sentence with the topic. Exercises 11 and 12 give students a choice of main-idea sentences. The final exercises, 13 and 14, require students to write out the main-idea sentence themselves.

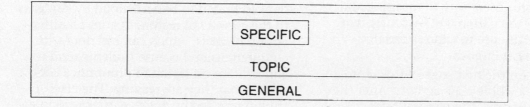

6. Writing practice: You can give students further writing practice in the following exercise:

   - Give students a list of five or six topics and ask them to write main-idea statements about each one.

   - From those statements, students should choose one about which they would like to write a paragraph. The main-idea statement then becomes the first sentence of the paragraph.

   - When students have completed their paragraphs, they should exchange them with a classmate and discuss the main idea. Are all the sentences in the paragraph about the main idea?

Unit 6: Finding the Pattern of Organization

1. Research has shown that readers comprehend and remember best those materials that are organizationally clear to them. However, many students are not familiar with the patterns of textual organization used in English and so have a more difficult time comprehending and remembering.

   The explanation given here for why recognizing patterns can help comprehension is similar to the explanation given for the advantages to reading faster in the introduction to Part Four. In both cases, the same basic factors are at work: The brain does not work well with random pieces of information that must be stored in the memory as so many separate items. It works more efficiently with information that has a recognizable order. Thus, to allow the brain to work well while reading, the reader must constantly look for order in the text, by grouping words according to meaning and by following the patterns of discourse that writers normally use to express certain kinds of ideas in English.

2. The activity on the first page of this unit is meant to be a whole-class activity. After the students try to draw the pictures from memory, have the class discuss the results and immediately introduce them to four common patterns in English, as given on pages 102–103.

3. Note that in almost every exercise, students are asked not just to identify a pattern, but also to write out the signal words and the details they signal. Although this may seem time-consuming and repetitious, it gives the students important practice that will help them gain confidence in their ability to recognize patterns and read for important points.

4. In an appropriate class context, you may want to point out to students (and do additional work on) the connection between the patterns present here and the patterns used in outlining for note-taking or preparing for writing.

5. In a writing/reading class, point out that the "signal words" for patterns can also be referred to as "transitional words." They are the signposts that writers use to mark the shifts and turns in their thinking and that readers should use to follow the writer from one idea to the next.

6. Writing practice: To give students further practice with patterns and the use of signal words, assign topics that fit clearly into each of the patterns and ask students to write paragraphs about each one, using at least three signal words per paragraph.

Unit 7: Making Inferences

1. All reading is, of course, inferential; the purpose of this unit is to make students aware of what it means to infer and how it is an essential part of reading. In these exercises, an answer that is different from the Answer Key is often possible. A correct answer is an answer that can be supported by the student with an argument based on the passage.

2. The dialogues in Exercises 1 through 10 are NOT intended to be read aloud by students to the class. Oral reading requires a different set of skills, which can interfere with comprehension because students tend to concentrate on trying to pronounce correctly what they are reading. The class should first do the practice exercise on page 133 together, so that you can emphasize using clues to guess the topic and location of each conversation. The students should work in pairs on the rest of the dialogues.

3. In Exercises 11 through 14, stress to students the importance of making clear and complete sentences in answering the questions. The last question, which asks students what they think will happen next in the story, can be the basis for additional writing assignments.

Unit 8: Skimming

1. Skimming is not, as is sometimes thought, a simple matter of reading very fast; it is selective reading, in which only certain parts of the text are actually read. To know what to select, students must call on all the reading skills previously practiced in this book. Thus skimming practice involves review of concepts included in all previous units.

2. These exercises must be timed in order to force students to work quickly through a text. Without the pressure of time, they will be tempted to read unnecessary parts and may be distracted from the purpose of the exercises.

3. As in the previous units, students should work in pairs to compare and explain their answers. This also helps students realize that there is no absolute right way to skim a text. What readers actually read while skimming depends on what they already know and on their interpretation of the text. In other words, it depends on what they are thinking; and, of course, no two people ever think exactly alike. Point this out to students and allow for different responses to the exercises.

4. Students can be given additional skimming practice in the classroom with multiple copies of a newspaper or magazine (preferably publications for students with easier text, such as *Student Update*). You may then divide the class into small groups and give each group a newspaper or magazine. The groups should skim the newspaper or magazine for articles of interest and discuss them.

Part Three: Thinking Skills

Learning to read well in English means learning to think in English. However, many students are used to translating as they read and have great difficulty thinking in another language. The exercises in Part Three are designed to help students make a transition from translating to thinking in English.

To complete the Thinking Skills exercises successfully, students will need to follow the way the ideas are presented in English. Correct completion could involve understanding English syntactic, semantic, or logical connections. The exercises gradually increase in length and complexity.

1. For students to get the most out of Part Three, be sure to go through the introduction carefully with the whole class. In fact, you will come to a better understanding of the thinking process involved in these exercises if you actually work on at least ten of them before introducing this part of the book to your students.

2. Keeping track of progress is an important aspect of this part of the book. As described in "Guidelines for Thinking Skills Exercises" on page 160, students should always write the date in the margin when they finish working so that they know how they are progressing. This also makes it possible for you to monitor students' work.

3. After checking their answers in the Answer Key on page 286, students should record both the date and number correct on the Thinking Skills Progress Chart on page 271.

4. Students should complete these exercises at their own speed. However, they should be encouraged to work as quickly as possible. If they work slowly, they may continue to translate as they read and will not develop efficient reading habits.

5. Students may look back at the paragraph if they wish, but they should not study it for long. Their first response is often the correct one.

6. Some students may have trouble at first in following the logic of these exercises. If so, assign several exercises in class to pairs or small groups of students. They should discuss and decide on the answers and on the thinking processes involved. Afterward, those logical processes can be further clarified in a whole-class discussion.

7. Students should not use dictionaries or ask anyone about word meanings while they are working on these exercises. They should

be encouraged to use the context of the paragraph to guess word meanings on their own.

Part Four—Reading Faster

Teaching students to read faster is a key part of any reading improvement program. There are two reasons for this. First, students in most academic settings are faced with an enormous quantity of reading in English. Many ESL/EFL students take three to four times longer than native-language students to complete reading assignments, which means that they have little time left to assimilate what they have read.

The second reason for learning to read faster is that it leads to better comprehension. When reading faster, the eyes cannot focus on every word; they must focus on groups of words together. This makes it easier for the brain to reconstruct meaning. Furthermore, since reading faster forces the reader to skip unknown or nonessential words, the brain can concentrate better on the general meaning of the text.

(This aspect of reading is explained in the introduction to Part Four, "Why Read Faster?" For a more complete explanation of the rationale and methodology for teaching faster reading, see *A Short Course in Teaching Reading Skills*.)

Be prepared to meet some resistance on the part of your students! Breaking them of the habit of word-by-word reading is not always easy. The habit may be of long standing and may be connected with the student's insecurity about his or her ability to understand English. If this is the case, do not push too hard for immediate change, but try to build up the student's confidence and willingness to take risks. Other students may be reluctant to read faster because attitudes toward reading in their native culture lead them to feel that reading word by word is the only real way to read. With these students, you may need to spend extra time discussing the nature and diverse purposes of reading in English.

Why read faster?

1. It is important to have a thorough grasp of the rationale behind reading rate improvement so that you can explain it in terms the students will understand. For this reason,

you should go through the students' introduction carefully first and, if necessary, consult other reference books for clarification.

2. Notice that the reasons given here for improved comprehension with faster reading are similar to those given in the rationale to Part Two, Unit 6: Finding the Pattern of Organization. Both explanations are based on a fundamental understanding of how the brain works in receiving and storing information—that it works most efficiently when the information can be grouped into some kind of order. This is the basic reason for reading faster. When people read faster, their eyes sweep over larger pieces of text. That gives them more data to use in grasping the author's meaning, which makes it easier to build up comprehension and retain information.

3. Along with discussing the rationale for reading faster, it is important to discuss with students the diverse ways of reading. Students may, in fact, need to be reassured at this point that not all reading must be fast. There are times when slow reading is appropriate, such as when they are reading poetry, complex technical material, instructions, or other material dense with essential information. More often than not, however, slow reading is the only kind of reading students do. They need to understand that learning to read faster will give them more flexibility.

How to read faster

Check your reading habits.

1. Some of your students may have a habit of moving their lips or following the text with their fingers while they are reading. These students should be alerted to this habit, of which they are often unaware, and helped to understand that it slows them down as they read.

2. While working on the Reading Faster passages, students should not write the meanings of words in the text. This only reinforces the habit of translation and drastically slows down reading. You may need to reassure students that it is useful to write down new vocabulary, but not during faster reading sessions.

Skip over unknown words.

1. You may be familiar with the use of cloze passages to determine reading ability or to teach grammar and vocabulary. The cloze passages here serve a different purpose: to convince students that they can understand the main points of a passage without reading every word of it. Furthermore, this kind of work with cloze passages encourages students to infer general meaning from partial information—a fundamental skill.

2. As always, students should know the rationale for these exercises before they begin. Do not ask students to fill in the blank spaces, because this would completely alter the purpose of the exercise in their eyes.

3. Stress the idea that unknown words can usually be ignored. Occasionally, it may be necessary to understand some words in order to comprehend the general meaning. When this is the case, the reader should continue reading and try to guess word meanings from the context. This skill is developed in Part Two, Unit 3: Building a Powerful Vocabulary.

4. If you wish to provide students with additional practice with cloze passages, choose a suitable text and blank out every seven or five words (the more frequent the blanks, the more difficult the exercise). The text should not contain difficult vocabulary or complex ideas.

Timed readings.

1. Examples C and D introduce students to the procedures they will follow for all the Reading Faster passages. They will have more success with the passages if they learn to time themselves. This allows them to work independently at their own pace.

2. Students should be instructed to preview all the passages for timed reading, starting with Examples C and D. If they have not yet done Part Two, Unit 2: Previewing and Predicting, you will need to introduce the concept of previewing to them.

3. Note that students should time themselves only while reading the passage, not while answering the questions! In answering the questions, students may need to be reminded that they should look for the best

answer *according to the text*. After completing each passage, students should correct their own work using the Answer Key on page 287.

Timing procedure.

1. When the class is ready to begin Example C, the students write the starting time on the line at the top of the passage. They then start reading and read as quickly as possible with understanding. If there is a large clock visible in the classroom, the students can use it to read the time. If not, write the starting time on the chalkboard. (Many students prefer to use their own watches, which often have timing devices on them.)

2. As soon as they have finished reading, students write the finishing time on the line at the end of the passage. If there is no clock, students should signal when they finish and you can write the time on the board.

3. Students then turn the page and circle the best answers to the questions (according to the text) without referring back to the passage.

4. After they have finished, they check their answers in the Answer Key on page 287 and write down the number of correct answers. This is their comprehension score.

5. Students then calculate their reading time by subtracting the starting time from the finishing time. Using this reading time, they find their reading rate on page 272.

In doing Example C, students often have questions about the timing procedures. Review the procedures before the students go ahead and do Example D. Make sure that the procedures are clearly understood before you start your students on the first unit of Reading Faster. The reading rate for Example D is students' initial reading rate.

Reading Faster Passages

1. After students have gone through the introduction and before they start the Reading Faster passages, reexamine with them their answers to the questionnaire in the introduction to the book. By now, students may have gained some insight into the reading process and changed some of their views of

what makes for good reading habits. In reviewing the questionnaire, students will, in effect, be reviewing some of the important aspects of reading covered so far.

2. Students are more likely to improve their reading rate if they set goals for themselves after they have established their initial rates. Many students find that they can double their rate by the end of a semester. A class discussion may help each student decide on a realistic goal. He or she should then be reminded of that goal and pushed to try to achieve it.

3. Remind students regularly about previewing. They may also need to be assured that previewing will not slow down their reading. The few seconds they spend on previewing (it should only take a few seconds) will save them reading time afterward.

4. These timed reading passages should not be used for other purposes (discussion, comprehension skills, or grammar) during faster reading sessions. If students think they may be held accountable for what they are reading, they will not feel free to take risks and experiment with rate-building strategies.

However, after all the students have completed a passage, it may be used in another context of the reading class. Many of the passages provide interesting material for intensive reading lessons and general class discussion.

5. Make sure that students record their reading rate and comprehension score on the Faster Reading Progress Chart on page 273. This visual record helps students evaluate their progress.

6. As they chart their progress in reading rate improvement, students may notice that their rate varies with the type of passage. They may have a slower rate on the passages of expository prose than on the narrative passages. They should be reassured that readers naturally react differently to different kinds of writing, especially when the content is also new. In fact, the more familiar the subject, the easier it is to read—and so reading rate and comprehension are higher.

7. For additional practice materials for timed reading, consult the bibliography in *A Short Course in Teaching Reading Skills*.